D1126055

Additional Praise for *How a Second Grader Beats Wall Street*

"I have a very strong feeling that sometime in the not-to-distant future I will happily be working for Allan Roth's son! If you buy only one how-to book this year, this is the one! Allan Roth is a National Treasure."

—**Mike Causey**, senior correspondent, FederalNewsRadio.com

"Allan presents in a very clever way why a second grader can outperform most investors, professional and individual. He demonstrates why smart investing is both simple and also why it is not easy for adults to execute because of behavioral mistakes to which they are prone."

—**Larry Swedroe**, author of *Wise Investing Made Simple*

"Successful investing should be a matter of choice, not chance. Follow this book's advice and your probabilities of success are 100% in your favor."

—**Paul Merriman**, author, *Live It Up Without Outliving Your Money!* (Wiley), and publisher of FundAdvice.com

"Allan Roth gets an A+. It is no surprise that a 2nd grader beats Wall Street because everything we need to know about beating the pros is taught in the first grade. That is when we learn to add and subtract. And after subtracting the high fees and commissions that the pros charge, their results fall far short of a simple market return."

—**Richard Ferri, CFA**, investment advisor and author of *The ETF Book*

"Pablo Picasso spent a lifetime learning to paint like a child. Investors might be wise to do the same. Allan Roth's *How a Second Grader Beats Wall Street* reminds us that the most important investment principles are actually simple truths that we lose sight of as our lives and investment approaches grow more complicated. By returning to the basics, we can both simplify our finances and improve our investment results."

—**Don Phillips**, Managing Director, Morningstar, Inc.

"Allan Roth shatters the Wall Street myth that investing is too complicated for ordinary investors. Using his son, Kevin, as an example, Allan shows us, in his easy-to-read writing style, how we can construct a simple personal portfolio that is almost certain to outperform the vast majority of investors. If you have been looking for an easy-to-understand book about how to invest successfully—this is it."

—**Taylor Larimore**, co-author of *The Bogleheads' Guide to Investing*

"Using just a bit of logic and a dash of arithmetic, Allan Roth lucidly explains why low-cost index funds should be the investment of choice for 2nd graders as well as their parents and grandparents."

—**John Allen Paulos**, mathematics professor at Temple University and the author of *Innumeracy* and *A Mathematician Plays the Stock Market*

"Kevin, the second grader, is really smart and cool! He knows what it took me decades to learn. A smart strategy is to diversify broadly across US stocks, international stocks and high-grade US bonds using low-cost, tax-efficient index funds. He even taught me how individuals can increase their fixed-income returns without incurring higher risks. By following Kevin's advice, we, too, can be smart investors. But we may never be as cool as Kevin!"

—**William Reichenstein**, Powers Chair in Investment Management at Baylor University

How a Second Grader Beats Wall Street

Golden Rules Any Investor Can Learn

Allan S. Roth

John Wiley & Sons, Inc.

Published by John Wiley & Sons, Inc., Hoboken, New Jersey.

Published simultaneously in Canada.

For general information on our other products and services or for technical support, please contact our Customer Care Department within the United States at (800) 762-2974, outside the United States at (317) 572-3993 or fax (317) 572-4002.

Wiley also publishes its books in a variety of electronic formats. Some content that appears in print may not be available in electronic books. For more information about Wiley products, visit our web site at www.wiley.com.

Library of Congress Cataloging-in-Publication Data:

Roth, Allan S., 1957-
How a second grader beats Wall Street: golden rules any investor can learn/Allan S. Roth.
p. cm.
Includes bibliographical references and index.
ISBN 978-0-470-37594-5 (cloth)

1. Portfolio management. 2. Index mutual funds. 3. Investments. I. Title.

HG4529.5.R67 2009

332.6–dc22

2008041525

Printed in the United States of America

10 9 8 7 6 5 4 3 2 1

To investors, like my son, Kevin, who
know the truth of simple arithmetic

Contents

Acknowledgments

Writing this book has been the closest thing to what I imagine childbirth is like to experience. From the excitement of getting the contract and advance, through months of discomfort, nausea, and maybe even a little weight gain from stress eating, all the way to the pain of bringing forth the finished product. As I reflect on this process, I know with certainty that I would never have gotten through it without an immense amount of support.

This section must first start with my deep appreciation to a legend—Jack Bogle, who did three things for me. First, he brought us all the tool to make competing with Wall Street an unfair game—the broad low-cost index fund. Next, by using his tool and harnessing the power of compounding, I accumulated enough funds to leave corporate America and pursue my dreams. Finally, he provided me with encouragement and guidance in the pursuit of my own little cause—to stop the flow of funds from the consumer to Wall Street.

Jack Bogle is a legend, but no legend exists without help. Jack's right-hand man, Kevin Laughlin, does so much to help the Main Street investor. He has given me years of wisdom and pored through earlier versions of this manuscript suggesting countless changes that have made this book much better. In many ways, Kevin wrote this book with me. Jack's small team does a great deal for us consumers.

Another special word of thanks goes to Paul B. Farrell, columnist for DowJones/MarketWatch and author of some of my favorite books. Paul's seven "Lazy Portfolios" were developed by some of the most brilliant and successful investors in the United States. Imagine the proud dad I was when he added my son's portfolio as the eighth. Paul, you understand the brilliance of simplicity.

Writing is difficult for a left-brained math geek like me. I was encouraged by people who, not too long ago, were total strangers. Some of my favorite and most respected writers befriended me and gave me constant encouragement. These include Jonathan Clements, formerly of the *Wall Street Journal,* and Jason Zweig, who replaced him. Eric Schurenberg, managing editor of *Money* magazine, has taken the time to read my work and has helped me to develop as a writer. Other brilliant writers like William Bernstein and Dan Solin have generously given me the benefit of their experience and guided me through the process.

I would never have become a writer had it not been for Mike Boyd and the great people at the *Colorado Springs Business Journal.* Mike asked me to write a column for the paper, and I thought it would be fun to do for a few months. That was about five years ago and I'm still writing.

Other media types have also contributed greatly. Jeffrey Pritchard, who writes a wonderful blog, AllFinancialMatters.com, has helped me enormously. Mike Causey of Federal News Radio is a kindred spirit and constantly preaches the brilliance of simplicity.

I'd like to express appreciation to my talented friend, Laurie Anderson, who developed the illustrations in this book. In my view, a picture is worth a thousand words, and her graphics make this book much more powerful. The *Colorado Springs Business Journal* was also generous in allowing us to base some illustrations on their work. Venkat Reddy, the dean of the College of Business at the University of Colorado at Colorado Springs, taught me to teach. These skills have been critical in writing this book.

I appreciate all of the help from the good guys in investing, and I must also make mention of the countless friends and clients who gave of their time to read this manuscript. I've been poisoned with all of the financial jargon of the industry and needed them to point out where I was using psychobabble that had meaning only for us professionals. Dozens of people, like Jeff Hundt, Charlie Rollman, and Steve King, helped me make this closer to a jargon-free book.

I often learn more from people I disagree with than from those who share all of my views. For this reason, I'd like to thank Marv Tuttle, CEO of the Financial Planning Association. His ability to deal with dissent by keeping the dialogue continuing in a productive way is something I will always strive for.

By far the largest data source for information in this book was Morningstar, Inc. Their assistance and ability to turn large amounts of data into simple, understandable information helps investors make better decisions.

My publisher, Joan O'Neil, and everyone else at John Wiley & Sons have been wonderful to work with. I am deeply grateful to my editor, Bill Falloon, for his willingness to take a big chance with a first-time author, as well as his superb editing. Emilie Herman, development editor, and Laura Walsh, associate editor, have always had time to walk me though the process and have given me great ideas now incorporated in this book.

While I started by acknowledging Jack Bogle, I must end by thanking my family, because writing this book was truly a family affair.

I want to thank my son, Kevin, first and foremost, for all that his very presence has brought to my life. Becoming a dad in midlife has definitely proven to me that the old adage "better late than never" holds water. I would also like to thank Kevin for listening to his old dad give investment lessons, and actually enjoying them. He in turn gave me some important lessons that made me realize the ways in which I made things more complicated than they needed to be. But most of all, I want to thank Kevin for all the ways he makes his dad so proud.

Finally, no one has done more to make this book happen than my wife, Patty. Not only has she put up with me and supported me for the past couple of decades, she has helped me every step of the way in writing this book. She is a brilliant writer and has edited every single page in this book, as well as every article I have published. I believe this book comes alive because of her. Living with me is hard enough, so also working with me qualifies her for sainthood. I am indeed a lucky man.

Introduction

The Seeds of Financial Success

Throughout history, wiser individuals than I have extolled the virtues of the child's perspective. Be it religion, society, or, in this case, investing, there are lessons we adults can learn from the uncluttered and uncomplicated minds of children.

In *How a Second Grader Beats Wall Street,* we'll look at what the uncluttered mind of my second-grader son, Kevin Roth, was able to accomplish with some money from his grandparents and some direction from his dad. We'll explore some simple techniques that can work wonders in your own portfolios, such as moving up financial freedom by 10 years or more. That's a decade closer to pursuing whatever makes you happy. And you can do it by cutting through the baloney that Wall Street wants us to believe and returning to basic simplicity.

It all started when Kevin was still in kindergarten. I set a goal that by the time he was in second grade, I would teach him to build and maintain an investment portfolio that would beat Wall Street. I'll confess that I didn't consider this to be a daunting challenge at the time. In fact, I actually thought I had set the bar pretty low. This was Wall Street, after all, home of the "new age economy" of the 1999 tech bubble and "AAA-rated risk-free subprime mortgage notes."[1] As Warren Buffett put it "First, many in Wall Street—a community in which quality control is not prized—will sell investors anything they will buy."[2] Well, Kevin and I did design the portfolio in second grade and it did beat the professionals of Wall Street. Paul Farrell, of Dow Jones MarketWatch, now includes Kevin's portfolio in his list of eight "lazy portfolios" that consistently beat Wall Street. The second-grader portfolio is side by side with some of the world's best investors, such as David Swensen, chief investment officer of Yale University's endowment fund, and William Bernstein, investment advisor and author of many great investing books, including one of my favorites, *The Four Pillars of Investing* (McGraw-Hill, 2002). You can see all these portfolios and their current performance at www.marketwatch.com/lazyportfolio.

It was not the success of Kevin's portfolio that surprised me, as he merely used the simple principles that consistently work in investing. What *did* surprise me were the large advantages that a kid has over an adult when it comes to investing. What started out as a journey to teach my son simple principles of investing instead turned into an incredible joint learning experience. And what I learned is that *everything we need to know about investing, we've learned by second grade.* It's what we learn *after* second grade that turns out to be so destructive.

Before we get to that, let me first give a little background. Five days after my wife Patty turned 40, with me four months behind her, we learned she was expecting our son. At this point in our lives, we figured the ship had sailed on having children and that maybe we would do like many of our friends and get a couple of dogs to give our cat, Hoover, some siblings. We were sure we would be the oldest couple at our natural childbirth class, but we weren't. In fact, we were simply part of a growing social trend known as *GWK,* or Geezers with Kids.

There is an interesting shift in the family dynamic that occurs when an only child is born to middle-aged parents. We've often felt like some hybrid of a parent and a grandparent. I certainly don't remember my parents regularly getting down on the floor and playing with me as parents do now, nor do I remember being included in things that were considered to be adult territory. But strangely enough, Kevin and I have found a mutual interest in the adult territory of investing. In fact, it is his uncomplicated perspective on something that we adults have made very complicated that has provided me with a wonderful window on the power of a fresh perspective.

For starters, money is obviously more critical to adults than it is to second graders. To a child, money is only as important as what can be bought with it. It's a means to an end—something that's used to obtain candy or a new video game. Adults care about money in a material and an abstract sense; historically, we adults have placed enormous value on accumulating as much of it as we can. To us, money is a new house or car, but it is also freedom or security. In addition to that, adults are barraged constantly with helpful "expert" advice on the next hot investment, so as to increase our supply of money. Accordingly, we take all of this knowledge, apply what we believe to be thoughtful analysis, and somehow manage consistently to outsmart ourselves. Yet we don't learn from our investing mistakes, and that pretty much guarantees we'll continue to repeat them. This book will delve into the silly behavior we adults seem hell-bent on repeating, even though it only leads to sabotaging our retirement.

Just as an example, we adults tend to follow the herd, thinking there is safety in doing what everyone else does. We bravely *invest in the stock market after a bull market* and then *panic and sell after the bear arrives.* Kevin, on the other hand, doesn't even have a clue that the investing herd exists, let alone want to follow it. That's a huge advantage over you and me.

Together, Kevin and I developed some "golden rules" about investing. These rules will help anyone to unlearn some of the things we think we know about investing. By following the golden rules presented in this book, we can simplify our thinking and stop doing the things that needlessly set our financial goals back.

What will these golden rules do for you?

1. Show you why the debate between active and passive investing is just plain silly.
2. Move up your financial independence by a decade, and dramatically increase your spend rate during retirement.
3. Show you how to go beyond indexing, which owns the entire market, and actually beat the market by using the one advantage the small investor has over the large institution. Yes, we have an advantage in fixed income!
4. Show you how to reengineer your portfolio so it will be more tax efficient, because your portfolio is probably designed backwards, causing you to pay taxes needlessly. A little portfolio reengineering can save a bundle.
5. Give you a simple tool that, in a couple of minutes, will allow you to know whether a product with a 447-page disclosure document has something in it for you.
6. Guide you to the low-hanging fruit in your portfolio that is likely sitting right in front of you. It's a sure way to increase returns whether the market goes up, down, or sideways.
7. Show you that common sense isn't all that common and how you can profit from second-grader logic.
8. Assist you to unlearn what you know about investing and be able to think in the crisp terms that only a child can.

9. Make you feel better about paying the high price of gasoline. Many of us can save more from investing than we could from winning free gasoline for the rest of our lives.
10. Help you understand why we owe a great debt of gratitude to active investors and Wall Street.

It is my hope that this book will provide you with many *aha!* moments that will bring a clarity to your investing that may increase your long-run return by 4 percent annually or more! I also hope you will realize that *common-sense investing* isn't actually all that common.

What This Book Is, and Is *Not*

This book isn't about a kid who either got lucky or did anything complex in investing, or who is a prodigy of some kind. Kevin's success had nothing to do with luck or brilliance, and everything to do with simplicity and low cost. His U.S. stocks beat Wall Street, and so did his international stock portfolio and his bond portfolio. The most important thing, however, is that they must continue to do so. It's a mathematical certainty.

Neither is this book one of those self-discipline books about spending less today so you can have more tomorrow. Don't get me wrong; I happen to believe that this is an essential part of reaching your financial goals. Saving, however, involves giving up some immediate gratification, such as not buying that big-screen HDTV, in return for having more later on in life. Like dieting, saving involves making some sacrifices.

What this book *is* about is building up wealth without having to make additional sacrifices. As long as you have money to invest, this book is about making it grow. Not at the long-term rate you'll get from the vast majority of Wall Street's highly paid financial wizards, but at a real (inflation-adjusted) rate that will double or triple it.

What do you have to sacrifice now for that faster growth? Absolutely, positively *nothing!* In fact, a sign that you are doing it right is that you find yourself with more free. And if a second grader can explain the logic, it's something all of us have the ability to do; we just need the willingness to apply some simple logic to question what we are currently doing.

Kevin's Accomplishments— Kid Handily Beats the Street

In Wall Street speak, Kevin designed a portfolio that beat the S&P 500 by 4 percent annually. In fact, in 2007, he earned nearly 2.5 times the S&P 500 index. Most Wall Street firms would be thrilled to have this performance, but few firms ever will. As long as the laws of simple arithmetic hold, Kevin's portfolio will continue to outperform Wall Street:

- Over the two-year period, his portfolio has grown 34.1 percent, which equates to a 15.8 percent annual return, according to Morningstar.[3]
- He bested the S&P 500 common benchmark by 2.23 percent annually, and did so with less risk.
- Kevin's portfolio joined the eight portfolios Paul Farrell tracks that include billion-dollar portfolio managers, famous authors, and money managers—some of the world's best investors.

Most high-performing portfolios take a lot of risk. Not this one. The securities in the second-grader portfolio take on far less risk than the portfolios of the Wall Street firms. The second-grader portfolio doesn't use sophisticated risk-management techniques to outsmart the market. Those same sophisticated techniques led to hundreds of billions of dollars of Wall Street losses and the collapse of Wall Street icons like Bear Stearns, Lehman Brothers, Wachovia, and AIG.

How did Kevin do it? It depends on whom you ask. Let's take a look at a couple of different explanations.

Wall Street Explanation

If Wall Street had designed this portfolio, it would say it used modern portfolio theory to design a portfolio on the efficient frontier that beat the S&P 500 index by 4 percent annually. Furthermore, the portfolio was designed to provide a superior risk-adjusted return as measured by the Sharpe ratio, with a lower standard deviation than the market. The portfolio was built by using thousands of underlying securities, screening for different asset classes with low correlations with each other, and stock styles that do not always move in tandem. It utilized the teachings of Nobel Laureates in economics such as Harry Markowitz, William Sharpe, and Daniel Kahneman. The portfolio takes the essence of their findings and applies them in a practical manner that is quantifiably guaranteed to outperform other investors. Some of these theories are complex, but they end up being incredibly simple to implement.

Kevin's Explanation

While the Wall Street explanation sounds impressive and complex, the truth is that Kevin accomplished this by using simple common sense and a little second-grade arithmetic. His magic portfolio is simply:

Vanguard Total Stock Market Index Fund (VTSMX)	60%
Vanguard Total International Stock Index Fund (VGTSX)	30%
Vanguard Total Bond Market Index Fund (VBMFX)	10%

Exhibit I.1 Annualized Performance of Second-Grader Funds

	1 yr	3 yr	5 yr	10 yr
Vanguard Total Intl.	15.52%	19.13%	23.45%	9.44%
Vanguard Total Stock (U.S.)	–5.49%	8.90%	13.80%	6.25%
Vanguard Total Bond	6.92%	4.51%	4.35%	5.72%

Annualized returns as of 12/31/2007.

With these three funds, you can own virtually the entire global equity market and the U.S. investment-grade bond market. Now, this portfolio certainly isn't right for everyone, but a version of it with different allocations should be the building blocks for most investors. We just have to resist adding in too many additional blocks.

These funds earned quite respectable long-run returns in a time when the stock market resembled a rollercoaster. They survived the Internet bubble, and the subprime mortgage fiasco, as well as Enron's and WorldCom's (Exhibit I.1).

How has the portfolio done versus the S&P 500 index? Look at Exhibit I.2 and judge for yourself.

Exhibit I.2 The Second-Grader Portfolio Handily Beat the S&P 500 Index in Every Time Period

Second grader portfolio handily beats S&P 500.

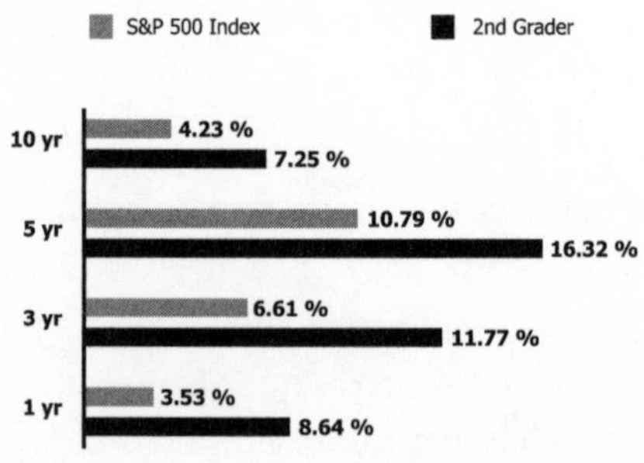

Through 12/31/07

As I finish this book, the market is clearly in bear territory and the numbers above have deteriorated. The impact of the subprime mess ended up being more devastating and far-reaching than we could have ever anticipated. And clearly, Kevin's portfolio is down. In Kevin's short life, he has experienced the Internet bubble where cash supposedly didn't matter, and years of easy credit where we lent trillions of dollars to people who never had a prayer of ever paying it back. Keep in mind, however, that the advice in this book is even more valuable in down markets because:

- Kevin's long-term performance versus the S&P 500 index has actually increased during this down market.
- Kevin is unlikely to panic and sell, as many investors do. He has other things on his mind besides his portfolio. This gives him a huge advantage that we should try to emulate.
- Kevin is able to buy in at lower prices. Unlike many adult investors, he likes to buy when prices are low.

Yes, Kevin's portfolio is down, but he's not watching the talking heads on television and following an aged-old adult tradition of panicking and selling low. He's not rationalizing how "this time it's different." In fact, Kevin rarely thinks about his portfolio. This is an advantage that his dad, and all of us adults, will find hard to replicate. And even Kevin will lose this advantage as he grows up.

How does Kevin beat the S&P 500 index in any market? For now, I'll just leave you with the hint that Wall Street likes to compare its performance to the S&P 500 index because it's not the entire market. In fact, it's not even the total return of a portion of the market.

Of course, there is much more to this book than simply talking about three funds. There are alternative funds to use as building blocks that have lower costs and even more diversification. These are some risky asset classes that may actually decrease the overall risk of our portfolio. If you are willing to do just a little work, you can even replace the bond fund and bump your return while lowering risk. Finally, there are some things you can do with this portfolio that will increase return no matter what the market does.

Successful use of this book means increasing your returns by 3 to 4 percent annually. This may not sound like much, but each 1 percent may, on average, move your financial goals up by four years (much more on this in Chapter 13). We are talking about giving you 12 to 16 years of your life to pursue whatever it is that makes you happy. And if you are already retired, the wisdom of a second grader can increase the amount of your portfolio that you can safely spend by as much as 50 to 70 percent annually! Both Jack Bogle and Albert Einstein talk about the power of compound interest; this book will show how harnessing this power can simply change your life.

Reading this book will show you that investing isn't rocket science. Wall Street experts want you to believe that it is, so you will be dependent on them and fund their lavish lifestyles. This book will show you how to cut the cord that transfers our wealth to Wall Street. For those who don't believe simple is better, remember that both Albert Einstein and Sir Isaac Newton, considered to be perhaps the two smartest humans in history, were known to state that brilliance lies in simplicity rather than complexity.

Get ready to unlearn all of the psychobabble you've been taught regarding investing. Our second grader will show you how to replace it with simple common sense. And we will show you why common sense isn't actually all that common.

Embracing the simple second-grader wisdom will shield you from the "helpers" that I call Wall Street that merely want to transfer your wealth to them. And by *Wall Street,* I mean *everybody* who's after your money, not just the large brokerage houses. I've seen many independent planners, insurance companies, and mutual fund companies do things that make me cringe. They all share one thing in common: They fail to pass a simple smell test from a second grader.

If you are successful in applying the golden rules in this book, you will achieve your financial goals far sooner than you imagined. That alone is a pretty good reason you should give it a try. But let me offer a word of caution: Simple investing is really easy for a second grader, but not so easy for us adults. We have to overcome something even more likely to rob our wealth than Wall Street. We have to overcome our own emotions, because our emotions consistently steer us toward the path that leads only to giving away our hard-earned nest egg.

I hope you enjoy the simplicity and messages from the pages that follow. Much of the wisdom lies in the beginning of each chapter describing a conversation with Kevin. The 13 conversations were actually compiled from many more than that and condensed down. I also have taken a bit of creative license with them to better illustrate how simple it is to be a successful investor.

As you read this book, remember the phrase, "Simple investing isn't easy." Good luck in your process of unlearning the many complicated mental models that we have all blindly accepted as true.

Disclaimer and Data: "Why Do We Need This, Dad?"

Why do we need this? Well, primarily because we live in a litigious society. Even in a book about simple investing, you *never* want to leave home without the proper disclaimers. Therefore, in the interest of disclaiming, I have done my best to accurately capture information and offer advice that I believe will work for most people, if they dare to implement it. None of the advice, however, takes into account the individual reader's specific circumstances and should not be taken as such. As there is nothing simple about taxes, and though I touch on taxes in this book, seeking proper expertise on your individual situation is strongly, and I mean *strongly,* recommended. In short, getting into a simple portfolio is easy, but getting out of a complex portfolio is not. I always recommend gaining a full understanding of any investment product purchased and the entire long-term investment strategy.

Throughout the book, I've listed data sources in the text and on the graphics. Morningstar has provided much of the data. All data is believed to be accurate, but such accuracy is not guaranteed. And, of course, past performance is no guarantee of future performance.

Chapter 1

The Claw Will Take Your Money

"10 − 2 = 8"

"We live in a great and free country," I told my 8-year-old son Kevin, as we sat eye-to-eye at the kitchen table one day in what I hoped was one of those father/son bonding moments. I continued by explaining that we are so prosperous because of a beautiful thing called *capitalism*. And that one of the benefits of capitalism is that if we don't spend all of the money we have, we can invest it in companies. "Our money will actually grow," I said, miming a tree growing with all the dramatic flair a CPA can muster.

"How fast will it grow?" asked Kevin. I estimated that owning stocks has resulted in about a 10 percent annual growth, meaning that every dollar invested would be worth $2 in 7 years, $4 in 14 years and almost $7.50 in 21 years.

Kevin was amazed and excitedly blurted out, "If I invest all the money from my grandparents, I can buy anything I want when I'm older!" I'd hooked him.

At this point, I had to clue him in on one more thing. I explained that in order to see their money grow, most people who invest pay about 2 percent per year to helpers. That means instead of $7.50 in 21 years, he'd only have about $5.00, I told him.

"What do the helpers do?" asked Kevin.

The answer, of course, was *absolutely nothing.* If the stock market earned 10 percent and the average investor paid Wall Street 2 percent, that left only 8 percent for investors. This is simple arithmetic any second grader can do.

Upon hearing this news, Kevin looked a little less excited. If there's one thing every second grader has a clear grasp of, it's what is and isn't fair. Being a second grader and therefore one of the "go-to" guys in determining fairness, Kevin decreed, "That doesn't sound fair." He astutely noted that if he didn't have to pay the 2 percent, then he could keep the entire 10 percent, affirming we really were from the same gene pool.

I then explained to him that we always have to pay something to invest, but we could cut that 2 percent down to 0.2 percent. Realizing that he would get to keep nearly the entire 10 percent that his money would grow, Kevin perked up again—although he still wondered aloud, "Why do people pay two percent when they don't have to? That sounds like 'the claw' to me."

Kevin was referring to an arcade machine where you put a quarter in and direct the claw scooper over a bunch of prizes in the hopes that it will pick up the prize you're aiming for. (See Exhibit 1.1.) After all, snagging some cool stuffed animal for only a quarter was virtually irresistible. For a few weeks, Kevin would spend a portion of his allowance trying for his

Exhibit 1.1 The Claw Always Wins

The Claw is a game few will win.

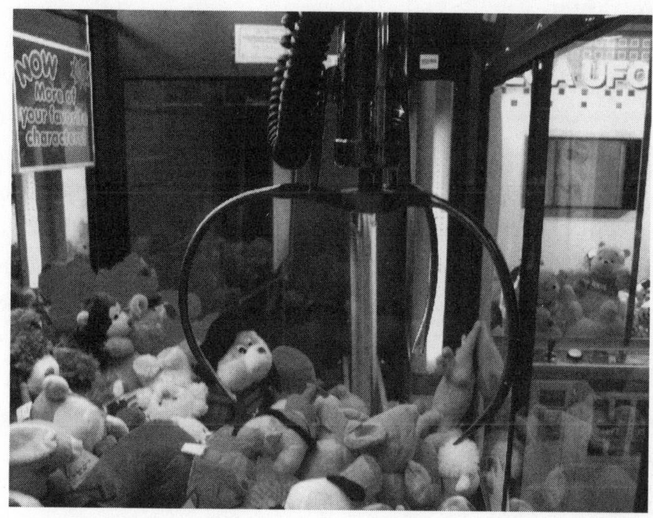

grand prize. He got nothing. After feeding it a few dollars, Kevin had an *aha!* moment. "This game is a ripoff!"[1] he said, as he came to the painful realization that he wasn't going to get that prize he had repeatedly aimed for. He hasn't played the claw game since.

I've often wondered why adults keep feeding quarters to Wall Street. In response to his question, I could have launched into some scaled-down explanation of the efficient market hypothesis, but instead I just thought of Charley Ellis's timeless investing book, *Winning the Loser's Game* (McGraw-Hill, 3rd ed., 1998) and recited the book's famous message (with a small tweak to appeal to Kevin):

> Paying Wall Street is a loser's game. Your odds are probably better with the claw.

The Common Sense of Kevin's Math

If you have any investing experience, you may be thinking that I've just skipped the whole debate between active and passive investing.

Active management refers to the use of a human element—such as a single manager, co-managers, or a team of managers—to actively manage a stock portfolio. Active managers rely on analytical research, forecasts, and their own judgment and experience in making investment decisions on what securities to buy, hold, and sell. Warren Buffett and Bill Miller, for example, have long-term track records of beating the market.

Passive management is an investment theory that states that it is impossible to "beat the market" because stock market efficiency causes existing share prices to always incorporate and reflect all relevant information. People who ascribe to this are generally followers of the *efficient market hypothesis* (EMH). According to the EMH, this means that stocks always trade at their estimated fair value on stock exchanges, making luck responsible for investors either purchasing undervalued stocks or selling stocks for inflated prices. Burton Malkiel's famous book, *A Random Walk Down Wall Street,* advocates passive management.

Can I just make the assumption that the expenses associated with active investing (the 2 percent I mentioned earlier) don't add any value? As you'll see, we don't actually need to explore this active-versus-passive debate, because the answer is merely dependent on second-grade arithmetic. There are countless papers, books, and experts all around us that claim to beat the market. After all, they state, it's not about the lowest cost; it's about getting the highest return. The arguments for active management have two things in common:

1. They are emotionally appealing.
2. They fly in the face of simple mathematics.

Sticking with the theme of simple math, let's examine the simple $10 - 2 = 8$ equation by looking at the U.S. stock market.

The U.S. Stock Market

The U.S. stock market is comprised of roughly 7,000 individual stocks with a total value (market capitalization) of roughly \$17.5 trillion. Wall Street revenue from the services it provides is roughly \$350 billion[2] (which just happens to be about the size of the U.S. deficit[3]). The Wall Street take is about 2 percent of the value of the U.S. market.

While Kevin won't have the lessons to construct the whole portfolio until Chapter 2, let's take a look at how Kevin's total U.S. stock index fund will perform in a year with a bull market return, average market return, and bear market return with an expense ratio of 0.2 percent, and compare it to the professionally managed Wall Street U.S. portfolio. Exhibit 1.2 illustrates the return of the Wall Street portfolio versus Kevin's portfolio in an up year in the market.

Exhibit 1.2 Net Investor Returns—Up Stock Market

If the stock market earns 10% and the average investor pays 2%, the average investor earns 8%.

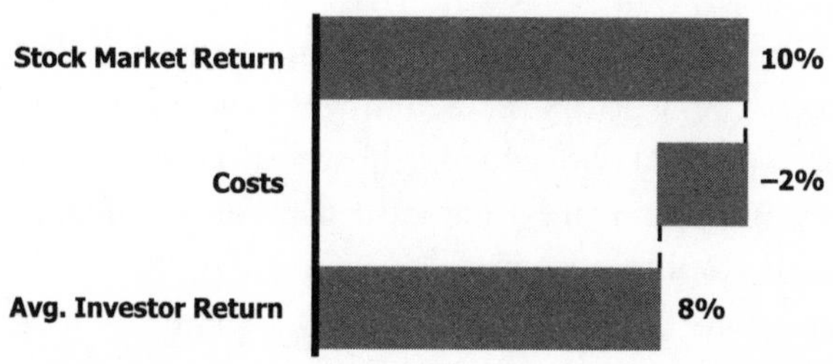

Second grader portfolio earns 9.8% besting the avgerage investor by 1.8%

Exhibit 1.3 Net Investor Returns—Down Stock Market

If the stock market loses 10% and the average investor pays 2%, the average investor loses 12%.

Second grader portfolio loses 10.2%, besting the average investor by 1.8%

Kevin also earned the 10 percent of the U.S. market but only paid 0.2 percent in expenses (to Vanguard). Thus, he earned 9.8 percent, which is a full 1.8 percent more than the average investor earned. Will this work in a down market as well? The answer is an unequivocal *yes!* In a year where the stock market loses 10 percent, the average investor will lose 12 percent. Because Kevin pays 1.8 percent less than the average investor, he again earns 1.8 percent more. See Exhibit 1.3.

What does this extra 1.8 percent in annual earnings mean? Let me put it a couple of different ways:

1. At an 8 percent annual return, Kevin's dollar invested would be worth over $21 in 40 years, when he's his old man's age. At 9.8 percent, however, it will be worth over $42. In other words, that extra 1.8 percent of annual return nearly doubles his portfolio's final value.
2. We adults may not have as many years to benefit from the power of compounding as Kevin does, but I've found that my average clients can reach their financial goals by a year sooner for every 0.25 percent they can lower expenses in

their portfolio. This means that 1.8 percent is worth about seven years to us adults. And, as you will soon learn, most adults can boost return by far more than this 1.8 percent, thus reaching our goals that much sooner.

An important item to note is that Kevin's advantage isn't dependent on whether the market goes up or down; it's dependent only on the difference in expenses that he is paying versus the Wall Street average expense.

A second important item is that this argument of simple arithmetic is not dependent on the efficient market hypothesis. It doesn't matter one iota whether stocks are efficiently priced or wildly misvalued. The only thing that matters is that all investors—you and me—cannot be above average and that 10 − 2 *must* equal 8! So, forget the debate about the efficient market hypothesis and remember the *second-grader hypothesis* that 10 − 2 = 8. Of course, this is adapted from Jack Bogle's *cost matters hypothesis.*

The International Stock Market

The same simple arithmetic of investing that worked for the U.S. stock market must work in the international stock markets as well, right? International markets have their versions of helpers who get their take of the action. The argument that international markets are less efficient than the U.S. market happens to fly in the face of contrary data. According to Morningstar, the Vanguard Total U.S. Stock Market Index Fund (VTSMX) has bested 77 percent of its peers over the past five years. That's pretty impressive, but the Vanguard Total International Index Fund (VGTSX) bested 86 percent of its peers.[4]

Granted, we could debate the point of whether international markets are less efficient, but the argument also happens to be irrelevant. The world stock market has a total value of roughly $40 trillion and, while coming up with the total fees charged by the worldwide helpers is more difficult, there is no reason to believe it should be any less than 2 percent. So, the

Exhibit 1.4 Kevin versus Wall Street International Portfolio

	Bull Market	Average Market	Bear Market
Wall Street Stock Portfolio			
Stock Market Return	30%	10%	−10%
Wall Street Take	−2%	−2%	−2%
Average Investor Return	28%	8%	−12%
Kevin's Stock Portfolio			
Stock Market Return	30%	10%	−10%
Kevin's Expense	−0.2%	−0.2%	−0.2%
Kevin's Return	29.8%	9.8%	−10.2%
Second-Grader Advantage	1.8%	1.8%	1.8%

concept remains the same. If Kevin owns the international markets at the lowest costs, he *must* beat the average professionally managed global portfolio that has higher costs. See Exhibit 1.4.

The Bond Market

I'll explain a bit later in the book why everyone needs some fixed-income investments (bonds)—even a second grader with a very long investment horizon. For now, let me say that every argument made for keeping fees low in the stock market applies just as stringently in the bond market. That is, the average bond investor will get the average bond return before expenses. Thus, owning the entire bond market at the lowest costs must yield a return that beats the more expensive professionally managed portfolios.

The Arithmetic of Active Management

As much as I'd like to claim that this simple mathematics is the brainchild of Kevin's and my brilliance, it isn't. A fellow by the name of William Sharpe, the winner of the 1990 Nobel Prize in Economics, wrote a famous paper called "The Arithmetic of Active Management."[5] In it Sharpe states, "Properly measured, the average actively managed dollar must underperform the average passively managed dollar, net of costs." He also notes that the proof is "embarrassingly simple."

It's simple enough that an 8-year-old can understand it, yet somehow very difficult for us adults to grasp. *We adults seem to buy into the expectation that* our *active manager is really good, so we will be among the few who beat the market. Of course, if my manager is so good that he can beat all the other managers, then why isn't he working for the billion-dollar investors?*

Can My Professional *Really* Beat Yours?

One reason that ignoring simple mathematics seems preferable to most adults is that we strongly resist thinking of ourselves as average. And if by some wild chance we *are* average, can't we just find a money manager who is above average? Whether we are in the casino or playing the stock market, it's virtually impossible to resist thinking of ourselves as a Doyle Brunson or a Warren Buffett.

It seems intuitive that paying a professional investor to pick the right stocks and mutual funds should add value. The logic goes that someone who constantly studies the market should be able to outperform individuals who "play" the stock market. This might have actually been true at one time when there were but a handful of professional investors, and stocks were largely owned by individuals. In 1945, only about 10 percent of U.S. stocks were owned by institutions. So it's not hard to imagine that the small population of professional investors might be able to add value when trading with a large population of individual investors.

Today, however, 80 percent to 90 percent of the stock market is owned by professionals such as pension plans, mutual funds, and insurance companies.[6] Information flows much more freely and instantaneously, thanks to the wonder of the Internet. *Anyone* can listen in on a company's earnings report, rather than just a few selected analysts as was the case in the past.

When it comes to picking an investment professional, the following analogy may click for you: *If you needed heart surgery, you wouldn't go bargain hunting for a surgeon*. This analogy breaks down when you consider the nature of both professions. Unlike medicine, or almost any other profession, investing is a zero-sum game. That is, one surgeon's success has no impact on another's. Investing, however, is precisely the opposite. If my mutual fund manager purchases a stock from yours, my manager's gain (or loss) comes at a direct cost (benefit) to yours—for every investor who beats the market in a given year, there is another who's lost by the same amount.

If we take a step back, we realize it all comes down to paying our professional more and more money in the hopes that he outsmarts someone else's professional. It's a flawed model, much like the one in Exhibit 1.5. No matter how much money

Exhibit 1.5 Active Investing Model

Paying a team of professionals to outsmart other professionals is a flawed design.

we pay to get the best rowers, we're still going in circles. Paying more to get the best rowers may just make us dizzy, but you can bet it's making the rowers rich! The harder they row, the faster they spin, and they will make progress only when the rules of simple arithmetic are repealed.

Following the track record of the professionals perpetuates this flawed design. Statistically they are every bit as likely to underperform as the individual investor. Luckily, this depressing trend has not seemed to dampen the spirits of any of the professional investors I have spoken with. They all claim to beat the market, just like in Lake Wobegon, where we are all above average.

Why We Play a Loser's Game

If active investing is so illogical, then why do we adults practice it regularly? Traditional economics dictates that we would act in a rational manner to increase our wealth. Unfortunately, traditional economics fails to take into account that we are feeling animals who happen to think, rather than thinking animals who happen to feel.

Behavioral finance is a fascinating new field of investing that is a combination of psychology and finance. It shows that we consistently act in ways that result in lower economic gains. It shouldn't be surprising that we are willing to dismiss common sense and hold that the laws of simple mathematics don't apply to us. Maybe they apply only to, you know, the *average* people, not those of us who are above average.

As a practicing financial planner, I have individuals come to me all the time who have played the beat-the-market game with high expenses. As we go through this book, I'm going to give you some real-life examples that will make you cringe.

These people usually have two things in common:

1. They have absolutely no idea how much they are paying for their portfolio. When you look at the costs of your

portfolio, such as the expense ratio of your mutual funds, and then throw in some hidden trading costs, you'll discover the painful reality that most people are needlessly paying thousands of dollars a year for their portfolio. Curiously, these are often the same people who are very cost conscious in other areas of their lives. If only they could transfer that penny-watching to their investing.

2. In at least 95 percent of the cases, their portfolio has vastly underperformed the comparable low-cost indexes. That is to say, the higher fees they paid for the professional have resulted in lower returns. Clearly, their attempt to disprove the equation $10 - 2 = 8$ has failed miserably.

When I show clients how they underperformed the low-cost comparable indexes, I typically get one of two responses. The first type of knee-jerk response is *"Get me out of here, quickly!"* They have used their logical brain and understand the opportunity they have to cut costs and earn more for themselves going forward. This epiphany often comes with much self-flagellation. I try to impress upon them that they are among the few that actually questioned how their portfolio has performed, and that's a good thing. I do my best to make them feel better, but a motivational coach I am not.

The second type of response is the one I find the most fascinating. I call it the "You don't understand!" approach. In trying to convince me that I don't understand, they'll become quite upset, resolute in their belief that my benchmarking can't be right. To these people, it was very important that their perception of being above average remained intact, and I was raining on their parade. Far from looking to me for wealth building direction, they instead were looking to me for confirmation of their brilliance and I wasn't cooperating. In my experience, people often place the benefit of the psychological gain they receive from their investing decisions over any economic gain they could achieve by halting their attempt to disprove second-grade arithmetic.

I used to think of it as a personal failure when I was unable to convince individuals how much economic gain they could have by changing course. Didn't I just show them how they lost out on tens of thousands of dollars in return? How could they benefit by continuing to chase whatever hot, flavor-of-the-month stocks came their way?

Then the obvious occurred to me, like realizing those glasses I was looking for were on my head. Those "above-average" people who believe they know more than the rest of us keep the market efficient, and here's how. They, along with the "professionals" of Wall Street, think they know more about a company than other people. Armed with this superior knowledge, they will then buy or sell that stock to someone else, typically one professional selling the stock in the company to another professional. Did I mention that both professionals are being paid by us to be smarter than each other? Anyway, that causes the market price of the security to change, which keeps the market going.

So, the investors who believe that they can pick stocks, or at least pick a professional who can pick stocks, better than the average Joe, fill an important need. Without these people trying to disprove arithmetic, markets wouldn't work, and the low-cost investor couldn't get a free ride off of their delusions and harness all that the market has to give.

Ultimately, the logic becomes more flawed with the belief that we can pick people who have access to managers who can beat the market. Using private money managers would be an example. That's rather like rejecting the argument that $10 - 2 = 12$ in favor of the argument that $10 - 3 = 13$. All we are doing is adding another layer of costs.

Kevin Doesn't Play That Game

Kevin knows that $10 - 2 = 8$. In spite of how much we want to believe it, $10 - 2 \neq 12$. While he hasn't read Sharpe's "Arithmetic of Active Management," he does know that if the market return is

10 percent and the helpers take 2 percent, then there is 8 percent left for the investors. He knows that if the helper gets a 0.2 percent fee rather than a 2 percent one, there is more left for him. He doesn't understand the efficient market hypothesis and doesn't need to. All he cares about is that he came out ahead. It's that simple.

I posed this question to Kevin: "Which would you rather have: the belief that you are making a lot of money, or actually making a lot of money?" He fixed me with a gaze that pretty much said, "You're kidding, right?" and answered that he'd rather *make* the most money, not *think* that he had. *Duh,* Dad.

The second-grader portfolio sheds those bulky rowers and cuts costs to the bone. It's completely different from the Wall Street version. It's a simple, far more logical and streamlined model where an 8-year-old can effortlessly row past the professionals (see Exhibit 1.6).

Exhibit 1.6 Second-Grader Investing Model

The simpler design is superior.

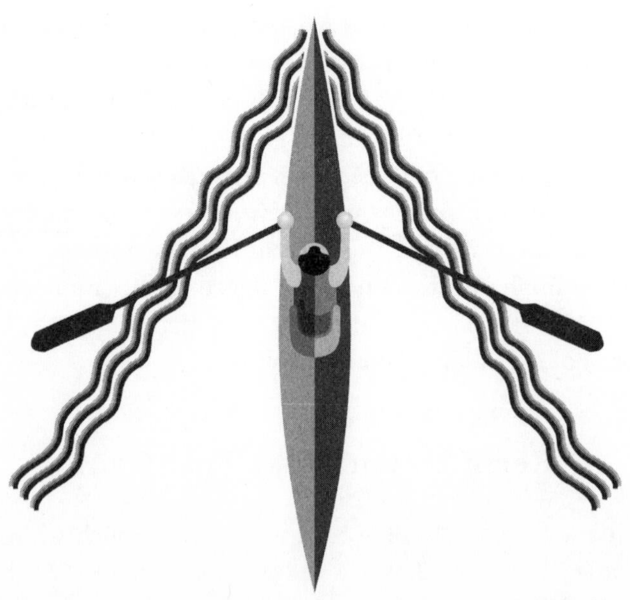

In short, Kevin finds believing in Santa Claus more plausible than many of the investing assumptions held by adults. "It's just silly," explains Kevin. "How could people not know that ten-minus-two equals eight?"

Applying the Golden Rule: 10 − 2 = 8

We haven't yet reached the *how-to* advice, but Kevin's lesson on simple arithmetic shows that if the basis of your investment plan goes against simple arithmetic, you are on the losing end of the claw game. Sure, there are a few highly skilled investors out there, Warren Buffett for instance, but your odds of finding the next Warren Buffett are not good.

Find out how much you are paying in costs. If you are investing directly, go to www.morningstar.com and look at the expense ratios of your mutual funds. If they are greater than 0.5 percent, you, too, are trying to disprove second-grade math. In Chapter 5, I'll show you what your odds are, but for now, I'll just say the odds are you don't know the odds.

If you are using an advisor, money manager, financial planner, or any other helper, my advice is to ask that person how much you are paying. Make sure you ask the question, "How much am I paying in total?," rather than just how much he is making from you. As much as your helper won't like this, get him to put the answer in writing, and make sure it's in terms of both percentage of assets and total annual dollars.

Always remember that market return less costs equals the average investor return. If your costs aren't the lowest available, then mathematics will not be on your side and you should expect an uphill battle. Your Wall Street advisor may make a compelling pitch as to why the strategy will work, but if it goes against the golden rule of simple arithmetic you are likely making someone else rich.

So take Kevin's advice and stop playing a loser's game. Don't feed quarters to the Wall Street claw.

Chapter 2

Own the World

"Don't Put All of Your Eggs in One Basket"

Now that Kevin understood the need to keep costs low, he felt ready to put the money he'd received from his grandparents someplace, but where?

This was one of Kevin's favorite lessons, because it began with a Happy Meal at McDonald's followed by a trip to the Wal-Mart toy department. I explained that he could own a little piece of companies like Wal-Mart and McDonalds. Kevin's eyes lit up like a Christmas tree at the thought of profiting from every toy bought at Wal-Mart, and every Happy Meal cooked at McDonalds. It would have been nice to leave things at that. After all, Wal-Mart and McDonalds are American icons, no need to worry, right?

I bit the bullet and decided to explain to Kevin that when I was his age, there were some really big companies that seemed like *they* would endure forever. I told him about a store named K-Mart, which was like the Wal-Mart of 1965. I also told Kevin about Pan-Am and Eastern Airlines, which were the biggies in my youth and had essentially invented the airline industry. I told him that if I had invested in these three companies way back when, I would have lost every dime.

I saw Kevin begin to deflate like a balloon, and quickly asked him to think of an Easter basket piled high with colorful eggs and what would happen if he dropped it.

"Bye-bye, eggs."

"But wait," I said to his crestfallen little face; "there is a way to spread your eggs across the entire world. And if something bad happens to Wal-Mart or McDonalds, you'll still have thousands of other companies." I told him that, in investing jargon, this was called *diversification*.

"Well, okay," Kevin hesitantly responded, "but I'll still own some McDonalds and Wal-Mart?"

"You betcha," I said.

"I'll own some of Burger King and Mattel?" asked Kevin.

"Absolutely," I replied. I told him that spreading our eggs as widely as possible would allow him to own a piece of nearly every big company in the entire world.[1]

"How do we do that?" asked Kevin.

I explained that there were companies that go out and buy stock in companies, known as *mutual funds.* Some buy stock in a handful of companies and charge a lot of money. Some buy stock in thousands of companies and have very low costs.

Now came the moment of truth. "Which type would you rather own?" I asked.

Without hesitation, Kevin said in an excited tone, "I want to own the world and only pay a little!"

That's my boy!

The Common Sense of Spreading Our Eggs

Mutual funds that own thousands of individual securities at the very lowest costs are known as *index funds.* Index funds were brought to the public by investment maverick Jack Bogle, the founder of Vanguard. In essence, index funds recognize the simple arithmetic of active investing and realize that 10 − 0.2 is a heck of a lot better than 10 − 2. Of course, there are index funds that charge as much as active funds, but Kevin and I were in agreement that buying those was just plain silly. Good index funds also recognize that owning the entire market is a lot less risky than owning a handful of stocks. In essence, index funds lower risk and increase returns by refusing to play the same claw game that Kevin now boycotts. Following are some of the differences between active and indexed mutual funds:

Active Stock Mutual Fund	Stock Index Fund
Typically charges about 1.5% per year plus another 1% in what are known as *hidden trading costs.*[2] You may even pay an upfront fee for the privilege of buying the fund in the first place. For the most part, the fee goes to the firm that sold you the fund. The monies you pay go to the professional stock pickers in hopes that they are better than the stock professionals others picked.	Also professionally managed, but takes a distinctively different approach by owning the entire market.
	The largest index funds own the entire U.S. or international stock markets and thus don't incur high fees for researching individual stocks.
Because the managers constantly buy and sell stocks within the fund, they pass on tax gains even when the owner doesn't sell the mutual fund.	The index funds that own the entire market don't have to trade individual stocks, so they tend to be very tax-efficient.
	Because they own the entire market, you eliminate the market risk that actively managed stock funds have of substantially underperforming the market, as most typically do.

I typically explain to clients that investing is about measuring risk and increasing that risk only if they can expect a long-term higher return. For example, investing in the stock market is riskier than leaving our money in a savings account backed by the U.S. government's FDIC (Federal Deposit Insurance Corporation). In the long run, however, we typically get a higher return in the stock market than we do with our savings account. That higher return is compensation for taking the risk that is the price of admission for investing.

We can also increase risk without increasing our long-term expected return. This could be accomplished by, say, going to Las Vegas. Personally, I do not go to Las Vegas to invest; I go to speculate or gamble. Increasing risk without increasing return is *speculation,* and has no place in investing.

I try to illustrate speculating to my clients by giving them the example of buying a handful of stocks. Sure, they would be quite fortunate if, a few years back, they had invested everything in Apple or Google. On the other hand, they would be broke if they put everything in once-solid companies like Enron, WorldCom, or Bear Stearns. If they buy a few-dozen companies, they may get lucky and outperform the market, or unlucky and perform badly. I never hesitate to point out that buying a couple of dozen companies is not going to increase your expected return but will increase risk. That, of course, is *speculation,* not investing.

The common response I receive after delivering my speculation lecture is that we don't pick random companies. We research the companies or have others research the companies. That's when I throw out one of my own studies of the top investment managers with the best track records.

The Ultimate Investment Club

A *Money* magazine[3] article once went to the top 24 money managers, whom they dubbed "the ultimate investment club."

These were the money managers with the best long-term track records. *Money* asked them for their top stock picks, and those managers offered a total of 34 stocks traded on U.S. stock exchanges. Over the next 12 months, those 34 stocks picked by the best of the best lost about 2.4 percent in value at a time when the total U.S. stock market went up by 11.5 percent. In other words, the experts underperformed the market by nearly 14 percent!

While it's certainly notable that the best of the best performed so badly versus the market, it's even more important to note that a portfolio of only 34 stocks could produce a return that differs so greatly from the market's. The point is that owning 34 stocks or even a couple hundred is not enough to reduce risk from the total market return and can easily vary by more than 14 percent—and that's without the fees those top managers would have charged.

In all fairness, *Money* has come a long way since that issue in 2003 and now writes about many of the techniques preached in this book. I, in fact, am a subscriber.

What about Mutual Funds?

I knew people who felt pretty well diversified back in March 2000, when the Internet bubble was about to burst. They owned dozens of mutual funds from several fund families, and were feeling financially invulnerable. What happened, of course, is that they lost a fortune; far more than the devastating enough loss that the market suffered between then and October 2002. They didn't realize that nearly every fund they owned was heavily invested in dot.com and tech companies. They confused owning a large number of mutual funds with being diversified in the market. They might have just as well owned a few dot.com companies directly.

Own the Entire World, Starting with the United States

Now that I've spent all this time showing what we all seem to do wrong, let's get back to building a second-grader portfolio. There is one way, and only one way, to build a stock portfolio that is guaranteed to beat the average dollar invested. For the U.S. stock market, that one way is to buy the entire market in proportion to the value of each company.

There are a couple of ways to do this. You could go out and buy shares of thousands of different companies listed on U.S. stock exchanges, making sure that you are buying far more GE and Exxon than you are a small, locally based company. This may work for Bill Gates and even all those overachievers on the Forbes 400 list, but if you don't have a few billion dollars to play with, there is a better way to go. For those of us not so fortunate to have all of the money in the world, the practical solution would be the index fund we discussed earlier in this chapter. Many investors associate indexing with the S&P 500 index, which is essentially composed of the largest 500 companies in the United States.

For reasons we will discuss in Chapter 3, Wall Street likes to use the S&P 500 as a surrogate for the U.S. market. I happen to think it's not a particularly good index fund and don't recommend it for my clients. While it's a good way to own a large chunk of the U.S. stock market, it misses out on thousands of smaller U.S. companies. It also suffers from what I call the *Google effect.* On March 23, 2006, Standard & Poor's announced Google was being admitted to the S&P 500 index. It made the announcement after the stock market had closed that day. Now, just because the stock market is closed doesn't mean people can't trade stocks. Wall Street has invented something called *after-hours trading,* where people can buy and sell stocks after the market closes. In after-hours trading, Google went up a whopping 7.3 percent that night.[4] That's because investors knew that all of the many large S&P 500 index funds had to go out and buy Google pronto. Demand for the stock drove the price higher.

Thus, it's reasonable to assume that any new entrant to the S&P 500 index will come at an inflated price since the S&P 500 index fund will buy only after the price has gone up. Conversely, any company being booted from the S&P 500 index will likely suffer a price decline before the S&P 500 index fund dumps it.

There are some pretty easy ways to build the rest of the U.S. stock market around the S&P 500 fund, but I'm a strong believer in the *KISS principle* (keep it simple, stupid) and the wisdom of Occam's Razor, a principle that states that (all other things being equal) the simplest solution is the best.

In constructing a U.S. portfolio, take a look at Exhibit 2.1. This is how Morningstar breaks down the roughly 5,000 or so U.S. companies with their famous "style box."

On the left, we have what are known as *market capitalization measures.* Large-cap companies are the Exxons and GEs of the

Exhibit 2.1 Morningstar Style Box™ and Allocation of Stocks

Morningstar allocation of the stock market.

23%	24%	23%	70% Large
7%	6%	7%	20% Mid
3%	4%	3%	10% Small
33% Value	34% Core	33% Growth	

country, and these are generally the companies in the S&P 500. The mid- and small-cap companies are the thousands of other companies most of us have never heard of.

The numbers represent the percentage of the stock market value represented in each category. Roughly 70 percent of the value of U.S. companies is comprised of large cap, 20 percent mid-cap, and 10 percent small cap.

On the top are what is known as *value, core,* or *growth* companies. While there are many technical measures to classify a type of stock, value companies are those that are beaten up and trading at lower valuations. Warren Buffett is probably the best-known value investor. Growth companies, on the other hand, are the darlings of Wall Street and trade at very hefty premiums. Core companies are in between value and growth. Morningstar pretty much divides the three classifications by a third each.

Using this box to build a diversified U.S. portfolio, we could come up with the following:

23%	Large-Cap Value Index
24%	Large-Cap Blend Index
23%	Large-Cap Growth Index
7%	Mid-Cap Value Index
6%	Mid-Cap Blend Index
7%	Mid-Cap Growth Index
3%	Small-Cap Value Index
4%	Small-Cap Blend Index
3%	Small-Cap Growth Index

While this would indeed be a wonderfully diversified portfolio, some of the smaller index funds can get rather expensive. Also, because a total portfolio needs to keep these same allocations over time, we would need to rebalance every so often as one fund grew faster than another. I'm going to go out on a limb and say that Kevin wouldn't want to keep calculating each of these and doing the constant rebalancing. Luckily, he doesn't need to.

A much better way to buy the U.S. stock market is to own a total U.S. stock index fund. It not only owns the S&P 500 stocks, it also owns the thousands of smaller corporations that make up the rest of the U.S. stock market. It's free from the Google effect in that it would have owned Google both before the announcement of its admission to the S&P 500, as well as afterward.

I explain to people that owning one total U.S. stock index fund is the most diversified U.S. stock portfolio one can have, irrespective of the number of funds one has. That's right: It's impossible to add a second U.S. stock fund that would improve diversification as it could only begin to overweight one of the style boxes or industry sectors.

Thus, it always owns the entire market in each style box in each sector and is never out of balance. It's the essence of simplicity. By owning different classes, this fund is the ultimate in *modern portfolio theory,* which optimizes expected returns for the given amount of risk one wants to take. For example, because small-cap value stocks don't always move in perfect tandem with large-cap growth stocks, owning the whole market reduces the total risk of owning only one asset class.

It not only comes with the lowest fees around, it provides yet another bonus: extreme tax efficiency. As it happens, the average mutual fund is constantly buying and selling the stocks in its portfolio, which causes it to realize any capital gains it may have earned on those stocks. The fund manager can ignore the tax implications of his frequent trading, but you can't—you have to pay taxes on gains from those sales. It's bad enough if your mutual fund goes down in price, but getting a 1099 from a mutual fund company showing a capital gain and leaving you with a tax bill is just adding insult to injury. A total U.S. stock fund is far less likely to generate a capital gain, because it doesn't actually buy and sell stocks. It could technically happen if people withdrew money from these funds in droves, but is far less likely than a Wall Street actively managed mutual fund or stock portfolio.

There are a couple of different ways to index. The traditional index fund is a mutual fund, in which an investment company pools funds from investors and then invests those funds. A new way of index investing was introduced about 14 years ago, known as *exchange traded funds* (ETFs). I could write a whole separate book on the technical differences and similarities between index mutual funds and ETFs, but basically the differences between the two are really structural. An index fund in either form offers the same benefits. Exhibit 2.2 is a comparison of one index mutual fund to one exchange traded fund on the items that matter to the investor.

Exhibit 2.2 Comparison of Index Mutual Fund to Exchange Traded Fund

Name	**Vanguard Total Stock Market Index Mutual Fund (VTSMX)**	**Vanguard Total U.S. Stock Market Exchange Traded Fund (VTI)**
Stocks held	Thousands of U.S. companies according to their total stock value.	Thousands of U.S. companies according to their total stock value.
Costs to buy and sell	None, if bought directly through Vanguard.	Brokerage commissions similar to buying a stock, e.g., $7 per trade.
Ongoing annual fees	0.15%	0.07%
Bottom line	Because no commissions are charged on each purchase, this form is superior for the investor in accumulation mode who is purchasing small amounts every month or so.	Because this form has lower annual expenses, this form is superior for investors who are making a lump sum investment.

The bottom line is that it matters less whether you own an index mutual fund or an index ETF. What does matter is that you must own the entire market in one simple index fund that provides the:

- Highest level of diversification
- Lowest costs
- Highest tax-efficiency

Exhibit 2.3 offers a few good ways to own the entire U.S. stock market that meet all of these criteria.

I challenge anyone on Wall Street to show me a more diversified U.S. portfolio than this. The funds in Exhibit 2.3 are the most diversified U.S. holdings bar none, and are designed to give you higher returns, pay less taxes, and lower your risk. What's not to love? Okay, I'm getting a little emotional here—I just need a moment to collect myself.

Exhibit 2.3 Total U.S. Index Funds

Total U.S. Stock Market Index Choices	**Symbol**	**Expense Ratio**	**Investment Minimum**
Vanguard Total Stock Market Index Fund ETF	VTI	0.07%	1 share
Fidelity Spartan Total U.S. Market Index Mutual Fund	FSTMX	0.10%	$10,000
Vanguard Total Stock Market Index Mutual Fund	VTSMX	0.5%	$3,000
iShares Dow Jones U.S. Index ETF	IYY	0.20%	1 share
State Street Spider Dow Jones Total U.S. Market ETF	TMW	0.20%	1 share

Next, Own the Rest of the World

Some of the most patriotic Americans you are likely to find are in the primary grades. Unfettered by partisan politics, Kevin unequivocally believes that the United States is the greatest country in the world. Yet great though we are, we are only one of many countries.

I grabbed our world globe from the bookcase, sat down at the kitchen table, and spun it around a few times. I asked Kevin which country was going to have the hottest stock market next year. Looking at me quizzically, he said, "I don't know."

I confused him even more by telling him that was the right answer. "The right answer is not knowing the answer?" Kevin asked.

"No," I said, "the right answer is *knowing* you don't know the answer."

Kevin's gaze was silently saying "*Ooookkaaay,* Dad. No more caffeine for you." But in fact, Kevin doesn't know, I don't know, and neither do any of the gurus on Wall Street. What separates Kevin and me from the Wall Street whiz kids is that we actually *know* that we don't know what next year's hot market is.

The Easter basket analogy of spreading your eggs out is just as relevant when talking about owning the rest of the world. And second-grader arithmetic and diversification works overseas in exactly the same manner as it does in the United States.

We could certainly use the Morningstar nine-style box and make sure that we are in every sector in every country, and could easily build an international index portfolio with dozens of funds. But there's a simpler way to own the entire rest of the world with one fund with the lowest costs and highest tax-efficiency: an international index fund. Exhibit 2.4 lists some of the international indexes available to investors.

As much as I hate to admit it, none of these are as good as owning the entire world. iShares MSCI EAFE index and the Fidelity Spartan Total International index fund own only Europe,

Exhibit 2.4 International Index Funds

Total International Index Choices	Symbol	Expense Ratio	Minimum Investment
Fidelity Spartan Total International Stock Market Index Mutual Fund	FSIIX	0.10%	$10,000
Vanguard FTSE All World Excluding U.S. ETF	VEU	0.25%	1 share
Vanguard Total International Stock Market Fund	VGTSX	0.32%	$3,000
iShares MSCI EAFE Index Fund ETF	EFA	0.32%	1 share
State Street Spider All World Excluding U.S. ETF	CWI	0.35%	1 share
Vanguard FTSE All World Excluding U.S. Mutual Fund	VFWIX	0.40%	$3,000

Australia, and the Far East and miss out on emerging markets and Canada. The Vanguard Total International Stock Market Fund misses out on Canada, which somehow got left out as the indexes were defined. The Vanguard Total International Stock Market Fund also has a tax disadvantage, because the IRS won't let any foreign tax credit be passed through to the holder. Vanguard is addressing this issue by restructuring this fund to directly own investments. Still, all of these funds are good ways to own the rest of the world. Kevin and I chose the Vanguard Total International Index Fund, because it was the broadest index with the lowest costs at the time. Today, the Vanguard and State Street FTSE All World indexes are superior in that they include both emerging markets and Canada. I do think the Vanguard FTSE All World Ex-U.S. (VEU) is superior here, because it has the lowest costs and avoids any front-end charges.

Also, unlike the total U.S. stock index fund, these foreign index funds don't own small-cap stocks. Thus, there is a little

Exhibit 2.5 Small-Cap International Stock Funds

Total International Index Choices	Symbol	Expense Ratio	Minimum Investment
iShares MSCI EAFE Small Cap Index	SCZ	0.40%	1 share
iShares FTSE Developed Small Cap Ex-North America Index Fund	IFSM	0.50%	1 share
SPDR S&P International Small Cap	GWX	0.59%	1 share

hole in Kevin's portfolio. I'd like the international portion of his stock portfolio to include about 10 percent small-cap stocks. Since it's a small portion of his entire portfolio, we skipped it. Recently, however, new ETFs have been started to fill this hole. Some of these are listed in Exhibit 2.5.

In full disclosure (imagine this from a financial planner), these are very small and brand-new ETFs and they are in a part of the market that is likely to be very volatile. Kevin isn't the only one who hasn't yet put these in his portfolio; I haven't either. I'm just getting ready to stick my toe in the water.

Own the Entire Bond Market

The final chapter of my diversification lesson to Kevin was that, in addition to buying the companies, we could lend money to the companies. In fact, we could even lend money to the U.S. government.

I explained to Kevin that you have a lot less risk when you lend money to others, because they have to pay it back before they can spend it for their own stuff.[5] And because we have less risk, we get a bit lower return.

By this time, Kevin was getting a clue that the first investing option I told him about was usually the less desirable one. And in this instance, the first option was lending money at 6 percent and paying someone 1 to 2 percent for nothing. It also meant placing all of his eggs in one basket. He figured a second choice

Exhibit 2.6 Total Bond Index Funds

Total Bond Index Choices	Symbol	Expense Ratio	Minimum Investment
Vanguard Total Bond Market Index ETF	BND	0.11%	1 share
Vanguard Total Bond Market Index Mutual Fund	VBMFX	0.19%	$3,000
iShares Lehman Aggregate Bond ETF	AGG	0.20%	1 share

was coming, and it was. This choice would allow him to do his patriotic duty and lend to the U.S. government, or lend money to Enron or United Airlines and still be in good shape eggwise.

Kevin guessed, as you probably did too, that there was an index fund that could do all that as well. Exhibit 2.6 shows some good ways to lend money by buying broad bond index funds.

For those of you thinking there is a fourth lesson here, to lend money to companies worldwide, I chose to pass on it. My reasoning is that the bond portfolio should be the cushion and make us more comfortable by lowering the swings in our portfolio. Because foreign currency swings are so big, international bonds can swing more widely and, thus, don't provide the cushion we are looking for. I'll discuss this further in Chapter 7.

I can't say Kevin looked all that heartbroken about skipping the lesson on foreign bonds. Or, if he was, he consoled himself by hopping on his bike and cruising the neighborhood.

A True Story of Diversification

A client came to me with a portfolio full of expensive funds that had underperformed the market. Her employer's retirement account was particularly troublesome. It was brimming with pricey mutual funds that seemed only to be financially enriching the broker. Now the option of

(Continues)

(Continued)

quitting her job and rolling these funds into a low-cost IRA did not seem all that advisable, so I searched for another option.

That option involved mustering all the tact I could (which, let's just say, isn't all that much), and approaching the broker on the account. I suggested that he could charge my client 0.5 percent per year and offer her low-cost index funds. Much to my surprise, he agreed and the client bought a total U.S. stock index fund and a total international stock index fund. I explained to the client that when she left her employer, she could own these same funds without paying the broker that extra 0.5 percent per year.

Everyone seemed happy and I basked in the afterglow of one of my few successful negotiations with an expensive broker. Unfortunately, I wasn't glowing for long. About six months later, the broker called me in a panic. With anxiety dripping from every word, he said we needed to change the client's accounts immediately. When I inquired why, the broker explained he had just been written up by his firm's compliance department. Since the stated reason for a compliance department to exist is to protect the client, I naively deduced that something must have been done that wasn't in the client's best interests.

The broker went on to explain that the firm's investment policy was that no more than a third of a client's portfolio could be in any one security. He stated that owning only two securities was considered too risky for the firm. Feeling relieved, I went on to explain that a total U.S. stock index fund owns thousands of individual stocks in proportion to the U.S. stock market. In fact, I explained, owning this one fund was the most diversified an investor could be in the U.S. stock market. Even owning hundreds of stocks and mutual funds would actually be less diversified. I assured him the same was true for the international stock index fund.

There, problem solved, or so I thought. Having presented this sound logic, I felt confident that the broker would say he'd go back to his compliance department. Instead, the broker again shocked me by repeating that we still needed to sell some of these funds and buy a third fund, because firm policy dictated that, to reduce risk, no more than a third of one's portfolio could be in any one security. That's when I asked him, "According to your firm, which portfolio would be considered more diversified?"

- Three very small individual company stocks that trade very infrequently, also known as micro-cap bulletin board stocks? The total value of all of the shares could be about $40 million.
- Two index fund securities that own thousands of individual stocks around the world? The total value of all of the shares of these stocks is about $40 trillion, which happens to be a million times that of the three individual companies mentioned above.

Without hesitation, the broker responded that the three tiny companies would meet the firm's diversification standards and solve this compliance issue. My brain was actually cramping from the illogic. At that moment, I realized Kevin's understanding of diversification was far superior to this firm's, which held billions of dollars in clients' assets and employed hundreds of sophisticated MBAs like me. I wanted to scream; so I did.

The Final Lesson: Think Long-Term

Kevin now understood that diversification meant spreading his eggs out across the world. But there was one more lesson on diversification we needed to have. That is to diversify over time.

I started out by explaining that stocks don't always earn 10 percent *every* year, and even bonds don't always pay what we think they will. I told him that his stocks could fall by 35 percent in one year. "I thought you said my stocks would grow at 10 percent per year," Kevin responded anxiously. It was at this point that my wife Patty's "mom radar" went up. She gave me that look that said, "What did you do to make Kevin so upset?"

I urged Kevin to turn that frown upside down and reminded him that what I actually said was that stocks have grown by 10 percent per year, but not every year. Sometimes they can lose 35 percent, or they can gain even more than that during a year. "Well," Kevin suggested, "what if I just invest in a good year and take the money out in a bad year?" Before I answered his question, I had to admit, ironically, that's exactly what most of us adults try and fail to do.

If only it were that easy. If only we all began each new year knowing whether it will be a good or bad one for the market. But, like our exercise with the globe, I reminded Kevin that there were two types of investors when it comes to predicting next year's stock market:

1. Those who don't know.
2. Those who don't know they don't know.

He thought that sounded funny, and it probably would be if the second category of investor wasn't always stirring the pot. I explained to Kevin that we didn't need to worry about the seesawing of how much we make or lose year to year. We could spread our eggs not only all over the world, but also over a long period of time. That way, it wouldn't matter so much if we picked a bad year. Over a 20-year period, the stock market has always bested inflation. So if we invest now and diversify over a long period of time, the market isn't so risky. In fact, it can be a veritable snooze.

"So I can still get my money to grow by nearly ten percent per year?" Kevin asked. That boy of mine is pretty single minded (can't imagine where he gets it).

I assured him that he could, or awfully close to it, and Kevin was back on board.

Finally, We Build the Portfolio

Kevin seemed more jazzed about the stock index funds than the bonds, probably because of the higher returns. Not a problem; since an 8-year-old generally has a long investment horizon, he's on the right track.

I tried to direct him toward just a little of the bond index fund, since it provides a bit of safety. I told Kevin that investing only 10 percent in bond index funds could really cushion a bad year and lessen his losses. He remained unconvinced.

"What if you could do that and it wouldn't take much from your overall long-term return?" I asked Kevin.[6]

"If I can get almost the same amount, then ten percent is okay," said Kevin. "But what do we do with the other ninety percent? Should we just split it in halves and put half in the United States and half in the world?"

That's not a bad idea, but let's examine this a bit more.

The U.S. stock market comprises roughly 45 percent of the world stock market value. The more technical way to say this is that the United States is 45 percent of the world market capitalization, whereas international stocks comprise about 55 percent.

Now, if we apply the rule where we spread our eggs as widely as possible, then, I explained to Kevin, we need to divide the remaining 90 percent the way the U.S. and world markets' capitalization is divided.

The lesson was almost done, which is good, because so was Kevin's attention span. Explaining any more about investing on that day, at that time, was going to be like herding cats. Yet we were so close to completion, and I still wanted to convey to Kevin that he is going to spend most of his money in U.S. dollars, rather than euros or yen or any other currency. I even wanted to go into the fact that American companies have operations internationally and international companies have operations in the United States.

Instead, I just said, "What do you think about keeping most of our eggs here in the United States?"

Remembering that he had three funds, and *really* wanting to go out and play, Kevin applied basic arithmetic and said, "How about putting two-thirds here in the United States and one-third in the world?" Our portfolio was done, and Kevin was out the door before I could say, "Great job!"

The *second-grader portfolio* was born:

10%	Total Bond Market Index Fund
30%	Total International Stock Index Fund
60%	Total U.S. Stock Index Fund.

Exhibit 2.7 Second-Grader Funds versus S&P 500 Index Annualized Returns

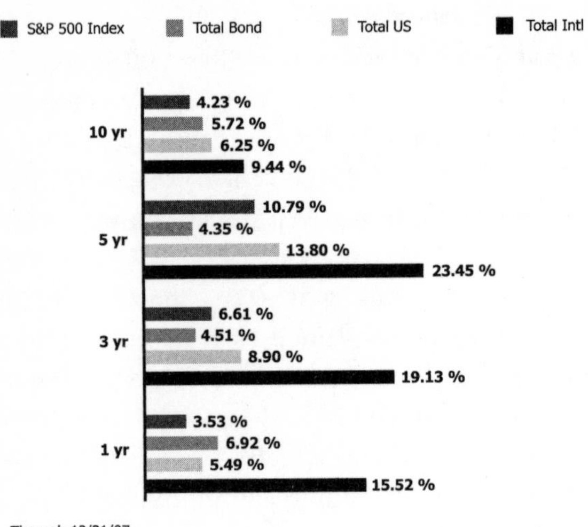

Later in the book, we will explore alternatives to the pure second-grader portfolio, but, for now, let's look at the performance of the basic three second-grader funds. I can tell you that very few professional managers have done as well as the second-grader portfolio, and these returns aren't bad considering they occurred during an Internet bubble, subprime mortgage crises, the price of oil quadrupling, and the U.S. budget deficit skyrocketing. The performance of each of these three funds has soundly beat the S&P 500 index for nearly every period of time, as shown in Exhibit 2.7.

Is The Second-Grader Portfolio Right for You?

The quick answer to this question is that it probably isn't. But a variation of this portfolio may be perfect for you. Kevin has a very long investment horizon and can stay in the stock market for at least a couple of decades. My investment horizon is much shorter, and yours is likely to be shorter as well. Thus, the amount of bonds may need to be drastically increased from the 10 percent level Kevin decided to invest in.

The amount of risk you need (and are willing) to take can vary greatly from Kevin's portfolio. But you can do it with different mixes of the exact same funds and be just as diversified. Exhibit 2.8 offers some examples.

Exhibit 2.9 shows the historic performance of the three second-grader weightings. Because the returns of bonds have been similar to stocks over the past 10 years, the long-run performance of these three weightings has also been similar. I don't think that this is likely to happen over the next 10 years, as equities tend to outperform bonds for the long run. Exhibit 2.9 shows the historic performance of the three second-grader weightings for the period ending 12/31/07.

We will further explore what portfolio is right for you in Chapter 9, when I discuss building the portfolio. The point is

Exhibit 2.8 Second-Grader Portfolio for Different Levels of Risk

	High Risk	Medium Risk	Low Risk
Total Bond Index	10.0%	40.0%	70.0%
Total U.S. Stock Index	60.0%	40.0%	20.0%
Total International Stock Index	30.0%	20.0%	10.0%
	100.0%	100.0%	100.0%

Exhibit 2.9 Annual Performance of Second-Grader Portfolio

	1 yr	3 yr	5 yr	10 yr
Second-Grader High Risk	8.64%	11.77%	16.32%	7.25%
Second-Grader Medium Risk	8.07%	9.46%	12.87%	6.76%
Second-Grader Low Risk	7.49%	7.04%	8.94%	6.25%

that this simple second-grader portfolio will work for any level of risk. All you need to do is adjust the level of risk you are willing to take.

A Couple of Alternatives

Most readers will think the funds I listed have very low expense ratios. After all, these funds have costs as low as 0.07 percent annually. While this is a tiny fraction of the average mutual fund, U.S. government employees have access to investment funds averaging an astonishing 0.015 percent, or nearly five times lower! The government's retirement vehicle, called the Thrift Savings Plan (TSP), offers funds with these ultra-low costs as well as with brilliant simplicity to build a second-grader-like portfolio.

Congress may be okay with allowing other employers to offer complex and expensive 401(k) plans, but they seem to have the best 401(k) plan in the nation for themselves. If you are a U.S. federal employee, go to www.federalnewsradio.com and look for advice Mike Causey offers on building a second-grader portfolio.

A second alternative to the retail funds I've mentioned can be found in the DFA fund family. This fund family recognizes the research showing that smaller companies and value companies (the lower-left box of the Morningstar Style Box) tend to outperform larger companies and growth companies (the upper-right side), over the long-term. This is commonly known as the *Fama and French Three Factor Model,* after its developers, Eugene Fama and Ken French.

I happen to be a fan of DFA funds, but there are a couple of things to be aware of. First, the higher historic returns from small-cap value investing are not a free lunch. They are compensation for taking greater risk. Thus you don't want to put all of your eggs in small-cap value stocks, representing only about 3 percent of the stock market. DFA does have more broad funds as well. Also, DFA funds generally can be purchased only through financial advisors. While DFA itself generally has low fees, advisors can add significantly to the total costs being paid.

The bottom line is that DFA can also be used to build a broad global portfolio with a little titling toward small-cap and value stocks. Just remember that it's the total costs that count, so, if you go this route, take into account the fees your advisor charges. Also remember, while small-cap and value stocks have far outpaced the market over the past 10 years, there is no guarantee they will continue to do so.

Applying the Golden Rule of Diversification

At the end of the day, it's not the number of mutual funds or ETFs you own that make a diversified portfolio; it's the number of securities *within* each of these funds that ultimately determine diversification. With only three index mutual funds, we can own many thousands of securities that own the whole world.

Wall Street portfolios will be more complex, but in no way will they be more diversified. The Wall Street portfolio in essence tries to defy simple arithmetic and ends up with:

- Higher expenses
- Higher taxes
- More risk
- Lower returns

Owning only three index funds can truly spread your eggs over the entire global basket and make competing with Wall Street such an unfair game—for them. If you own the entire market, not only are you mathematically certain to beat Wall Street, you will do it with less risk. It's the ultimate in the lesson we all learned as kids: "Don't put all of your eggs in one basket!"

Chapter 3

The Advantage of Having Wall Street Marketing Blinders (and Where Can I Get Some?)

"I Don't Watch Cramer; I Like SpongeBob"

Kevin built his portfolio with the widest diversification and lowest costs, and now all that was left to do was—nothing. Upon realizing this, he got that "I just got 100 percent on my spelling test" look, but was still puzzled by something.

"Why do people pay so much to invest when they get nothing for it?"

That was an easy question, and I thought I had an easy answer:

- Investors have no idea that they are paying 2 percent or more.
- Investors think they are getting something in return for the fee they pay.

When I saw Kevin's confused gaze, I realized that my easy answer did not exactly clear things up. Luckily, we had just come from a friend's birthday party where a magician was the main act. I tried another approach.

"Remember how the magician pulled the rabbit out of the hat?" I asked.[1]

"Sure," said Kevin. This particular magician had been making the rounds at his friends' birthday parties, and by now he understood that it was an illusion. It's simply a trick, but for the life of me I still don't know how he did it.

"Do you think some of the kids believed it was real?" I asked.

"Well, maybe the smaller kids," he replied. I explained that when it comes to investing, Wall Street is a master magician that can create illusions like a lion appearing out of thin air.

Kevin looked at me in amazement and asked, "But it's not real, right?"

"Of course not," I assured him.

I took Kevin over to the TV and channel-surfed until we landed on some financial shows. Channel after channel showed portfolio manager after portfolio manager bragging about their accomplishments and making new forecasts. Each one made it very clear that following his advice was the one path to getting rich.

"What's the S&P 500?" Kevin asked. "Why does everyone say they beat it?"

I explained to Kevin that these were the master magicians I told him about, and that these shows all created an illusion.

"Oh, like pro wrestling?" asked Kevin. I had to admit, that wasn't a bad analogy.

"Sorry Dad," Kevin said, "but this is kind of boring." Away he went to the sitting room, where he plopped on the couch and turned on *SpongeBob SquarePants.*

The Common Sense of the SpongeBob Strategy

I particularly like comparing watching *SpongeBob SquarePants* to Cramer's *Mad Money.* One's a cartoon character that never knows what's going on in the market, and the other is a human cartoon character who rants about buying and selling and encourages others to engage in foolishness. Kevin at least knows the *SpongeBob* characters aren't real, which is more than I can say for some of Cramer's followers betting their nest egg. This, of course, is my opinion, though I can safely say that Jim Cramer's endorsement won't appear on the jacket of this book.

At this point in his life, Kevin still believed in Santa Claus and his ability to cover the earth in one night in his reindeer-driven sleigh delivering presents to every good boy and girl. This was easier for him to believe than something as ridiculous as $10 - 2 = 12$.

Yet, we adults do it all of the time. We do it because we want to believe it, and we do it because Wall Street has a much larger marketing budget than Santa Claus. Their well-funded illusions make Santa Claus and the Tooth Fairy look like amateurs.

While I admit I have no idea how the magician pulls the rabbit out of the hat, I've been studying the Wall Street illusionists for some time. And like any top-hatted magician who refuses to reveal his secrets, Wall Street is just as unwilling to reveal its secrets—but *I* will. Here are three tricks every illusion is based on.

Trick #1: Don't Tell the Investors How Much They Are Paying

It is quite common in my financial planning practice to have people come to me without a clue of how much they are paying for their portfolio. Many actually think they aren't paying anything. Others know they are paying their money manager something like 1 percent of their assets, but think that's all they are paying.

Wall Street's power has allowed money managers to be very successful in limiting the transparency they must provide to the consumer. The consumer can be paying the following fees without realizing it:

- Fees to their advisor in the form of commissions, paid as a percentage of assets or even on an hourly basis.
- Front-end or back-end loads to buy and sell a mutual fund or insurance investment.
- Ongoing fees known as the *expense ratio.* The expense ratios of many funds often include expensive marketing fees, though Wall Street prefers to use the more obscure term *12b-1 fees* for these expenses.
- Ongoing hidden fees no one has to disclose, such as brokerage fees and buy/ask spreads incurred by mutual funds that churn the stocks in their portfolio.

All of these fees can really add up; by some estimates, the average mutual fund can cost the investor as much as 3.3 percent annually.[2] Whether it's actually 2 percent or 4 percent isn't the issue. The issue is that these expenses are detracting from our returns and we don't even know it.

Everything we eat these days comes with "the box." The box clearly reveals how many calories and fat grams, and how much cholesterol, and just about anything else you'd want to know about, is contained in our food. As educated consumers, we now expect access to that information. Yet, when it comes to investing your nest egg, it would be difficult for even Stephen Hawking to figure it out. Jeffrey J. Diermeier, CFA, president and CEO of the CFA Institute, recently stated,

> Fees should be so transparent that paying them should be like writing a check out of a checkbook. When I

write a check, I look at all the other items I am writing checks for and ask myself, is this a good expenditure of my money? Without such transparency, investors have no idea how to make good choices.[3]

We investors have no clue as to what we are paying for our investments, and even worse, there is no easy way to find out. We keenly feel the pain whenever the price of gasoline goes up by a nickel, but we keep blindly paying the Wall Street machine, unaware of its true costs.

Trick #2: Tell the Investors They Are Beating the Market

I was talking to a money manager who was proudly telling me that this was yet another year he beat the market. Since he knew I was an avid believer in low-cost diversified index funds, he just had to get that dig in. So, I asked, "How do you define the market?"

I got the answer that I always hear: the S&P 500 index. "That's the accepted measure," he quickly replied.

I *wanted* to tell him that Kevin's simple index fund portfolio earned 2.5 times the return of the S&P 500 index. I *wanted* to say that this was yet another year when Kevin's portfolio solidly trounced the S&P 500 index. (See Exhibit 3.1.) I didn't, because I want those money managers to keep bragging. I'll freely admit my selfish motivation: I never know when I'll need more material for another book.

Exhibit 3.1 The Illusion of Beating the Market Applied to Owning the Market

	Kevin's Return	S&P 500 Index	Kevin's Outperformance
2006	17.73%	13.62%	4.11%
2007	8.64%	3.53%	5.11%

By defining *the market* as the raw S&P 500 index, Kevin's portfolio beat the market in a big way. According to Wall Street logic and accepted measures of the market, Kevin's own-the-whole-market strategy triumphs. Of course, this conclusion is illogical, but no more so than what professionals do every day by comparing your return to something wrongly called *the market*.

At this point, you may be asking how a set of three index funds designed to get the return of the markets, less some small costs, can beat the S&P 500 index? There are two parts to this trick.

First, as mentioned in Chapter 2, for all practical purposes the S&P 500 stocks are essentially the largest 500 companies based in the United States. The index doesn't include the thousands of mid-sized and small companies based in the United States or any of the foreign-based companies. Thus, the first part of this trick is to compare apples to oranges: the least risky stocks (those in the S&P 500) to the manager's portfolio.

The second (and by far most powerful) part of the trick is that the S&P 500 index conveniently strips out the dividend portion of the return. Let me illustrate by using a single fictitious stock, let's call it Wall Street Marketing Corporation, and give it a ticker symbol of WSMC.[4] Let's say that WSMC starts the year trading at $100.00. Over the next year, WSMC pays out a $2.00 dividend and the price of the stock goes up by $8.00 to $108.00. It's pretty easy to see that an investor who held WSMC made a total of $10.00 for the year. The investor received a $2.00 dividend and the price of the stock went up by $8.00. Thus, the $10.00 return based on a $100.00 starting price yields a 10 percent return.

The same thing happens with the 500 companies listed in the S&P. On average, they pay a dividend of 2 percent, so your total return will be 2 percent paid to you in the form of dividends, plus whatever the increase in the price of the index will be. If the price of the index increased by 8 percent and you earned a 2 percent dividend, your total return would again be 10 percent. But what if your money manager shows you that he got you an 8.5 percent return, and beat the S&P 500 by 0.5 percent?

Not only did the money manager compare his global portfolio to the least risky stocks, he also compared his total return to only a part of the S&P 500 return. That's like comparing apples to *parts* of oranges. So, the Wall Street trick is to define the market as something they all can beat. I guess if you set the bar low enough, it's easy to beat. In other words, if you can't raise the bridge, lower the water.

The Illusionist's Assistant: The Media

Much of the media are also key allies to this grand illusion. Everyone loves reading a story or viewing a video on how to get rich. So, it's only reasonable that the media give the public what they are looking for. It doesn't really matter much whether the information is inaccurate or misleading.

I once read an Associated Press column in the local paper at the end of the year with the usual drivel about how the average mutual fund beat the market, using the raw S&P 500 index as the market. I emailed and called the reporter to explain that he was comparing global returns to a portion of the S&P 500 returns, noting that his conclusion could wrongly lead people to dump low-cost index funds and feed more money to Wall Street. He was polite, seemed appreciative, and appeared to understand my point.

Even though he didn't publish a correction, I felt good about the exchange—until the next year, when this same reporter did the same comparison. I'm sure you're familiar with a popular definition of insanity as doing the same thing over and over again and expecting different results. Perhaps I had finally crossed that line between tenacity and insanity, because I wrote the reporter just before the close of the following year, and asked him if we was going to *again* do the story comparing the total returns of global portfolios to partial returns of the S&P 500.

At least the story didn't appear *that* year.

Have you been told you beat the market? Look for some of these Wall Street tricks to create the illusion:

- Have you seen any data supporting this, or are your advisors expecting you to take their word for it?
- If there is data, is it accurate?
- Are they comparing your returns to the right indexes?
- Did they strip the index of its dividend?
- Are they including new money invested during the year as part of your returns?
- Have they adjusted your returns for taxes?

Trick #3: Sound as if You Know What You Are Talking About

I love reading Wall Street propaganda. It sounds so impressive and comforting. Take the following:

> Many of our individual and institutional clients come to us with the same pressing need: a disciplined process to integrate their resources, commitments, and risk parameters into a unified financial blueprint. Typically, this begins with comprehensive analysis and guidance on portfolio construction, including a focus on the tax impact of each asset class with the goal of optimizing after-tax returns. It may include complex issues relating to a family business and monetization strategies to facilitate liquidity and diversification for concentrated holdings. And where business interests are closely tied to family wealth, we may blend corporate and personal financial strategies.[5]

Sounds good, right? It's seductive, and I certainly understand why many investors would entrust their nest egg to someone with such a "disciplined process." This statement, however, came from the web site of Bear Stearns the day *after* it was announced it was being bailed out by JP Morgan in a U.S.

government-backed effort to avoid bankruptcy and risk a collapse of global financial markets. *Ouch*. This was the firm that in 2005 was rated #1 for the best sales force by *Institutional Investor.*

Now let's take a look at the most admired securities firm in 2007 according to *Fortune* magazine. In 2008, it released a company report highlighting its $4.2 billion in 2007 net income and noted it produced this record profit "without relaxing our vigilance on risk." This firm increased its total long-term capital to $145.6 billion from $100.4 billion the previous year. The total value of its common stock was over $35 billion.[6] Only months after releasing this glowing report, Lehman Brothers' vigilance on risk resulted in their filing for bankruptcy. Yes, Kevin's net worth is greater than the combined value of Lehman Brothers common stock, which is, of course, zero.

It's easy to kick someone when they are down, and I feel awful for the employees and shareholders of Bear Stearns, Lehman Brothers, and all of the once great giants. Nonetheless, it provides an excellent example of just how easy it is to talk a great game. And impressive talk is a lot easier to achieve than impressive performance.

I'd rather see Wall Street give an honest explanation of why the market does what it does each day. For instance, as the stock market opened on April 1, 2008, recession was all over the news, along with:

- The Bear Stearns government bailout.
- UBS writing down $19 billion; CEO resigns.
- U.S. financial crisis worsening.

How did the stock market react to all of this bleak news in the first trading day of the new quarter? It went up more than 3.5 percent, in what was the best start to the second quarter in many decades. Why? One pundit put forward the following argument:

> Wall Street began the second quarter with a big rally Tuesday as investors rushed back into stocks amid optimism that the worst of the credit crisis has passed and that the economy is faring better than expected.[7]

However, Stephen Dubner wrote on the Freakonomics web site:

> Stocks Surge, Reasons Unknown; May Be Nothing More Than the Random Fluctuation of a Complex System

April 1 demonstrated nothing more than the stock market's utter unpredictability. It does this to us daily, not just on April Fools' day. In fact, the only thing associated with the market's daily ups and downs that is predictable is the pontifications of analysts who attempt to explain the often unexplainable.

Marketing: The Auto Industry versus Wall Street

To see how masterful Wall Street is in selling using these three tricks, let's compare their marketing to that of the automobile industry. I once thought the auto industry defined effective marketing. They successfully took a mode of transportation and sold it as part of our personality. Most of us believe that "we are what we drive." Are you a Mercedes or a Ford?

It turns out that owning the Ford is much more likely to make you a millionaire, but I am digressing here. The point I'm trying to make is that when you buy that luxury or sports car, you at least know what you are paying for it. There is a sticker right on the window that shows the price. That same sticker also shows how much we are likely to pay each year for gasoline. It looks something like Exhibit 3.2 and shows us how much pain we can expect when filling up the gas tank.

Wall Street, however, is far cleverer than the auto industry, not to mention less regulated. They provide no sticker for

Exhibit 3.2 EPA Fuel Economy Label

We know roughly the cost of running our car before we buy it.

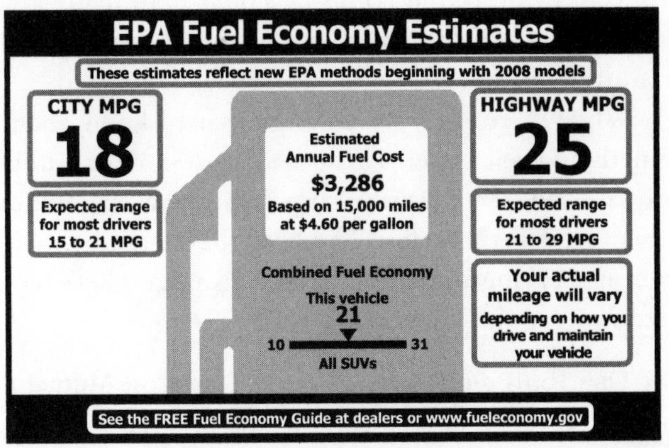

Exhibit 3.3 Alpha Bet Mutual Fund Disclosure

We have little idea how much our investments cost us.

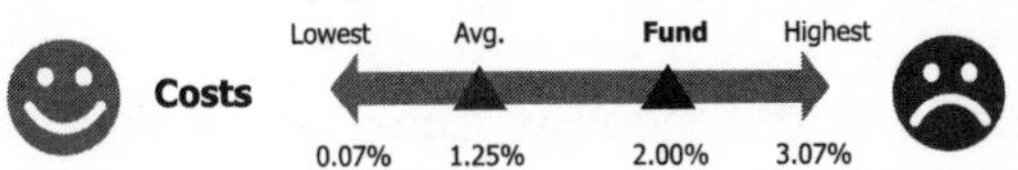

For every $1,000 invested, you will pay $200 over 10 years.

your investments, so you'll have no idea what you are paying for and, thanks to the master illusionists, no idea of what you are getting. Can you imagine Wall Street giving a mutual fund disclosure like that in Exhibit 3.3? That might involve your actually knowing what you are likely to be paying, and just what you have, without poring through the thick prospectus.

I remember a rumor circulating years ago that someone had invented an engine that could power a car on only tap water. The rumor went that an oil company bought the formula and then hid it from the rest of the world to protect its profits. Obviously, the company could have made a far bigger profit by patenting this engine, so I'd bet pretty heavily this rumor was false.

While there isn't such an engine that I know about, there is something even better! If you had a $200,000 portfolio, would you save more by lowering costs from the average or by getting a car that ran on water? Think of the pleasure we would get from not paying those outrageous gas prices. Let's look at how much you could save with each:

Car That Runs on Water:	**Low-Cost Mutual Fund:**
15,000 miles ÷ 21 miles/gallon × $4.60/gallon = $3,286	1.75% savings × $200,000 = $3,500

As much as it hurts every time we see what that gas pump takes from our wallets, we would save more by reducing what Wall Street takes from us!

Why We Keep Playing a Game We Can't Win

When Kevin played the claw game, he fed the machine quarters and got nothing back in the way of stuffed animals. The excitement was gradually replaced with the knowledge that all he was doing was losing his money. After a few weeks, he learned it was a loser's game and he stopped.

However, we adults keep playing the Wall Street version of the claw game. Why? Because we don't get the feedback that Kevin received. Kevin saw his quarters go into the machine and nothing come out. That was plenty of information for him to make an assessment.

We investors don't have the benefit of seeing our $350 billion[8] being fed to Wall Street and are only being told that we are paying something. For whatever reason, it seems to be fine with our financial market regulators that we don't have a right to know what we are paying in plain and simple English. I don't get it, but I'm a financial planner, not a political analyst. (And forget about trying to explain politics to Kevin, because that would involve my understanding it first.)

Get Real

Parents who take a young child shopping with them know the power of candy. If he stays next to Mom or Dad, doesn't touch anything, and doesn't have a fit in the toy aisle, there will be the reward at checkout. The reward comes at checkout because that's where the evil retailers *put* all the candy. While at the checkout counter one day, Kevin noticed that the price of his favorite candy had gone up. When he asked me why, I explained to him that the company that makes the candy sometimes has to increase the amount of money it pays to its employees, and has to pay more for all of the stuff that goes into the candy. That means they have to raise the prices to us, which is known as *inflation*. "But now I can't buy as much with my allowance," Kevin noted. I was fearful this would lead him to ask for a raise, but that didn't come yet.

The same goes for investing. First, we need to *get real* in terms of inflation-adjusted earnings. If we earn 8 percent and the prices of the things we buy go up by 10 percent, we are worse off. Let's look at an investor's returns in real, inflation-adjusted returns, and compare the actual return with perceived returns.

Let's say that a portfolio of 60 percent stocks and 40 percent bonds will earn a long-run return of about 8 percent (10 percent for stocks and 5 percent for bonds). Further, let's say that inflation will be at about 3.5[9] percent. This means that the portfolio will earn a real return of about 4.5 percent (8.0 percent less 3.5 percent). Now let's assume they give up 2 percent in fees, rather than the 3 percent average that some estimate. The result: a 2.5 percent net real return for our investor. Next, let's look at how much goes out to taxes. Naturally, the IRS taxes us on before-inflation-adjusted dollars. By my estimates, the portfolio will be drained another 2 percent by taxes and thus produce a real return of a measly 0.5 percent.[10] For those following along, yes, they are barely keeping up with inflation.

If this were made explicitly clear to us, we would all have the *aha!* moment that Kevin had with the claw arcade machine and realize that we were being ripped off. But, by some accounts, average investors think that they are beating the market by 3 percent.[11] If that's the case, there is a vast reality disconnect here, in which investors who believe they are earning a real return of 7.5 percent are in reality earning only a meager 0.5 percent return above inflation (Exhibit 3.4).

To illustrate this to people, I ask them if they've ever had any of their friends come back from Las Vegas thinking they have won money. The usual response is something like "All the time!" And when I ask people I know who are coming back from Las Vegas the same question, I typically get about two-thirds of them claiming they won money.

In reality, we know they don't build those billion-dollar casinos to give money away. In fact, one of my favorite sayings is "The two types of people that come back from Las Vegas are losers and liars." Of course, they're really not liars if they genuinely believe they've won money. The point is that we should never underestimate our ability to believe what we want to believe.

Exhibit 3.4 Actual Investor Return versus Perception

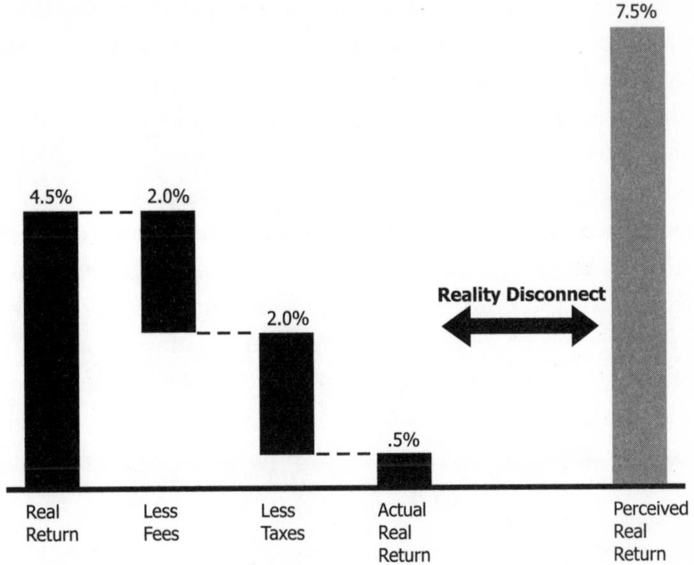

When it comes to games of chance, Las Vegas has nothing on Wall Street. When we go to Las Vegas, which I love to do, by the way, we know how much we started with and how much we are coming back with. We know how much we are betting and when we've won and when we've lost. This is exactly the same information Kevin received when he was playing the claw game.

However, the Wall Street game is much harder to figure out. We have no idea of whether we're winning, losing, or breaking even—because we are constantly being told that we are paying less, and doing better, than we really are. Oh, and there are always those money managers of ours who are *all* above average and beating "the market." The depressing result is that we keep transferring our wealth to Wall Street and the IRS.

The Wall Street Game and the Sad Results

If logic holds, then the more expensive the mutual funds, the poorer the performance when compared to the lower cost funds. Yet, there are plenty of examples where expensive funds have performed well for a good period of time. So, I embarked on my own research on the impact of costs on performance.

Exhibit 3.5 shows the Morningstar domestic equity performance of the 20 top mutual fund families compared to the disclosed expense ratio. Remember that the expense ratio is only one of the costs of a mutual fund, but that's all I had to work with. The Morningstar performance rating is on a one-to-five-star rating, with five being the highest performance.

Exhibit 3.5 Cost versus Performance for the 20 Largest Mutual Fund Families

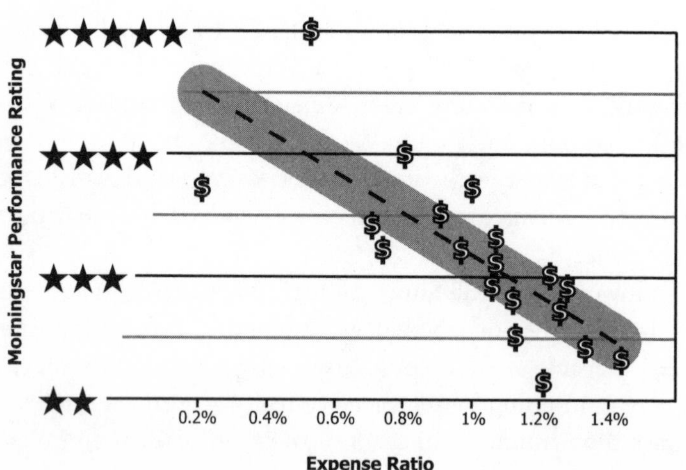

SOURCE: Morningstar.

A three-star fund is about average and the average mutual fund typically underperforms the market, if one defines the market correctly.

The "$" represent each of the fund families and the heavy line shows the trend. In what will probably not be the biggest *aha!* in this book, the lower-fee funds perform better than the highest-fee funds. In fact, just the stated costs were able to explain about 59 percent of the fund family's performance. This confirms Jack Bogle's famous statement, "You get what you don't pay for."

Now the downward trend is important, but perhaps the most important part of this chart is the mutual fund families in the lower right-hand side—you know, the ones that have expense ratios greater than 1 percent and have performance below three stars.

If we could all grasp, metaphorically speaking, that the stuffed animal is not coming out of the arcade machine, and act as logically as Kevin did with this knowledge, we would stop investing in those funds and they would go out of business. We don't, because they have marketing might in creating the illusions. It turns out that lower-performing fund families typically pay advisors to go out and sell them. A recent study entitled "Assessing the Costs and Benefits of Brokers in the Mutual Fund Industry"[12] found that those funds sold by advisors underperformed those that were bought directly by the consumer. And in the knock-me-over-with-a-feather category, those advisors were merely selling the funds they could make the most money on.

So, the lower-performing fund families do what any good illusionist would do. They find their four- or five-star funds from among their dozens of dogs, and promote the heck out of them. When they no longer perform well, they find the few that performed well recently, and do the same. With dozens of funds, it's a virtual mathematical certainty that at least a couple will do well.

The Story of Headline News: Active Beats Passive!

Remember the so-called debate between active versus passive investing we discussed in Chapter 1? Well, it's really not so much of a debate, because we know that the arithmetic must hold that the average dollar invested in the market can only get the market return, before costs and taxes. However, if investors understood this, they'd stop feeding Wall Street, so it's very important to the Wall Street illusion to keep this debate alive.

Whenever I see a study showing that active investing beats the market, I chuckle a bit. And it's usually pretty obvious how they are trying to prove that $10 - 2 = 12$. A few years ago, however, I read a fascinating paper in the *Journal of Financial Planning,* the periodical of the Financial Planning Association (FPA), which is largely composed of certified financial planners. This paper[13] showed that the average active mutual fund had in fact beaten the market by 2 percent annually, and had done so with less risk. It claimed that all previous measures of performance were inaccurate and that Jack Bogle, the man who brought indexing to the general public, was exposed, much like the emperor wearing no clothes. The paper produced empirical results with some pretty impressive charts and graphs. In fact, the *Journal* was so impressed that they gave it an award.

I kept thinking to myself, how could the average mutual fund be above average anywhere outside of Lake Wobegon? The math just didn't seem to add up. As luck would have it, I was at a conference where the study's author was speaking and arranged to discuss it with him. I asked him the Lake Wobegone question and he noted that this wasn't part of the study. When I indicated that I'd be interested in seeing the data that he used to reach his revolutionary conclusions, the author told me the data was confidential.

It turned out that the source was a well-respected firm, Lipper Analytics, and that the data used by the author was not in the least confidential. The author's methodology was fatally flawed, and would have required knowledge of future mutual fund performance for 30 years into the future. It would be the equivalent of my saying I could beat the index if I had a working crystal ball that would allow me to buy a lot of the funds that did well and very few of those that didn't. True, yet completely useless.

Rarely has a study had such a documented flaw. Chalk it up to my naïveté, but I was pretty sure this would be easy to have corrected. Instead, the *Journal* was unresponsive. Only after much hounding on my part did the *Journal* finally agree to undertake an official "challenge" and form an "Appeals Committee." I felt vindicated, but as I mentioned earlier, I'm a bit on the naïve side. It seemed to me that all they had to do was call the analyst at Lipper (and I had kindly provided the telephone number) to verify the methodology flaw. Instead, the committee upheld the paper's conclusion, with one member stating, "A two percent annualized difference is headline news in the active/passive debate."[14] They did toss me a bone in the form of encouragement to write a paper to continue the debate. Yeah, thanks, I'll get right on that.

Finally, I bluntly asked the FPA's Board why they pounded on claiming the consumer has a right to accurate information, and yet went to such great lengths to avoid making a call to Lipper to see whether they had published fatally flawed headline news that could harm the consumer. They eventually made that call and retracted that award-winning paper.[15]

The moral to this story is not that the Financial Planning Association or certified financial planners are evil. Actually, I think my fellow CFPs are among the best in the profession. The point I'm trying to make is that even the good guys of the profession must continue the active/passive debate to leave open the question as to whether $10 - 2 = 8$. If the good guys are creating this illusion, can you imagine what the rest of Wall Street and the media are doing?

The Secret of Kevin's Immunity to the Wall Street Illusion

When it comes to investing, Kevin has some huge advantages over you and me in regard to the Wall Street Illusion.

First, *Kevin doesn't get solicitations from helpers.*

I get about five calls, emails, and letters a day from helpers willing to make a fortune for me. Some of these strangers call to tell me about an oil well that is guaranteed to turn a tidy profit for me. Others send me fancy engraved invitations to my favorite hotel, the Broadmoor, offering me a free prime rib dinner and unlimited cocktails. Am I the only one who wonders why, if these investments are really so good, their marketers would need to spend a small fortune peddling them? I believe in the kindness of strangers, but these strangers are only slightly more reputable than the Nigerian prince who keeps sending me emails on how to turn my $10,000 into millions.

While we get these offers from strangers on a daily basis, thankfully Kevin is still part of a demographic that is flying under the radar. Because he is a minor, it would be illegal to solicit to him, so he has immunity from Wall Street and other helpers claiming they will make us rich. Besides, he doesn't even have an email address yet.

Second, *Kevin doesn't watch Wall Street shows.*

To the best of my knowledge, the only time Kevin has watched *Mad Money* with Jim Cramer or any other financial show was the time I made him. As you may recall, he quickly got bored and moved to another TV to watch *SpongeBob SquarePants.* Kevin hasn't had to buy into the illusion of beating the stock market, and he doesn't much care about the active-versus-passive debate. He finds ways of entertaining himself that are far less costly than buying into the Wall Street illusion.

Applying the SpongeBob Golden Rule

My advice is to reach deep down inside and find a way to resist the allure of Wall Street. Start caring about how much you are paying and how you are performing. For all the smoke and mirrors and fancy charts, the Wall Street wizards are unlikely to beat Kevin's portfolio, no matter how much they appeal to our emotions. Work toward lifting the curtain to see how much your portfolio is costing you and exactly how it is really performing.

Find out how much you are paying for your portfolio.

If I were an investment yoga instructor, I would advise my students to use this mantra: *costs matter, costs matter, costs matter.* Close your eyes, take a deep, cleansing breath, and let that phrase sink in. Keep in mind that we are probably paying more for someone to invest our money than we are to fill up our gas tank. We wouldn't go to a gas station that wouldn't tell us the price we were paying, so I recommend you find out how much of your portfolio is being drained by costs.

If you are using advisors, ask them how much you are paying in total fees and get them to put it in writing. Make sure they understand that you are not asking them how much they are making off you; it's far more important to know the total fees you are paying. If you are doing the investing yourself, the news is probably better on the expense front, though you may still be paying through the nose. I'd love to be able to give you a simple way to figure out all of your costs, but there really isn't one. There is virtually no transparency in the costs you pay. I *could* write a very technical book on how to calculate the following costs which you *may* be paying:

- Advisory fees
- Annual operating expenses including 12b-1 (marketing) fees

- Sales fees, often known as *loads*
- Soft-dollar costs
- Hidden fund-turnover costs

It's difficult to see the whole picture on fees, but going to Morningstar.com is a good place to start. There you can find the annual expense ratio and front- or back-end loads. If your fund has turnover of more than 50 percent annually, a safe assumption is that your soft-dollar and hidden turnover costs are also high.

Find out how your portfolio is really performing.

While finding the first part of the illusion—fees—is more complicated than splitting an atom, the second part of the illusion is a bit simpler to figure out. At the risk of seeming immodest, my advice is to benchmark your portfolio's performance to the second-grader portfolio. *Benchmarking* is a fancy name for comparing, which in this instance means your portfolio's return against the second grader's. Before you do this, I want to warn you that some pretty famous stock investors have come out on the short end of the comparison to Kevin's portfolio.

In fact, Paul Farrell, of Dow Jones MarketWatch, compared Kevin's portfolio against one of the world's best-known Wall Street experts. Jim Cramer, of the famed *Mad Money* show, has been picking stocks on TV for quite some time. I personally find him very entertaining. How has he done? In a column entitled "*Boo-Yah* This!," Paul Farrell calculated a return of 14.9 percent for Cramer, whereas the second-grader portfolio earned 19.5 percent.[16] Admittedly, Kevin would not be as entertaining on TV; just more profitable.

Marketing can easily create the illusion of award-winning performance and reality has virtually nothing to do with actual performance. I tell my prospective clients they can either have the psychological comfort of believing they are beating the market, and take at face value that they are earning above-market returns, or benchmark against the second-grader portfolio.

To benchmark your portfolio, take all of your investments and categorize them in one of three types of investments:

1. *Bonds:* individual bonds, bond funds, CDs, money markets, etc.
2. *U.S. stocks:* individual U.S. stocks or U.S. stock funds
3. *International stocks:* individual international stocks or international stock funds

If you are not sure of certain types of investments, I suggest you go to www.Morningstar.com and type in the security. Then click on "portfolio" to see what it's invested in. For example, the Dodge and Cox Balanced Fund (DODBX), as of the time of this writing, was invested as follows:

34%	Bonds (32% bonds and 2% cash)
53%	U.S. Stocks
13%	International Stocks
100%	

If your portfolio was allocated like Kevin's (60 percent U.S. equity, 30 percent international equity, and 10 percent bonds), your numbers would resemble Exhibit 3.6.

You can do this for your own portfolio by comparing your results to those of the second-grader portfolio, filling in your allocations for the ones used by Kevin, and doing some math. See Exhibit 3.7.

I regularly do this benchmarking for new clients, and I can count on one hand the number of times that their existing portfolio beat the second-grader portfolio, adjusted for their weighting in asset classes.

The bottom line is that not only are most of us lagging far behind the risk-adjusted version of the second-grader portfolio, we are also paying far more in taxes than this portfolio incurs.

Exhibit 3.6 Simple Benchmarking Calculation

2007 Return	Your Allocation	2007 Return		Calculation
Vanguard Total Stock Index (VTSMX)	60%	5.49%	=	3.29%
Vanguard Total International Stock Index (VGTSX)	30%	15.52%	=	4.66%
Vanguard Total Bond Market Index (VBMFX)	10%	6.92%	=	0.69%
	100%			8.64%

2006 Return	Your Allocation	2006 Return		Calculation
Vanguard Total Stock Market Index (VTSMX)	60%	15.51%	=	9.31%
Vanguard Total International Stock Index (VGTSX)	30%	26.64%	=	7.99%
Vanguard Total Bond Market Index (VBMFX)	10%	4.27%	=	0.43%
	100%			17.73%

Exhibit 3.7 Simple Benchmarking Calculation

2007 Benchmark— Your Portfolio	Your Allocation	2007 Return		Calculation
Vanguard Total Stock Market Index (VTSMX)		5.49%	=	
Vanguard Total International Stock Index (VGTSX)		15.52%	=	
Vanguard Total Bond Market Index (VBMFX)		6.92%	=	
	100%			____

2006 Benchmark— Your Portfolio	Your Allocation	2006 Return		Calculation
Vanguard Total Stock Market Index (VTSMX)		15.51%	=	
Vanguard Total International Stock Index (VGTSX)		26.64%	=	
Vanguard Total Bond Market Index (VBMFX)		4.27%	=	
	100%			____

Applying the Golden Rule of Marketing Immunity

Perception and *reality* are two very different things. As an adult,[17] I don't have the advantage that Kevin has. I can merely apply two lessons that get us a bit closer to achieving some of the marketing immunity of a second grader:

First, *people aren't out to make you rich.*

I get the daily calls offering "guaranteed" fortune-makers in a specific sector, or the more subtle promise of award-winning performance. Kevin doesn't.

There has never been a shortage of ways Wall Street has devised to separate you from your money, and new ways are being devised every day. Ask yourself why they would be contacting you. Wouldn't institutions be beating down the door to get in on these investments if the returns were real?

Determine which is most important to you: (1) feeling good about your investments, knowing that a sophisticated money manager is at the helm who gives you the perception that you are earning above-market returns, or (2) buying the entire market via a second-grader portfolio, and being guaranteed that each of your asset classes will beat the average dollar invested by those same sophisticated money managers.

Second, *simplify your investing.*

I have to admit that my portfolio is far more complex than Kevin's, mainly because of mistakes I've made in the past and the tax consequences I'd have in trying to correct them. I can't just give blind advice to clients and readers to sell everything and build the second-grader portfolio. There could be huge tax bills, including the dreaded Alternative Minimum Tax (AMT), that could hit you hard.

The best advice I can give is to *simplify* and get closer to a second-grader portfolio with whatever allocations are right for you. You can start in your tax-deferred IRAs and 401(k)s, as well as tax-free vehicles such as Roth's. You can buy and sell securities within each of these accounts without incurring a tax bill, as long as you leave the funds in that vehicle.

Always remember that what you aren't paying to someone or something else, such as fees and taxes, goes to you and will get you to your financial goals much sooner. It's your choice: Do you want to fund the financial goals of those on Wall Street, or do you want to fund your own goals? After showing Kevin pictures of the yachts near Wall Street, he for one has decided they're rich enough already.

Chapter 4

Adults Behaving Badly

"Don't Act Silly When Something Is Important"

Occasionally, I work from home. In his comings and goings, Kevin noticed that I looked at the stock market several times a day. He asked why I looked so often, and when I turned to give him an explanation—I realized that I didn't have one. I had absolutely no idea whatsoever why I looked so often. It's not like I ever trade based on what the market is doing, and my long-run investment strategy is certainly not dependent on constantly telling clients what the market was doing today.

I was stumped. This should have been an *aha!* moment for me, but apparently, not so much. Can you guess how many times I looked at the market today? In spite of Kevin shining a light on my irrational behavior, I realized that knowing we behave irrationally and changing that irrational behavior are two very different issues.

On another occasion, I was on vacation with my family in Las Vegas. As we walked through the casino, I thought I would get a little gambling in before we called it a night. I asked Kevin and my wife, Patty, to give me a few minutes to gamble at the blackjack table. They both watched by the gift shop, since Kevin was underage and couldn't be standing in the casino. With Kevin watching, I wanted to show off my gambling skills. I had memorized the blackjack odds table and felt I knew when to stay, hit, double down, or split. Naturally, I lost four hands in a row.

As I sheepishly made my way over to the gift shop, Patty gave me that "don't quit your day job" look. Kevin, on the other hand, looked quite perplexed. "That was really silly, Dad," he said. "You just threw money away."

Aha!

This chapter offers the twist of Kevin giving his dad a lesson in fiscal responsibility: Don't do silly stuff with money.

The Common Sense of Good Money Behavior

When I went to the Kellogg Graduate School of Management at Northwestern University way back in the early 1980s, I learned the standard economic theory of supply and demand. That is to say, we humans act in rational ways in order to maximize our wealth. I bought it hook, line, and sinker.

Lately, I can't figure out why I was so dumb to believe it for the next couple of decades.

A fellow by the name of Daniel Kahneman come along and won a Nobel Prize in economics back in 2002 for his work in what became known as *behavioral finance.* What I found amazing was that Daniel Kahneman won the Nobel Prize in economics even though his degree was in *psychology.* Tying the two together, Dr. Kahneman showed just how irrationally we all act with our money. He also pointed out that we are not very good at learning from our mistakes, which means, in keeping with author George Santayana's famous warning: "Those who cannot remember the past are condemned to repeat it."[1]

Jason Zweig's book, *Your Money and Your Brain,* explains that we really have two brains. Our *reflexive* brain gets the first crack at decision making, and is essentially based on intuition or how we feel. Our *reflective* brain, on the other hand, is more logical. The problem is that we usually don't know which part of the brain is at the helm when we make a decision.

Today, when I ask people what money means to them, I get descriptive words, such as:

- Freedom
- Security
- Survival
- Enjoyment

You take words like *freedom* and *survival* and you're likely conjure up all sorts of emotions that will, of course, result in otional responses. How could I have ever believed we were ical, rational beings?

Dr. Kahneman and Mr. Zweig both wrote about the same g that Kevin realized I was doing: acting silly with my money. s smart enough to realize my behavior at the blackjack table rrational, but human enough that I couldn't stop it.

n the coming pages, we are going to explore some silly investing behaviors, including some more from yours truly.

Fear and Greed—Buying High and Selling Low

The word *value* is defined as "benefits minus costs." That is to say, if we derive more pleasure from something than what it will cost, we make a logical, rational decision to buy it. To avoid being too technical, I explained this concept to Kevin using the metaphor of buying his favorite candy. The candy had a price hike in the store, and by still buying it he derived less value from it.

$$\text{Value} = \text{Benefits} - \text{Costs}$$

Next, I asked Kevin whether he would want to buy more of something if what he wanted went *down* in price. "Of course!" said Kevin. Then I asked, if it went up in price, whether it would make him less likely to buy. He said something in the affirmative, but I could tell by his glazed-over expression that he was hoping I would get to the point soon. The point was, as I explained to Kevin, that we adults act just the opposite when it comes to the stock market.

"No way!" he exclaimed.

I countered with my best *Wayne's World* imitation and said, "Yes way," and then pulled out a chart of the last bull and bear market cycle (Exhibit 4.1). In it, you can see that the stock market more than doubled in price between 1996 and March 2000. I explained to Kevin that investors' reactions to the price doubling were to buy more stock at record levels.

About two-and-a-half years later, the stock market had a half-off sale in October 2002 from the pricing in March 2000. I explained to Kevin that one could essentially buy a piece of every stock in America for half-off what it once cost.

"Wow—did everyone go out and buy some?" asked Kevin. Not exactly; in fact, that was when more people were selling the stock they had. Can you imagine if people shopped the way we invest? A sale like the one in Exhibit 4.2 might even confuse Santa Claus.

Exhibit 4.1 Vanguard Total U.S. Stock Index Fund (VTSMX)

Fear and greed make us time the market to buy high and sell low.

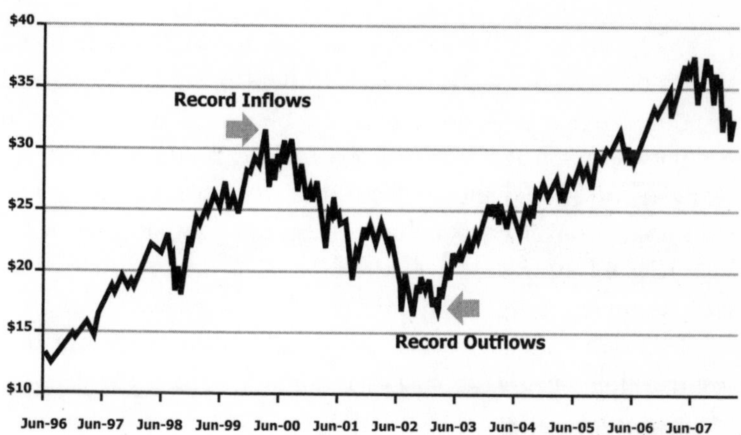

Exhibit 4.2 If Only Retailers Had It as Easy as Wall Street

Imagine if we shopped the way we invest.

We've Doubled Our Price Sale

Customers rush in to buy all they can.

50% Off Sale

Customers rush to return all they bought at the first sale—returning at the lower price.

It was easy to explain to him how buying high and selling low was not going to make his money grow, even if he did it in index funds. It was much harder, however, to explain to him *why* adults behave in this manner. Money isn't as tangible to

Kevin as it is to you and me. He didn't look at his money from Grandma as something he could actually go out and *spend.* He is spared the dilemma of whether to buy that shiny new car with a windfall or put it toward retirement since, obviously, Kevin's not old enough to drive and how many second graders are thinking about retirement?

To us adults, though, who *are* thinking about retirement, seeing the size of our nest egg shrink is painful. The human response to pain is to do whatever is perceived as necessary to get it to stop, or at the very least mask it. So the solution for many is to sell and move everything to cash and—*voila!* The pain stops. Conversely, watching our stocks go up is pleasurable. The human response to pleasure is to want more, which translates to buying more stocks after they have done well.

In looking at financial pleasure and pain, it turns out that losing a dollar causes about twice as much pain as the pleasure we get from making a dollar. This is known as *loss aversion.* That is why staying in the market when it is down is the most difficult behavior to master.

This human response to pain and pleasure has served us well since primitive times and works in most parts of our lives today. When it comes to investing, however, it fails us miserably. We all know that most mutual funds greatly underperform the appropriate index, but did you know that the average investor underperforms the average mutual fund by another 1.5 percent per year? A study by Geoffrey Friesen and Travis Sapp in the *Journal of Banking and Finance* showed that investor decisions in the timing of equities cost us a bit more than this.[2]

Behold the Brilliance of Hindsight

I know it's not good form for the author to brag, but I just have to share this: I have the ability to forecast the past with uncanny accuracy! With a little creative license, I can also make you think I knew it was going to happen. In the interest of full disclosure, what I'm not so good at is forecasting the future—especially in the short term.

When I ask people if it was obvious that the NASDAQ was overvalued at over 5000 back in March 2000, roughly 95 percent of people say *yes.* After all, how could a "new economy" really exist where cash flow didn't matter? Looking back, we can all see the folly that brought about the dot-com bust, but it wasn't so obvious back then. In actuality, if anywhere close to 95 percent of us knew the valuations were ridiculous, we would have sold and the value would never have approached that 5000 level.

There is no shortage of TV pundits out there explaining why the market did what it did today. And if we had the ability to turn the clock back (or TIVO), we would probably hear them using the same explanation for why it did just the opposite the day before. I've heard many a talking head explain that the market losses today were a result of higher oil prices. It seems a reasonable assertion until you consider that crude oil was at about $23 a barrel at the bottom of the market in 2002, and was pushing $100 in 2007, at the height of the five-year bull market.

So, the next time someone is explaining why something happened, remember that brilliance in hindsight doesn't translate into brilliance in predicting the future.

Forget Everything You've Heard About Optimism

I often illustrate this pitfall to people by posing a question about NCAA college basketball. What percent of the time does the collegiate basketball team down at halftime eventually come back to win in the second half? The typical response is somewhere between 30 percent and 50 percent of the time, though I often hear over 50 percent.[3] Now, you may be asking what the heck this has to do with investing, but give me a little slack here, and I'll explain shortly.

Being the exciting kind of guy that I am, I once counted thousands of college basketball scores over a season and (drum roll, please) the answer was just a tad under 20 percent. The purpose of this counting was to show statistically that we humans are generally optimistic, and my tedious counting ended up in a *Wall Street Journal* column written by the renowned Jonathan Clements.

When you think about it logically, the same team that got behind in the first half is the same team that shows up in the second half. They aren't two independent events, like a coin flip. So it makes perfect sense that only a small percentage of teams would come back to win.

Then why do we consistently overestimate the odds? In my opinion, it's due to the media—both news and Hollywood. We get fed a very unrepresentative sample. Which do you think makes a better story?

- The University of Colorado basketball team was down by 15 at halftime and came back to win in double overtime, or
- The University of Colorado basketball team was down by 15 at halftime and lost the game by 28 points.

The answer is obvious: The spectacular comeback is the one that makes the news. It's exciting and emotional. Who wants to see a rerun of a blowout? It's just not newsworthy.

The same thing goes for Hollywood. Have you ever seen a movie where the sports team starts out as the worst in the league and finishes just as poorly? Or how about the movie where the worst player on the team remains on the bench the entire season? The Dream Makers have our number and oblige us by cranking out movies where the team goes from worst to first and the worst athlete makes the winning play. They know we love an underdog and want to see him or her triumph at the end. Thanks for sticking with me on this sports detour; now I'm ready to make the leap to investing. The next time you read a business periodical or are watching TV, pay careful attention to any advertisement for a mutual fund. Everyone lists some sort of rating that shows the fund is *way* above average. For example, they may say this fund has a five-star Morningstar rating or handily beats the Lipper average.[4]

I confirmed with Morningstar that in fact there are just as many one- and two-star funds as there are four- and five-star funds. In fact, both have exactly 32.5 percent. I'll bet you the price of this book that you won't see a one- or two-star fund being advertised. Can you imagine an advertisement looking something like Exhibit 4.3?

Our tendency toward optimism is a good thing. It makes us more fun to be around, and even makes us heal faster and live longer. So, for the record, I'm all for optimism, with one little

Exhibit 4.3 A Mutual Fund Ad You'll Never See

Mutual fund companies advertise only their winners.

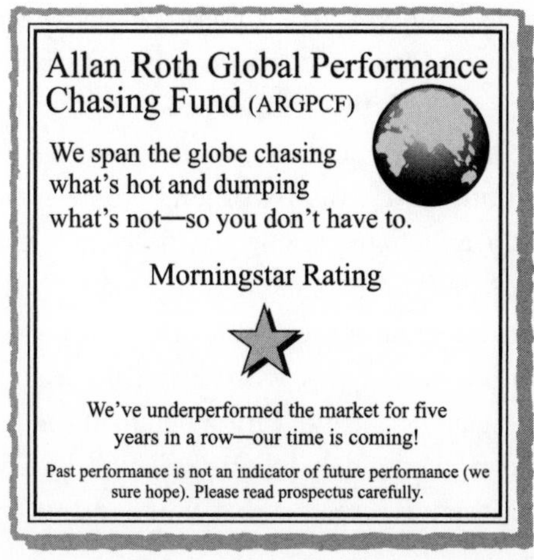

exception—in investing. In this particular arena, the optimism of thinking our odds are much better than they really are can hurt us badly.

The Curse of Overconfidence

When I give talks and am looking for a little audience participation, I ask for a show of hands of people who identify themselves as below-average drivers. I get very few people raising their hands. This is consistent with a study in Sweden that found that 80 percent of drivers believed they were in the top 30 percent of drivers.[5] In fact, we tend to think we are above average in almost everything we consider to be important.

Since investing is important, and because it's so easy to find those investments that have above-average ratings, it stands to reason that we would be overconfident when it comes to investing. Why wouldn't we be able to pick winning stocks or stock funds? At the very least, we can pick an advisor that can pick the right funds, can't we? Well as Kevin knows, we will be successful only when 10 − 2 = 12.

I haven't gotten around to this particular lesson yet, but some day I'll need to tell Kevin that, when it comes to investing, our male gender is at a disadvantage. Males tend to suffer more from overconfidence than our counterparts. We men tend to think we can pick the winners and sell the losers. This causes us to trade more frequently, which results in earning nearly 1 percent annually less than women.[6] There is no question that, on average, my female clients tend to get indexing and the arithmetic of investing faster than my male clients.

This isn't a formal survey, but can you guess which professionals I've found to be the very worst investors? Hands down, it's *physicians.* Don't get me wrong; I'm generalizing here and have some great physician clients that I hope still will be clients when they read this, yet there is a reason that they tend to be poor investors.

They tend to be very confident. To get that *Dr.* before your name, and the *MD* after, you have to beat some odds and make it through medical school and residency. To the best of my knowledge, they are among the very few professionals in America who are addressed by a title. You can bet that your four-year degree or MBA is not going to get *Bachelor* or *Master* before *your* name. In many ways, physicians are treated as professional royalty. And although they have every right to be confident about their intelligence and knowledge, it just doesn't translate to being smarter than the market. Exercising that excessive confidence can be costly.

Data Mining to Find Patterns in Randomness

It turns out that it is within the human condition to hate randomness. Many studies show that we like to be in control, or at least think we are.[7] That's why someone on a "hot streak" at the craps table believes his next roll of the dice is somehow related to his last one. Left to our own devices, we will find patterns for everything. This phenomenon is known as *data mining.*

Take a look at the two series of coin flips shown in Exhibit 4.4. Which series do you think has a higher probability of occurring?

Exhibit 4.4 Which Coin Toss Has a Higher Likelihood of Occurring?

It's human nature to find patterns in randomness.

Most people know that the odds are *exactly the same*—each has a 1-in-32 chance in occurring. The first series, however, seems to me more of a pattern. And when we see a pattern, we tend to think that this pattern will continue. Some of the patterns related to the stock market that we have found in the past include:

- *Dogs of the Dow*—buying the highest paying dividend stocks of the Dow.
- *August and September market slump*—bad months to own stocks.
- *Presidential election cycle*—the market performs badly after a presidential election.
- *Skirt length*—short skirt lengths predict bull markets.

They all seemed to form some pattern in our minds that, if they continued, could make us a bunch of money. Of course, they didn't continue. Why? If you search thousands of pieces of data and compare them to the stock market, you are going to find some that only by chance happen to give you some correlation (patterns) and offer no predicative information at all.

My particular favorite investing pattern was the "Dogs of the Dow" investing method. The Dogs were known as the highest-dividend-yielding stocks in the Dow Jones Industrial Index. *Highest yield* meant most beaten-up stock price; hence the name *Dogs.* It was discovered that owning these Dogs that no one else wanted actually resulted in stock performance that far exceeded the market. People following this fad called themselves *contrarians,* but as I hopelessly tried to explain, following a fad is just the opposite of being a contrarian. It didn't work going forward, as most herd-type behavior does underperform the market. John Allen Paulos, in his book, *A Mathematician Plays the Stock Market,* reveals the highest correlation ever found to the S&P 500: It was the amount of butter produced in the country of Bangladesh. Apparently, between 1983 and 1993, when butter production was up 1 percent, the S&P 500 was up

2 percent the next year. Conversely, if butter production was down 10 percent, you could predict the S&P 500 would be down 20 percent.[8] If you're wondering why it wasn't as popular as Dogs of the Dow, it is because no one could figure out why it would be so predictive. As silly as our behavior can get when it comes to investing, it's comforting to know we have our limits.

Data mining is used more prominently in technical analysis, which uses charts of past performance to predict the short-term performance of stocks, mutual funds and ETFs, and even the stock market as a whole. There are some really impressive-looking charts with cups and handles and stochastic oscillators to show momentum. The ironic thing about technical analysis is that the logical conclusion would be that, if they actually worked, they would no longer work in the future. When enough people have a tool to predict stock prices, it ceases to be of any use since the stock would have already reacted to this knowledge.

Anchoring to Something Meaningless

Anchoring is a mental bias where we set a reference price of a stock even though it may no longer be relevant. An example of anchoring is illustrated here:

> You are gifted $10,000 and decide to invest equally in two stocks:
>
> 1. You invest $5,000 in ABC by buying 100 shares at $50 a share.
> 2. You invest $5,000 in XYZ by buying 100 shares, also at $50 a share.
>
> A few months later, ABC is trading at $75 a share while XYZ is trading at only $25. If you were then told that you had to sell one of the stocks, which one would you sell?

The vast majority of people would sell the shares of ABC at $75 a share. The common reason is that they can lock in a gain and then wait for the shares of XYZ to come back to $50. In this decision, we anchored the purchase price of both companies at $50 a share.

I'm here to tell you that the correct economic decision is to sell the shares of XYZ and take the loss on your taxes instead of selling ABC and reporting a gain. If you don't agree, that's okay. I also have a hard time convincing CPAs that their client benefits more by *harvesting the tax loss.* Most of us, however, can't get past anchoring to the purchase price.

Before you think I'm holier than thou, and would never make such an emotional mistake, let me fess up to a couple of things. First of all, I have a little portfolio I call my gambling portfolio. That's right, I'm capable of thinking outside the index box. The same impulse that draws me to the blackjack tables in Las Vegas also draws me to have a little fun with my investing.

While I generally don't sell my winners because I don't want to pay the taxes, I did have one stock that went up several thousand percent. I convinced myself that I had to sell it as it was growing too large for my portfolio. Ultimately, I decided to sell about half of it. I had all sorts of justification in my mind, but the bottom line was that I bought a mental option by anchoring it at the price I sold the shares. If the stock price went down, I could pat myself on the back and feel good that I had unloaded half of it. And if the stock price went up, I could also pat myself on the back and feel good that I held on to half. Either way it went, I was getting patted on the back for my "brilliance." And, yes, I was aware that this was completely irrational logic—but, *dang,* it just felt good.

Anchoring, by the way, is very important to Wall Street. Wall Street would anchor Kevin's three-fund index portfolio against the performance of the three corresponding indexes and correctly say his portfolio has absolutely no chance of beating those indexes. That's how they get you to buy into the myth that indexing is guaranteed to be mediocre. If they actually anchored indexing against the average investor or, better yet, their clients' average return, they would be out of business.

Framing a Problem to Confidently Reach a Wrong Conclusion

How we tend to think of a problem impacts the choice that we make. Consider the following:

> Sue is very quiet and has little interest in other people. She rarely goes out. She is, however, very helpful and knowledgeable. She has a degree in English literature.

Is Sue a sales rep or a librarian?

Most of us confidently reply that Sue is a librarian. After all, doesn't she fit the personality of a librarian? Well, in all likelihood, Sue is a sales rep. There are roughly 1,000 sales reps for every librarian, so the odds are tipped in favor of Sue being the sales rep.

I framed the problem in such a way that I withheld some important information from you regarding the number of sales reps versus the number of librarians. Sorry about that! In my defense, however, I did it to illustrate the point that framing a problem can impact our decisions.

In investing, we frame things incorrectly all of the time. Examples include:

- We are happier with a 10 percent return when inflation is at 12 percent than we are with a 4 percent return in a year when inflation is at 3 percent. Translated, this means we'll take a 2 percent real loss over a 1 percent real gain.

- Some investors won't go with broad indexing because we know it has zero chance of outperforming the market. If we framed the decision that indexing must beat the average return of a dollar invested, we are far more likely to invest in the broad index.
- We are happier with our stockbroker when she gets a 15 percent return in a year when the market earned 20 percent than we are when she loses 5 percent in a year when the market lost 10 percent.
- We don't mind paying someone 1 to 2 percent to manage our money because these are small numbers and we don't actually have to write out a check.

Just as I probably got you to confidently predict that Sue was a librarian rather than a sales rep, Wall Street also helps us frame things in ways that lead us to believe we are making logical and rational choices. In reality, we are merely doing exactly what will transfer our wealth to them.

Mental Accounting Always Adds Up to What You Want

As a CPA, I've learned that debits must equal credits. While it's a royal pain when accounts aren't balancing, it does create a certain discipline. If people kept an accurate count of their activities while sitting at the Las Vegas gambling tables, I'm willing to bet that the two out of every three gamblers who believe they've won money would rethink that.

Mental accounting is how we trick ourselves into believing that we are doing better than we actually are. Just like the two out of three gamblers in Las Vegas, we tend to remember our brilliant investments and forget our *what-were-we-thinking* ones. That's because remembering our winners gives us pleasure and forgetting our losers stops the pain. And if remembering our winners brings pleasure, why not bring that pleasure to our friends and family by touting our winners and sweeping our losers under the nearest rug?

Confirmation Bias: Everyone Has a Right to My Opinion

Once we make an important decision, we like to feel good about it. We have a tendency to carefully review any information that supports our decision and dismiss any new information that leads us to believe we may have made the wrong choice.

Perhaps this is where the phrase *ignorance is bliss* came from; we don't like the feeling we get when information is presented that shows our choice may have been wrong, even when we have the chance to change that choice.

I noted earlier in the book that the reactions I receive from clients when benchmarking their portfolio against the second-grader portfolio vary greatly. Some investors are so distraught over the results that they will never accept the facts. That's *confirmation bias* in practice. Most people that do come to me, however, are not terribly surprised and ask for help. This may seem contradictory to confirmation bias, but those that come to me are not a good sample of the general investing population. They tend to suspect they have been underperforming and are ready to change course.

Heuristic Biases Get in the Way of Performing Even Simple Tasks

Our brain also takes mental shortcuts when we perform routine tasks. For example, read the following sentence:

> Finished files are the result of years of scientific study combined with the experience of years.

Now, read it again, counting aloud the number of *F*s in the sentence. Most people count three or four, but there are actually six. Our brain tends to read the *F* in *of* as a *V.* It's a mental shortcut that we take that leads us to an incorrect answer in a very simple task. In reality, we take many mental shortcuts that often lead us astray. It's very easy to present a set of simple choices where even mathematicians have been known to incorrectly calculate probabilities.

These heuristic biases are used against us frequently by Wall Street. Just as I did with the simple *F*-counting exercise, we are led to predictably take shortcuts and confidently make the wrong choices.

A Tale of Silly Human Behavior

A very intelligent and successful businessman once came to see me. It turned out that a key purpose of this visit was to educate me on investing. He *confidently* stated that he had an unfair advantage over other stock market investors. When I inquired how so, he showed me his portfolio comprised of individual stocks paying an average of a 14 percent dividend. The man noted that the stock market yielded only 2 percent and thus he started every year with a 12 percent advantage. By his *mental accounting,* he was soundly beating the market.

I asked if I could examine his statements and he kindly obliged. I looked at his performance over the past year, and he did indeed get a 14 percent dividend. The problem was that the value of the stocks themselves dropped by 12 percent. Thus, he netted only a +2 percent return over the past year. By comparison, the same proportion of U.S. and international stock portfolios earned 20 percent. So, in reality he lagged the market by a whopping 18 percent.

On his next visit, I showed him my analysis of his gross underperformance. I also tried to tactfully point out that he had managed to pay far more taxes than he needed to since he paid taxes on his dividends and deferred the losses on the value of the stocks.

"How can this be?" asked the man.

I tried to show some sympathy as I explained that when stocks yield several times more than the market as a whole, it was the market's way of saying that it didn't think these dividends would be sustained. I showed him several had recently lowered their dividends. He was visibly upset and kept explaining that my analysis had to be flawed (*confirmation bias*). I then showed him the "unrealized losses" clearly printed on his brokerage statement.

I pointed out that he had *framed* the problem by just looking at a part of the return, the dividends, and ignoring the capital appreciation. He was surprisingly very calm. But then he responded that he had technical charts to back his decisions (*data mining*). He went on to note that dividend stocks had recently performed quite well (*hindsight bias*).

I suggested that he had a great opportunity to sell the stocks and own the entire global stock market. Not only that, but he could move to the new portfolio without paying any taxes. "Of course," the man agreed, "but not until the prices come back to where I bought them." He was *anchored* to his purchase price and overly *optimistic* that he would quickly recover his loss.

I suggested that he do this right now and he immediately snapped back, "How much more can I lose?"

My answer, of course, was "All of it!"

I still keep in touch with this man, and by no means do I think he is the only one making these emotional mistakes. This was just the single example that covered so many human biases. I know many brilliant people who are some of the world's worst investors.

We all act silly with our money, and that includes me, as well. If you want to find the investors most prone to these human investing biases, that's easy. They are the ones who are bragging about their investment performance and don't know they are acting silly with their nest eggs.

Applying the Golden Rule of Not Acting Silly with Our Money

The first step of acting more rationally with our money is to admit that we are human, and as such have emotions that may prevent us from acting in our own economic best interests. It's easy for a second grader to see how silly his dad is acting; it's a lot harder to change our own behavior. Here are a few tidbits that may help you:

- *Fear and greed.* Stop yourself from giving into the human emotions that lead us to buy high and sell low. Set an asset allocation target of U.S. stocks, international stocks, and bonds. Write a contract to yourself that you will stick to your asset allocation. I'll provide an example at the end of this book.

  Remember that stocks are a better buy after they have declined than when they set new record highs. As Warren Buffett put it, "Be fearful when others are greedy and greedy when others are fearful."
- *Hindsight.* We are all brilliant at predicting the past. Don't let the recent past guide your future investing. Just because one investing style performed well in the last bear market doesn't mean it will do well in the next one. Whenever you hear a talking head on TV telling you why something happened and extrapolating to the future, remind yourself that this doesn't work. No one knows the future.
- *Optimism.* Remember that the odds are you don't know the odds. When you see an advertisement for a hot investment, think of all of the investments from the same firm or fund family that aren't being advertised. When the advertisement says, "Past performance is not indicative of future performance," believe it!
- *Overconfidence.* We are not all above-average investors, and very few of us will beat the second-grader portfolio. Be happy to consistently beat most investors by owning the entire market with the lowest costs and lowest taxes. You are unlikely to be or even find the next Warren Buffett.

- *Data mining.* A pattern that *has* predicted the future is very different from a pattern that *will* predict the future. There will always be another great *discovery,* like Dogs of the Dow, and it will be hailed as a contrarian strategy. Ask yourself: If everyone is following this contrarian strategy, how contrarian could it be? Are you merely following the herd?
- *Framing.* Any good talking head or financial salesperson can frame an issue by giving you certain information and leaving some critical information out. Ask yourself whether you are looking at the issue with the big picture in mind. Take a devil's-advocate view and ask your spouse or trusted friend to find a flaw in your logic.
- *Mental accounting.* Never underestimate the human ability to believe what we want to believe. Are you really beating the market? It may be painful, but compare your return to a weighted average of the three funds in the second-grader portfolio. I can't tell you how many people I've run across who truly believe they've bested the market, including the man that lagged it by 18 percent!

There are thousands of financial professionals figuring out how to use your emotions to separate you from your money. Here are some things you can do to protect yourself from them and even from yourself:

How to Keep from Beating Yourself[9]

1. Avoid the "sure thing."
2. Don't invest in what has been hot.
3. Think twice before you act.
4. Don't follow the herd.
5. Track your feelings.

Always ask yourself whether you know which part of your brain is in the driver's seat when making a decision. Is it your emotional, reflexive side or the more logical reflective side? You may never know, but considering these five points will increase the likelihood it's coming from your logical side.

After you've considered the steps to stop you from beating yourself, you are ready for the final test before you take action. Can you explain what you are doing to a second grader or would he think you were just acting silly?

Chapter 5

Can You Beat a Second Grader's Portfolio?

"I'm Not Going to Win All Three Spins"

After dinner, Patty, Kevin, and I sometimes play board games like Candyland and Trouble. When he was very young, we would always let Kevin go first (and win). My wife would likely let him go first and win until he was in grad school, but by second grade I thought it was time for one of those life lessons. So, to decide who got to go first, we used several games of chance—including dice, rock/paper/scissors, and picking the highest card. Our favorite was probably the simple spin-the-dial (illustrated in Exhibit 5.1).

Exhibit 5.1 Spinner: Who Goes First?

Each person has a one-third chance of going first.

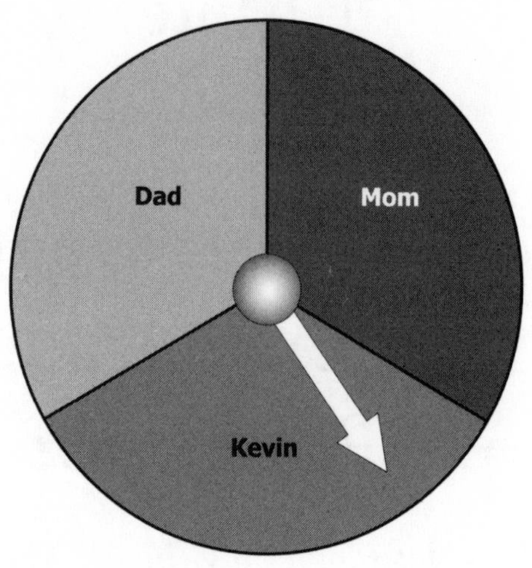

Kevin had just finished learning the basics of fractions and multiplication, so I asked him what he thought his chances were of beating his mom and me. Still not at the age where he could calculate without a visual, Kevin used his fingers and said "That's easy—I have a one-third chance of winning."

"Great," I said. "What are your chances of winning twice in a row?"

He thought about it, pulled out his trusty fingers, and then asked for some help. I assured him that all we needed was a little multiplication, and pulled out the whiteboard to illustrate how to solve the problem:

$$1 \times 1 = 1$$
$$3 \times 3 = 9$$

To be sure he had grasped the concept, I decided to test Kevin's knowledge. I asked him what his odds were of winning three in a row. He wrote 1/3 × 1/3 × 1/3, and then paused—he was stumped. I wrote the following:

$$1 \times 1 \times 1 = 1$$
$$3 \times 3 \times 3 = 27$$

That meant his odds were 1 in 27. "That's not very good!" Kevin exclaimed.

Before his attention span evaporated like steam in a shower, I gave Kevin a similar question on investing: If you had to close your eyes and pick one of three U.S. stock funds, one of three international stock funds, and one of three bond funds, what are your odds of picking ones that are in the top third for all three categories? He asked if it was the same as asking whether he could spin three winners in a row. "It's exactly the same," I told him. "Then that would be the same answer—it's one in twenty-seven," replied Kevin.

I probably could have gone on for hours about the relevance of that little exercise in mathematics to investing, but Kevin's interest had shifted back to the board game and whatever I said from that point on was going to sound like any adult in the Charlie Brown movies—*mwah-mwah-mwah.* Since I was confident that Kevin now understood some of the odds most investors will never understand, I handed him the dice and the game was on.

The Common Sense of Avoiding Bad Bets

One of the biggest criticisms of index funds is that they aim for mediocrity. Who wants to shoot for average, when tying the market is a bit like kissing your sister? Luckily, Kevin doesn't have a sister. I've already pointed out one flaw in this argument in that the argument is framed incorrectly. The better way to frame it would be that the broad index fund gives you a guarantee that you will *beat,* not tie, the average return of every dollar invested.

Still, I hear people say I never see index funds in the top 10 percent of performance for a 1-year period or even a 10-year period. Generally speaking, they are right, but as we will see in this chapter, not only can index investing result in top 10 percent performance, in the long run it can translate into top 1 percent performance. To put it another way, a typical portfolio has less than a 1 percent chance of beating Kevin's after adjusting for the allocation that is right for your risk level.

The Performance of Kevin's Portfolio

I've already shown you that the returns of Kevin's portfolio look great compared to the traditional Wall Street approach of comparing total returns to the raw S&P 500, stripped of dividends. Let's take a more valid look.

Morningstar does a great service to investors by comparing like funds to each other. It recognizes that an awful emerging-markets fund could easily beat a great large-cap domestic fund for a given period of time. That's because a bad fund in a hot sector can handily beat a great fund in a not-so-great sector. So, Morningstar changed its whole rating system to compare apples to apples. It ranks large-cap domestic funds against other similar funds, and the same for emerging markets and the like.

I'll grant you it's an imperfect system, but it's better than anything else out there. As part of its comparison, Morningstar ranks each fund against its assigned peers and gives it a percentage rank. A ranking of 1 means that it was in the top 1 percent and a ranking of 100 means it was in the bottom 1 percent. So, remember that a *low* ranking is good.

Exhibit 5.2 shows how the three funds in Kevin's portfolio did. The largest holding, Vanguard Total Stock Index, barely

Exhibit 5.2 Morningstar Fund Ranking—12 Months

Fund (Symbol)	**12 Month Return (%) Rank**
Vanguard Total Bond (VBMFX)	12
Vanguard Total Intl (VGTSX)	45
Vanguard Total Stock (VTSMX)	38

Period ending August 28, 2008.

Exhibit 5.3 Morningstar Fund Ranking—10-Year Period

Fund (Symbol)	10-Year Return (%) Rank
Vanguard Total Bond (VBMFX)	16
Vanguard Total Intl (VGTSX)	16
Vanguard Total Stock (VTSMX)	32

Period ending August 28, 2008.

performed above average, while the international and bond funds did quite nicely.

This data is hardly a compelling case for indexing, which is precisely why I am showing it. Others will show it and yet draw an incorrect conclusion. They will conclude that you are shooting to be a solid *C* student and imply that you can do much better. But let's see how those funds performed over a 10-year period (Exhibit 5.3).

You will see that all performed in the top third. Admittedly, Kevin didn't hold these funds for 10 years since he was only eight when we designed the portfolio. Does that mean I am guilty of performance chasing and picking the funds that historically performed the best? I think not, and offer the following as a rebuttal.

I have owned all of these funds for 10 years or longer. I didn't pick them because they performed well in the previous years; I picked them because their costs were low, they were the most diversified funds out there, and because 10 – 2 = 8. I was too stingy to give the 2 percent to Wall Street, and my personal patriotism doesn't demand that I pay more taxes than I need to. Finally, Kevin has now owned these funds for three years and all three are in the top third of their category.

As you can see, over a 10-year period Kevin's portfolio moved up to a solid *B* student, with all three funds being in the top third of the class. Perhaps with grade inflation, maybe now the top third of the class qualifies as at least an *A*–student.

Let's revisit our earlier lesson of second-grade math. I had asked Kevin to figure out what the odds were of going first in our games three times in a row. The odds of picking three different mutual funds, all performing in the top third, are figured by the exact same math:

$$1 \times 1 \times 1 = 1$$
$$3 \times 3 \times 3 = 27$$

That is to say, there is a 1-in-27 chance of selecting three funds that will each provide performance in the top third. That translates to less than a 4 percent probability, meaning that the second-grader portfolio is now in the top 4 percent, and beat out more than 96 percent of the class. I can tell you that I certainly give out *A*'s to more than 4 percent of my students in the university finance classes I teach.

The longer the second-grader portfolio goes, the higher its overall relative performance is likely to be. Will it ever get to class valedictorian? If you define valedictorian as Warren Buffett, probably not. However, if you don't mind being in the top 1 percent of the class over the long-run and graduating *summa-cum laude,* the second-grader portfolio may be for you. You may feel you are lucky enough to be in that 1 percent. If so, please know you have Kevin's and my appreciation for keeping the market efficient as your mutual fund tries to outsmart other professionals and trade stocks.

Odds Are You Don't Know the Odds of Your Portfolio

As I discussed in Chapter 4, it's human nature to be both optimistic and overconfident. We tend to overestimate the odds of any outcome we are looking for. So let's examine what the odds really are.

Before I do, I have to confess that I'm a quant-jock-nerd type and if there's one thing more exciting than counting thousands of basketball scores to calculate probabilities, it's building a spreadsheet. You can imagine how excited I was a few years ago when Jack Bogle's office enlisted my help in developing a *Monte Carlo simulation* to estimate the odds of an average-cost mutual fund beating the low-cost index. You say *spreadsheet* and I'm there!

As much as I'd like to brag about the complexity of a Monte Carlo simulation, it's just a computer program that simulates reality and runs that reality a thousand times or more to calculate possible outcomes. As with any model, the assumptions and the inputs have to be accurate or you end up with the old garbage-in, garbage-out scenario. Now, being the spreadsheet-loving control freak that I am, rather than just help Kevin Laughlin, Jack Bogle's very impressive research assistant, I actually *built* the Monte Carlo simulation.

I compared thousands of simulated mutual funds to thousands of simulated index funds. The results (shown in Exhibit 5.4) show the probability of an active fund beating an index fund, with the index fund having about a 0.23 percent total expense and the average mutual fund or separately managed account having a 2.00 percent expense ratio.

You will note that the odds go down the longer the period of time. That is to say, the longer you try to prove that 10 – 2 > 10, the worse your odds get. I liken it to sitting at the blackjack table—the longer I play, the lower my probability of walking away a winner.

I felt pretty good about the results. I compared them to Morningstar's historical results and they seemed to pass my smell test. You'll note that, over a 10-year period, the three

Exhibit 5.4 Probability of Active Beating Passive

No. of Years	Probability of Active Beating Passive
1	43%
5	29%
10	23%
25	13%

index funds in the second-grader portfolio beat 70 to 80 percent of their peers.

I proudly sent my results to Jack Bogle. Let's just say he was less than enthused. It wasn't so much the one-year results that he questioned; it was the long-term results. I even showed him results going out 100 years, in which a few of the active funds still beat the index.

I looked at those funds to discern a pattern and noted that they did have one thing in common. They were the stars in the first 5 to 10 years of the hundred-year period, and then seemed to underperform a bit for the remaining 90 years. I suddenly had one of those bolt-from-the-blue realizations that I called the *Magellan effect,* referring to the Fidelity Magellan Fund (FMAGX). Between the years of 1977 and 1990, the fund earned an average annual return of 29 percent versus 13.3 percent.[1] After this 14-year period, $1,000 invested would have been worth as follows:

Fidelity Magellan (FMAGX)	$35,339
Vanguard S&P 500 (VFINX)	$3,473

You will note that the money invested in the Magellan fund grew to be worth more than 10 times that of the S&P 500 fund. You may know the rest of the story. It turned out that after 1990, the Magellan fund lagged the index significantly over the next 18 years and wasn't exactly a stellar investment. But because its past performance had been so spectacular, it's still way ahead of the index and will probably stay ahead for many decades to come. If fact, even if the Magellan fund earned a zero return going forward from 1990, it would still be handsomely ahead of the S&P 500 fund.

So, I deem the Magellan effect to mean that, in reality, the odds of beating the low-cost index are even smaller than you think. Even though this is one of the few funds that beat the index over a 30-year period, very few investors actually got to participate during the time it did beat the market.

Just so you don't think I'm trashing the Fidelity Magellan Fund, it happens to have one of the lowest active fund expense ratios around at 0.53 percent. It also had a spectacular year in 2007, besting its category by 5.5 percent according to Morningstar.

Comparing an Active Portfolio to an Index Portfolio

It may look like I'm providing some ammunition for active investing advocates to use against indexing. A skilled investor should be able to pick a fund that performs in the top 12 percent over a 25-year period, right?

Not so fast. The odds we have looked at using the Monte Carlo simulation were the odds of one active fund beating one index fund. I don't know of any investor who has money in only one mutual fund or has only one private account manager. In fact, most people come to me with well over 10. So, I updated my Monte Carlo simulation to take into account both time and the number of funds one owns. That changes the odds significantly, much in the same way we examined Kevin's probability of winning the spin three times in a row.[2] Remember that I said the average active fund has a 42 percent chance of beating the index? For those active investors with 5 or 10 funds, the odds start declining. The probability of a portfolio of domestic funds beating the total U.S. Index fund is as follows:

1 Active fund	42%
5 Active funds	32%
10 Active funds	25%

So the odds start deteriorating a bit, as 10 active funds have only about a one-in-four shot of beating a low-cost index over a one-year period. Now we also don't invest for just one year—we invest over our lifetimes (hopefully). So let's look at the odds of a 10-fund portfolio beating the appropriate index over periods of time:

1 Year	25%
5 Years	9%
10 Years	6%
25 Years	1%

The way this reads is that someone with 10 or more mutual funds or private money managers on average has less than a 1 percent probability of beating the index over 25 years. Since fear motivates more than greed (loss aversion), I'll put it another way: If you are an active investor with 10 or more funds, your probability of failure is 99 percent. Feeling lucky enough to make this gamble with your nest egg?

Exhibit 5.5 shows more outcomes. You will notice the two patterns:

1. The more funds you own, the worse your odds get.
2. The longer you play the game, the worse your odds get.

Exhibit 5.5 Probability of Active Management Beating Passive before Taxes and Emotions

Active investing has a very low probability of beating passive investing in the long-run.

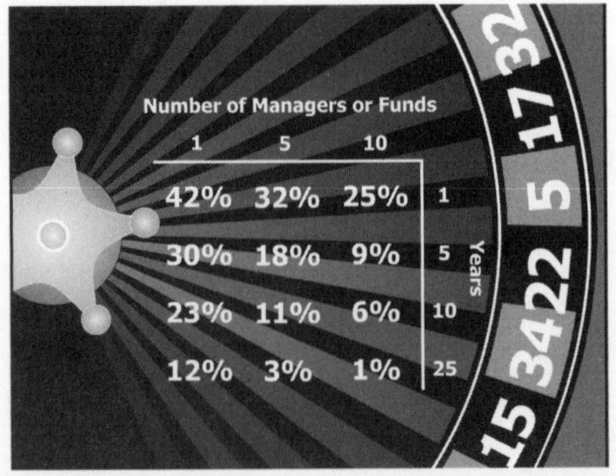

To return to the Las Vegas analogy, the longer I sit at the blackjack table, the lower are my odds of walking away a winner. By playing multiple hands simultaneously, I can decrease my odds further with each dealing of the cards. There's no limit to how fast we can lose money in Las Vegas or on Wall Street.

I'm Not Done Yet—The Odds Are Even Worse

With 10 mutual funds or separately managed accounts, you have less than a 1 percent chance of beating the low-cost index funds of the second-grader portfolio. But all of this is only using an expense differential of 0.23 percent for index funds, and 2.00 percent for active funds. Unfortunately for active investors, the odds get even worse on two fronts: taxes and emotions.

Actively traded mutual funds are very tax-inefficient in that they churn the underlying stocks in these funds. This means more taxes to the IRS, even if you don't sell a single fund. As mentioned earlier, a total market index fund rarely has to make a trade and is much less likely to incur taxable capital gains. By my estimates, a buy-and-hold strategy of total index funds can save over 1 percent annually in lower taxes. Not that I mind active investors doing more than their fair share to pay off our national debt. Of course, if you're investing within a tax-deferred IRA or 401(k), then you won't be paying this 1 percent penalty.

Additionally, while you now know that the average mutual fund underperforms the market, you may not know that the average investor *also* underperforms the average mutual fund. That's right—first we pay a *fee penalty* that reduces our returns, and then we get zapped with an additional 1.5 percent *performance penalty* (discussed in Chapter 4) caused by our poorly timed purchases and sales.[3]

This is a phenomenon written about and well described by *Wall Street Journal* columnist Jason Zweig. It appears that we investors put our dollars into a fund *after* it has done well, only to take our dollars out of that fund once its performance lags, and move on to the next hot thing just in time for *it* to underperform. Jack Bogle calls this a *timing and selection penalty.*

To see an example of how we chase performance, we can again look at the Fidelity Magellan fund. During the 14 years it earned an average annual return of 29 percent, its average asset size was about $4.4 billion. Unfortunately for investors, its average size afterwards was $58.3 billion while it underperformed the market. The vast majority of its investors showed up late to the party, earning none of the superior gains and all of the mediocre returns the fund has provided since 1990.

Admittedly, we can chase performance even with broad index funds. We can get into and out of the market daily with index mutual funds and as often as we want with exchange traded funds, since they can be traded throughout the day. As you recall, exchange traded funds are merely index funds that trade on stock exchanges that one can use to chase performance to one's heart's delight. So index funds don't eliminate the possibility of performance chasing and paying the 1.5 percent penalty. You can dodge this bullet by thinking like a second grader and buying the whole market and doing nothing.

Let's take one last peek at the Monte Carlo simulation. We won't penalize the active portfolio for taxes, as we will give it the benefit of the doubt that no one would be silly enough to do active investing in a taxable account. Let's just say that the active investor acts with human nature and pays the 1.5 percent penalty. So, now the average dollar invested has a 3.5 percent drag comprised of 2.0 percent expenses and 1.5 percent penalty for chasing performance. Running this in the Monte Carlo simulation against Kevin's 0.23 percent fees, while he watches *SpongeBob,* creates the odds listed in Exhibit 5.6.

Exhibit 5.6 Probability of Active Management Beating Passive, Including Emotions

Active investing is even more of a longshot when you add the human element.

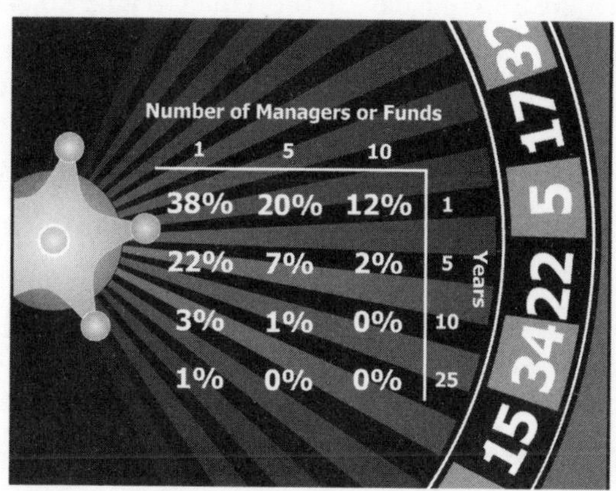
Number of Managers or Funds

1	5	10	Years
38%	20%	12%	1
22%	7%	2%	5
3%	1%	0%	10
1%	0%	0%	25

The results of the simulation show that the average investor, saddled with 2 percent expenses and an additional 1.5 percent penalty for timing things wrong due to emotion, has incredibly low odds of beating the buy-and-hold version of a second-grader portfolio. Owning an average of 10 active funds over a 25-year period yields an expected probability of beating the buy-and-hold second-grader portfolio at just a tad over 0 percent. That is to say, the average investor has almost as high a probability of beating the second-grader portfolio as of winning the lottery. Yet most investors will take their nest egg and keep playing the game they have virtually no chance of winning.

To relate why these odds are so low, imagine yourself sitting at a blackjack table in sunny Las Vegas. If you are a skilled player, but don't card-count, you can win about 49 percent of each hand you play. Now, you know, the longer you sit at the table, the worse your odds get of walking away a winner. If you play for four hours, your odds drop a ton. But if you decide to play three hands at each round, your odds drop three tons. So, an active investor with 10 mutual funds trying to beat the market is not all that different from the addicted gambler spending 20 hours a day at the tables trying to prove he can beat the odds.

Why We Make Those Sucker Bets We Have a 99 Percent Chance of Losing

Why do we take something as important as building our nest egg, and place a bet that's nearly certain to lose? There are two reasons:

1. *We don't know that we don't know the odds.*

As noted in Chapter 3, Wall Street and much of the media have a very powerful marketing machine that creates a perception far different from the realities of simple arithmetic. Much like the excitement we feel when we walk into a casino where lights are flashing and bells are ringing, we get the perception that everyone is beating the market and we have to get in on the action.

Wall Street trains us early to get this perception across. As of the time of this writing, Kevin was in fourth grade and came home with an assignment known as the "Stock Market Game™."[4] His assignment was to pick three stocks that would then be monitored using this game of simulated portfolio performance. The winner would be the student whose performance was the best over the next few weeks—ultra-short-term.

While Kevin's portfolio may have a 99.9 percent chance of beating most investors over a 25-year period, it has a goose-egg chance of winning this game over the next few weeks. The only way to win the game is to pick three incredibly risky stocks and hope they do well in the short-term. Such a strategy strays far and away from investing. It's gambling, pure and simple. I wanted to go with Kevin to school the next day and explain to the teacher that this was teaching anything *but* investing. Unfortunately, after some serious discussion with Kevin's mom, she—I mean I—changed my mind. Instead, I had Kevin close his eyes and pick three random stocks out of the newspaper stock listings. We both knew that this was a really dumb way to invest, but we also knew it wasn't real money.

Who are the sponsors of the Stock Market Game? As you might expect, according to their web site, they are Merrill Lynch, Wachovia Securities, A.G. Edwards, PNC Financial Services, and Morgan Stanley, as well as some industry groups and media. Call me cynical, but the parties above all seem to have a vested interest in making sure that future investors learn methods of playing the stock market by stressing the short-term odds of investing.[5] When all is said and done, someone in the class will probably think he is a Jim Cramer for picking three stocks that did well for a few weeks, and someone else will learn a lesson that investing in the stock market is bad because you can lose a lot of money. I'm not sure which of the two lessons is worse. I do know that Wall Street marketing has reached fourth graders and that Kevin is already losing his immunity to the Wall Street illusion.

Though not intended, I think the real lesson of the Stock Market Game is that the odds of winning it are high if you approach it in such a way that enriches Wall Street in the real world. We think because we performed well for a short period of time that we can sustain it over the long-run. We don't know how bad the odds are in the long-run.

2. *We don't want to know the odds.*

You know what they say about clichés: They're called *clichés* because they are so true. The one about ignorance being bliss is sometimes *too* true. Many investors know the second-grader portfolio isn't likely to get them rich over the next year or two. Some may be smart enough to hang up on the stranger who calls "guaranteeing" a windfall on an oil deal, but then will fall for the sophisticated sales pitch from someone managing large amounts of money. When we hear promises made based on what we *want* to hear, we suddenly suspend common sense. The feeling of excitement at the possibilities overwhelms us and we are carried forward with it. At this point, being committed to this decision, any data or logic that would show us how unlikely we are to outperform the simple portfolio is something that we don't want to hear, and therefore we don't hear it. All we want is confirmation that we are making the right decision. The last thing we want to hear is that we are making a sucker's bet.

How the Odds Play Out in the Real World

How do my calculations of the odds compare to real situations? Often, one of the first things I do when potential clients contact me is to benchmark their investments against the three asset classes in the second-grader portfolio. I change the asset allocations of the second-grader portfolio to those of the clients. That is to say, I compare a client's U.S. stock portfolio to the total U.S. index fund and then repeat it for international stocks and bonds.

How often has the client portfolio actually bested the comparable broad index benchmark over the past three years? I think I've seen it about 2 percent of the time. In reality, I think the odds are even worse than I've shown.

Applying the Golden Rule of Going with the Odds

As Mathew Emmert wrote in *Motley Fool,* "The best thing you can do as an investor or a gambler, is to know the odds of the game you're playing—because not knowing them will cost you."[6] Kevin knows his odds of winning three spins in a row are low, and that his odds of trying to prove that $10 - 2 > 10$ are even lower. He's not going to bet his allowance on it, much less his investment portfolio.

There are three things we investors can do to tip the scales in our favor when betting our nest egg. First, don't bet against simple mathematics. Each dollar of costs you are paying, whether you are seeing it or not, is handing off your wealth to somebody else. I don't know you, but I'm guessing most readers would rather keep their money than donate it to Wall Street billionaires. Even Mother Teresa would have passed on that cause. Every dollar you spend on your portfolio lowers the odds you will beat the simple second-grader portfolio. The *costs matter* mantra is so critical because the odds of rising above them are much worse than Wall Street wants you to believe.

Second, quit paying taxes that you don't need to. Active funds and separately managed accounts claim to be tax-efficient. Their constant churning, however, causes investors to pay far more in taxes than the second-grader portfolio, which rarely passes on a capital gain. I'm all for minimizing the U.S. deficit, but lowering taxes via index investing dramatically improves your odds.

Third (and as Jack Bogle advises), stay the course, whatever that might be for you. Emotions will sometimes tug at you, and sometimes drag you all over the map. Wall Street will bombard you with their glitzy, glamorous illusions, though I think *delusions* is closer to the truth. You will be told what the next hot sector or country will be and it will be hard to ignore. There will be other bubbles, such as the dot-com economy where cash flow doesn't matter, or buying financial institutions that make billions of dollars by lending people without jobs 110 percent of the value their house. Don't pay the 1.5 percent penalty that most investors pay by following the herd. If you can't stay the course, take Warren Buffett's advice: "Be greedy when others are fearful and fearful when others are greedy."

(Continues)

(Continued)

Remember that active investing is like smoking. It's *possible* to smoke two packs of cigarettes a day and live to age 100, but it is highly improbable. *Not* smoking, however, dramatically improves the odds of living longer and healthier. I try to instill in Kevin the need to make choices that will improve the odds of increasing both his health and his wealth.

You, too, can make choices that will improve the odds of increasing your wealth. Though it really is simple, it's far from easy. At least it doesn't appear to be for us adults.

Chapter 6

Beyond the Second-Grader Portfolio

"If Dad Says There's a Better Way, I Might Try It, but I'm Not So Sure"

Kevin's dad is somewhat of a math geek. You bring out the standard deviations, correlations, probabilities, and the like, and it's a party. Imagine my popularity in high school: Allan Roth—Most Likely to Wear a Pocket Protector. So, how was I now going to explain to a second grader that there *could* be a way to top off our portfolio and lower risk without lowering return?

I toyed with the idea of using the formula shown in Exhibit 6.1. Yep, and then we could segue into quantum physics. Even *I'm* not that out of touch with what it was like to be an 8-year-old, so I took a different approach.

Exhibit 6.1 Correlation

This formula would turn anyone away from investing.

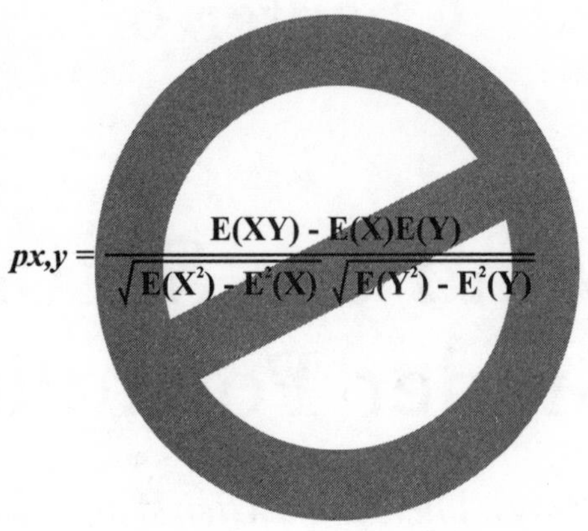

Instead, I asked Kevin to imagine that we lived in a simple world and that we had either a rainy year or a sunny year. (We had to pause here for a few minutes while Kevin lobbied for only sunny years in his imaginary simple world.) I then asked him to further imagine that there were two companies he could invest in: Golden Tan, Inc. made suntan lotion, and Rainy Day Umbrellas Corp. made umbrellas. During those sunny years, Golden Tan, Inc. would be going gangbusters and selling a lot of lotion—so much so that its stock would go up 30 percent. But in rainy years, its warehouses would be full of unsold lotion and its stock price would go down by 10 percent. Rainy Day Umbrellas, however, loved the rainy years. It would sell umbrellas like hotcakes, and its stock price would go up by 30 percent. In sunny years, however, no one was buying umbrellas and its stock would decline by 10 percent (Exhibit 6.2).

"So," I asked Kevin, "if you could pick only one company, what are your chances of picking the right one?" It seemed pretty obvious to him that half equaled 50 percent, so that was his answer—50/50. It was also obvious to him that he still had the other 50 percent and he didn't want to put it all in one

Exhibit 6.2 Correlations Redux

A better way to explain correlations.

Imagine that you live in a simple world where a year is either sunny or rainy and there is a 50% probability of either. You review two stocks. How would you construct your portfolio?

- Expected return-(+10%)
- Return on sunny years-(+30%)
- Return on rainy years-(10%)

Rainy Day Umbrellas (RDU)

- Expected return-(+10%)
- Return on sunny years-(–10%)
- Return on rainy years-(+30%)

SOURCE: Adapted from an illustration in Burton Malkiel's *A Random Walk Down Wall Street* (W.W. Norton & Co., 1999).

company—too risky. Good point, Kev. But since we were pretending and all, I asked him to calculate what his return would be if he invested half in each of the two companies. We came up with the returns shown in Exhibit 6.3.

He looked baffled for a moment, until he zeroed in on the bottom line. *Aha!*—10 percent rainy, 10 percent sunny. In a rainy year, Golden Tan lost 10 percent while Rainy Day Umbrellas gained 30 percent, yielding a total portfolio return of 10 percent. In a sunny year, the reverse happened, which also yielded a total portfolio return of 10 percent. Kevin had eliminated all risk and was assured of a 10 percent annual return in this contrived example.

Exhibit 6.3 Return of a 50 percent Investment in Each Stock

	Rainy Year	Sunny Year
Golden Tan Inc.	−10%	30%
Rainy Day Umbrellas	30%	−10%
Total Return (50% each)	10%	10%

NOTE: Rather than adding the two numbers, take half of each.

By now, Kevin had anticipated a follow-up what-if question that is going to have some relevance to investing. He asked, "So, is this something I can do in the stock market?"

"Sort of," I answered.

I went on to explain that there were some investments that kind of moved in opposite directions, but it didn't always happen. "Does one go up when the other goes down?" asked Kevin. Again, not really.

Resisting my math-geek urge to pull out the equation given in Exhibit 6.1, I wound things up with "Let's just stick to our three-fund simple portfolio for now." Kevin seemed relieved.

He did toss me a bone, though, by saying, "Maybe I'll try your way some day." He clearly has more tact than his old man.

The Common Sense of Not Explaining Correlations to an 8-Year-Old

I was trying to explain to an 8-year-old the concept of investing in asset classes that have lower correlations. Perhaps (as my wife kindly pointed out) I was overshooting just a bit; common sense should have told me a second grader doesn't want to know about correlations. At least I had planted the seed. Maybe that seed won't reach fruition for 15 years or so, but hey—I believe in planting early.

I'll wait a few years before I try this on Kevin again, but there are some lessons to be learned, even without pulling out that scary equation again. If we invest in asset classes that don't always move up and down together, we can lower our level of risk without giving up one iota of expected return.

I carefully constructed the Golden Tan and Rainy Day Umbrellas example to build a portfolio that earned a 10 percent market-like return and did so without any risk. Of course it's unrealistic—right up there with fairies and leprechauns and professionals that beat the market.

The Importance of Being Negative

Because the share prices of Golden Tan and Rainy Day Umbrellas always moved in opposite directions, I was able to construct a portfolio comprised of half of each and eliminate all risk by providing a guaranteed 10 percent return.

I promise not to have too much math in this book, but here are some basics on correlations. If two stocks move perfectly in tandem in the same direction, they are known as having a *perfect positive correlation* (or 1.00). An example might be Golden Tan, Inc. and Beach Sailboat Rental Corp.; theoretically, both would do well in sunny years and bad in rainy years.

Golden Tan, Inc. and Rainy Day Umbrellas stock moved in exactly opposite directions. That is known as being *perfectly negatively correlated,* or having a correlation of −1.00. Thus, all correlations fall between −1.00 and +1.00.

Let's pause to admire the beauty of investing in assets that have a perfectly negative correlation. In my fictitious example, the investor could be guaranteed a 10 percent annual return because we built the portfolio using two stocks that had a −1.00 correlation. No matter whether we had a sunny or a rainy year, a portfolio comprised of half of each stock gave us a 10 percent return, while owning each stock individually gave us an expected 10 percent return but with far more risk, given a range of −10 percent to +30 percent.

In reality, I don't know of any perfectly negatively correlated assets to produce a risk-free stock market return. In fact, for the most part, we are doing pretty well to get asset classes with low positive correlations, but the concept is still true that the lower the correlations of the assets in our portfolio, the less risk we have.

What Kevin Has Already Done Right

Before we go further in constructing a portfolio beyond Kevin's three-fund portfolio, let's look at what he's already done right with correlations, without even knowing it:

- *Bonds.* Quite often, bonds perform very well during times that the stock market plummets. Of course, those same bonds don't tend to perform so well during times the market soars. The correlation between the U.S. stock market and the U.S. aggregate bond market has been −0.27.[1] Because bonds or other types of fixed income have had negative correlations to the stock market, they act as stabilizers to our portfolio. There is also certainly no guarantee that bonds and U.S. stocks will remain negatively correlated, but there is reason to believe that the correlation will at least remain low. That is why even a second grader needs some bonds in his portfolio.
- *International stocks.* I explained to Kevin that we needed to spread our eggs across the world. Part of the reason I steered Kevin toward international stocks was the fact that the correlation with U.S. stocks is less than +1.00. It's quite true that, in our global economy, the correlation between U.S. stocks and International stocks has dramatically increased, but having any asset classes with less than a perfect correlation also mathematically lowers risk. The correlation between U.S. stocks and international stocks is +0.79. Nothing to write home about, but it does slightly lower risk.
- *Sectors.* Certain sectors of the stock market—such as utilities and energy—don't always move in tandem with the entire market. Their correlations are +0.47 and +0.59, respectively.[2] If we buy sectors with low correlations, we can lower risk. By owning all of the sectors in the U.S. market, the three-fund portfolio takes advantage of lower correlated sectors.

- *Styles.* Large-, mid-, and small-cap stocks will also not move in perfect tandem. The same is true with value, growth, and blend stocks. For example, the correlation between U.S. large-cap growth and U.S. small-cap value is +.74.[3] Because all of these sub-asset classes are already included in Kevin's three-fund portfolio, he automatically takes advantage of these correlations, without having to worry about that complicated equation in Exhibit 6.1.

Using Correlations to Go Beyond the Second-Grader Portfolio

My discussion of correlations with Kevin may have been ill-conceived, but actually I was trying to lead him to what's known as *alternative asset classes*—those assets that are not generally owned by the public equity markets and have low correlations with the U.S. stock market.

I think there are two alternative asset classes that add to diversification. These are real estate and precious metals. If done correctly, owning a small percentage of each in one's portfolio can lower the risk of the entire portfolio.

Real Estate

While the global value of the stock market is roughly $40 trillion, it happens to be far less than the global value of real estate. By some estimates, real estate has more than twice the value of the global stock market. It also happens to have a +0.60 correlation with the U.S. stock market over the past three years.[4] In the longer term, real estate has had an even lower correlation and, during the 2000-to-2002 bear market, real estate performed quite well.

It should be noted that you probably already own a substantial amount of real estate in an asset known as your home. It may not be a particularly diversified asset, but it is a real estate investment, nonetheless. But if you have far more invested in the stock market than the value of your own home, you may want to consider buying some of this alternative asset class. If you are like me, and don't have the disposition to buy rental properties and take on the headaches of being a landlord, you can consider buying a real estate investment trust (REIT). A REIT is a security that often trades on an exchange that owns real estate, such as shopping malls, office buildings, apartments, warehouses, and hotels. Some, however, own only the mortgages behind the real estate. REITs make their money from the rents they charge tenants and from the appreciation of their underlying real estate investments.

REITs are also either publicly traded on exchanges or privately sold to accredited investors. For the most part, I have found privately traded REITs too expensive for the majority of investors and tend to recommend publicly traded REITs. An added advantage of publicly traded REITs is their liquidity, in that they can be sold at any time. Privately placed REITs often don't have this liquidity.

As mentioned, REITs come in many different flavors, including those focused on residential properties, commercial properties, and even mortgages. Which do I prefer? I like all of them. That's right—the best way to own REITs is through a REIT index fund, which spreads the eggs of this alternative asset class as widely as possible and has the lowest costs.

How much should one invest in REITs? While this is purely a judgment call on my part, I recommend not going higher than 10 percent of the U.S. equity portion of your portfolio. That is, for Kevin's portfolio of 60 percent Total U.S. Stock Market Fund, we could go as high as 6 percent in a REIT and lower his exposure to the Total U.S. Stock Market Fund to 54 percent.

Exhibit 6.4 lists some REIT index funds to consider adding to your portfolio.

Exhibit 6.4 REIT Index Funds

REIT Index Choices	Symbol	Expense Ratio	Investment Minimum
Vanguard REIT ETF	VNQ	0.10%	1 share
Vanguard REIT Index Mutual Fund	VGSIX	0.20%	$3,000
StreetTRACKS DJ Wilshire REIT ETF	RWR	0.25%	1 share
iShares Cohen & Steers Realty Majors	ICF	0.35%	1 share
iShares Dow Jones U.S. Real Estate	IYR	0.48%	1 share

My recommendation is to add REITs only if you meet the following criteria:

- The value of your stock holdings is substantially higher than the value of your real estate holdings, including your home.
- You are investing in this asset class for the long run and won't move in and out based on how you feel or what the Wall Street gurus are saying.

Precious Metals

Back in 1980, I bought gold for something like $670 an ounce and silver somewhere around $20 per ounce. I bought these because prices had just plummeted and I was certain I would do well. Of course, this didn't even come close to keeping up with inflation and was one of the lowest-performing investments of my life.

Looking back, I bought gold and silver for the wrong reason: because I thought I was smarter than the market. In 2008, there is a new gold bug going around, and we are hearing the same statements that I heard back in 1980, that "gold is guaranteed to go up" and will soon be $10,000 an ounce. A recent investment club meeting on the topic of gold was sold out weeks in advance. I doubt many people would have showed up if the presentation had been given in 1999, when gold was trading at $253 per ounce. That, of course, is the time when people could have used the advice to buy gold.

The long-run reality is that precious metals prices tend to keep up with inflation and produce little real return. However, stocks that mine precious metals have done quite well. See, they can discover new deposits and develop new technologies to mine these metals. That's why I typically recommend owning the stocks rather than the metals themselves.

That precious metals mining stocks have the possibility of outpacing inflation and earning a real return isn't reason enough to buy them. The reason to buy them is that the correlation to the U.S. stock market tends to be relatively low. In the past three years, the correlation has been extremely high at +0.81. Over a longer period of time, however, the correlation has been much lower at +0.46 for a one-year period.[5] Precious metals stocks also did quite nicely during the bear market of 2000 to 2002.

There are not many choices in owning precious metals and mining stocks. Believe it or not, my preferred choice is not even an index fund. It's the Vanguard Precious Metals and Mining Fund (VGPMX). It has an expense ratio of 0.28 percent and owns about 40 individual stocks. As of the time of this writing, it was closed to most new investors.

In 2006, Van Eck launched a precious metals ETF known as the Market Vector Gold Miners. Its expense ratio of 0.55 percent is higher than the Vanguard fund and it has fewer holdings at 34. Nonetheless, it is a viable alternative to the Vanguard fund, especially considering that the Vanguard fund is currently closed to most investors. See Exhibit 6.5.

Owning this asset class is emotionally difficult because its volatility is extremely high. Morningstar lists the standard

Exhibit 6.5 Precious Metals Funds

Precious Metals and Mining Choices	Symbol	Expense Ratio	Investment Minimum
Vanguard Precious Metals and Mining Fund	VGPMX	0.28%	$3,000
Van Eck Gold Miners ETF	GDX	0.55%	1 share

deviation of the Vanguard Precious Metals and Mining Fund at 240 percent of the volatility of the Total Stock Market Fund. Thus, it takes either nerves of steel or the ability to ignore returns in order to stay in for a couple of decades or longer.

You may be asking how an asset class with a high volatility can actually lower the volatility of the entire portfolio. It turns out that the correlation of asset classes is more important than the absolute volatility of each asset. If we go back to the Rainy Day Umbrella and Golden Tan Inc. example, where one always went up by 30 percent and the other lost 10 percent, we built a portfolio that had no volatility and always earned 10 percent. If I keep the correlation at −1.00, but change the volatility to one gaining 50 percent and the other losing 30 percent, we still can build a portfolio that earns a constant 10 percent.

However, this works only if one owns this alternative asset class for a very long time. Most people will move in and out, and merely end up increasing risk and reducing return. Any good tool can be misused. (Case in point: me with an electric drill. If you removed all the spackle from my walls, they would look like Swiss cheese!)

Because this asset class is so volatile, I recommend that it be no more than 10 percent of one's international portfolio. I use our international allocation for this asset class because most precious metals and mining stocks are foreign, with VGPMX being 84 percent foreign, and GDX being 80 percent. So the alternative to the second-grader portfolio of having 30 percent Vanguard FTSE All-World Ex-U.S. (VEU) would be 27 percent

Just Say *No* to Hedge Funds

Hedge funds can mean just about anything, from leveraged portfolios to shoring the market to the ever-favorite derivative instruments such as products built from subprime mortgages. They can fit into a portfolio because of negative correlations with the stock market. Some of these funds can be great for large institutional pension plans with billions of dollars to invest, as large institutional investors have the ability to get in with low costs.

For anyone with less than a hundred million or so to invest, though, it's a very different story. The typical expense ratio is 2.0 percent and you will pay 20 percent of any positive returns the fund produces. As I see it, that type of fee arrangement has two problems. First, you will be paying an arm and a leg to get that asset with lower correlations, and it easily fails my cost–benefit test. More importantly, whenever you are paying someone 20 percent of the upside, you are giving them the incentive to take a ton of risk with your money. The hedge fund managers make a killing if they can double or triple your money, and the only way they can do that is by taking on even more risk. So, I guess we shouldn't be all that surprised at the multitude of hedge funds that have blown up. The fact that there is even weaker regulation than on mutual funds and industry performance data is scarce is yet another reason to avoid hedge funds.

VEU and 3 percent VGPMX or GDX. I recommend precious metals and mining only for those who I believe have a high risk tolerance.

The Sophisticated Portfolio I Couldn't Convince Kevin to Buy

With this lesson, I drastically complicated matters by adding two new funds to the three-fund portfolio. I admit that this is a 67 percent increase in the number of funds, but it still presents a relatively simple portfolio (Exhibit 6.6). I also admit that it's not for everyone.

Exhibit 6.6 Five-Fund Portfolio

	High Risk	Medium Risk	Low Risk
Total Bond Index	10%	40%	70%
Total U.S. Stock Index	54%	36%	18%
Total REIT Index Fund	6%	4%	2%
Total International Stock Index	27%	20%	10%
Precious Metals Stock Fund	3%	0%	0%
	100%	*100%*	*100%*

Note that this portfolio has only five holdings for the high-risk investor. As mentioned earlier, I am not recommending precious metals stock funds for anyone other than those who are willing to accept a high level of risk and have the fortitude to hold this security for at least a couple of decades. Thus, only the high-risk investor will have five funds while the rest can only have four.

Is the five-fund portfolio really better than Kevin's? There are a few answers to this question.

My answer is that it is theoretically superior because the majority of real estate and precious metals funds are not represented in the public equity markets. Overweighting these two asset classes versus the stock market actually produces a portfolio more representative of total global wealth. Because these two asset classes have low correlations to the U.S. stock market, we end up with a portfolio with a slightly higher risk-adjusted return. Remember that investing takes on higher risk only for the expectation of higher returns. Risk without higher returns is merely speculation or gambling.

That's one answer, but how have the two portfolios actually performed? There is some evidence that, over this time period, the REIT and the Precious Metals fund did help performance. (Exhibit 6.7)

There is no guarantee, however, that the correlations of REITs and precious metals and mining stocks to the stock

Exhibit 6.7 Annual Returns of the Second-Grader Portfolio

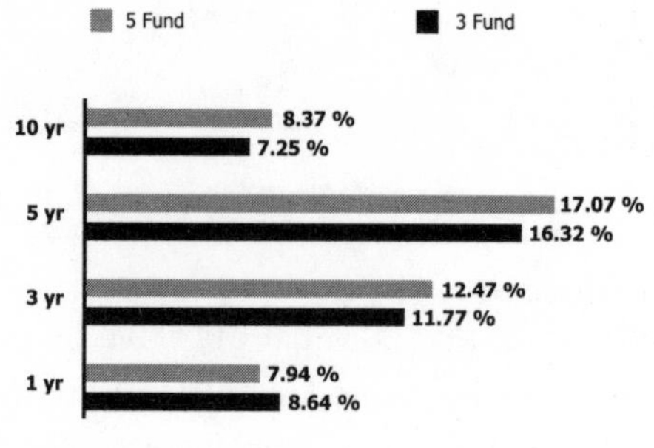

market will stay low. We want to be as negative as we can be, but correlations are constantly changing—as Richard Ferri points out in his book, *All About Asset Allocation* (McGraw-Hill, 2005).

Another thing to remember is that REITs and precious metals had a great 10-year run during this period. They handily beat stocks, as you can see in Exhibit 6.8. This is unlikely to continue indefinitely.

Before we throw in the towel on the alternative asset classes, remember that 10 years is an incredibly short period of time. Also remember that the main purpose of these alternative asset classes

Exhibit 6.8 Annual Returns of the Five Funds

	1 yr	3 yr	5 yr	10 yr
Vanguard Total Intl.	15.52%	19.13%	23.45%	9.44%
Vanguard Total Stock	5.49%	8.90%	13.80%	6.25%
Vanguard Total Bond	6.92%	4.51%	4.35%	5.72%
Vanguard REIT	−16.46%	8.08%	17.50%	10.23%
Vanguard Precious Metals	36.13%	38.01%	35.28%	23.42%

Annualized Returns as of 12/31/2007

is not to boost return, but to decrease risk. There does appear to be sound reasoning as to why real estate and precious metals move in different directions than the stock market, so I'm sticking with those two asset classes. Would I bet heavily that it will beat Kevin's three-fund portfolio over the next 10 years? Not a chance.

Applying the Golden Rule of Correlations

There are dozens of different sectors, styles, and types of assets we can use to produce complex correlation matrixes. We can then build those dozens of assets into a large portfolio, though doing that will (at best) achieve a portfolio that has no more of a risk-adjusted return than Kevin's three-fund portfolio. And Kevin's will be both lower cost and more tax efficient without cutting into his *SpongeBob* time. The beauty of the three-fund portfolio is that it automatically takes all of those correlations into account and simply builds the global portfolio without having to worry about standard deviations, correlations, Sharpe ratios, and the like. After all, we can enjoy our slice of the pie without knowing how it was made.

I recommend building a more complex portfolio with REITs and precious metals stock asset classes if, *and only if,* you understand why they should be a part of your portfolio—to lower overall portfolio volatility. That means you probably need about 10 years for the REITs and 20 years for the precious metals. That also means that if precious metals lose two-thirds of their value, *you can't panic and sell.* Keep REITs to no more than 10 percent of your domestic equity portfolio, and do not consider REITs unless the value of your stock portfolio is much greater than the value of your real estate. Keep the precious metals and mining stocks to no more than 10 percent of your international holdings, and go in only if you can commit to a long-term holding period.

Remember that the five-fund portfolio at most has a total of 9 percent of the total portfolio in these two new asset classes. That leaves at least 91 percent of it identical to Kevin's simple three-fund portfolio. This is fine-tuning Kevin's simple portfolio rather than making any major change.

Chapter 7

Bonds—Your Portfolio's Shock Absorber

"Don't Lend Money to Someone Who Won't Pay You Back"

As you may remember, I convinced Kevin to allocate 10 percent of his portfolio to bonds. He wasn't too crazy about earning less on his money, but I got him on board by telling him that the role of his bond funds was to provide just a bit of stabilization for his portfolio. I avoided using the word *stabilization,* of course, and instead went for the metaphor of his bop bag—you know, those inflatable bags with the sand at the bottom that you can punch or kick and generally knock over, only to have them bounce back up. I told him that the bonds do for his portfolio what the sand at the bottom does for his Spiderman bop bag—they allow it to bounce back up.

That made it a little clearer for him, but we still had a way to go. I explained to him that instead of owning a piece of thousands of companies, we were actually lending money to the United States. This includes U.S. companies and even the U.S. government. Once I had invoked the name of the *U.S. government,* I expected my little patriot to give me one of his enthusiastic *wows*, but he was having a hard time overcoming his lack of enthusiasm about earning only about 5 percent on his money.

"Can't I lend money out and get the same ten percent?" asked Kevin. I told him that he could, but it was likely that he wouldn't want to. Having run out of appropriate metaphors, though, I decided to punt and told him it was time to do his homework.

I thought about it the next day, and after dinner I gave it another try. "Do you trust all of the kids in your class?" I asked.

"Kind of," Kevin replied, "except for Randy." He filled me in on Randy and all the trouble he constantly got into. From what Kevin told me, I wouldn't be surprised if the principal had Randy's parents on speed dial. I asked him if he would lend a dollar to Randy.[1]

"No way!" was the adamant reply.

"What if he promised to pay you back one dollar and ten cents tomorrow?" I suggested, noting that this was a 10 percent return in one day.

Kevin continued shaking his head and saying *no,* because Randy was always borrowing stuff and never returning it.

I was on a roll now. I asked Kevin the same question about one of his closest friends. "Would you lend a dollar to Brittany, if she promised to pay you back a dollar and ten cents tomorrow?"

"Of course," he responded without hesitation, "she wouldn't even need to pay me the extra dime." My wife beamed at Kevin's cuteness or altruism (or both). As a dad, I was also proud; however, I realized I had a thing or two still to teach him about capitalism.

I explained to Kevin that we could invest in bonds that might pay 10 percent, but it would be like lending money to companies that sometimes behave more like Randy, and don't always pay back what is lent to them. We call these *junk bonds.* I went on to say that if we lend money to companies that are more like Brittany, in that we know them pretty well and they will be able to pay back our money, we only get a 5 percent return. This is because we know these companies behave much more like Brittany than Randy. We call these *government and investment-grade corporate bonds.*

"Oh, I get it," said Kevin happily. "I don't want the junk bonds because I might not get my money back."

And having gotten it, Kevin went forward buying a total bond fund of government and investment-grade bonds earning about 5 percent, yet with the knowledge that he was going to get his money back.

The Common Sense of Lending Money to Someone Who Will Pay You Back

A bond is essentially when an investor loans money to an entity (corporate or governmental) for a defined period at a certain interest rate. Bonds are used by companies, municipalities, states, and U.S. and foreign governments to finance a variety of projects and activities.[2] Bonds stabilize our portfolio's performance, and the mix of bonds with a global stock portfolio dramatically impacts the amount of risk we are taking.

This is a critical component of anyone's investment portfolio—even for the second grader who doesn't look at his portfolio, and especially for the adults who look all of the time.

While this is a tad oversimplified, bonds are issued by three types of organizations:

1. *U.S. government or agencies of the U.S. government.* Examples include Treasury bills or GNMA mortgage bonds. Some of these bonds are exempt from state taxes.

A Second Role of Bonds: Income to Live On

I discussed only the risk-mitigating role of bonds with Kevin. Most bonds pay a periodic interest payment that can be either received in cash or reinvested into our accounts. Kevin doesn't need the cash, because his parents provide him with a generous $2-a-week allowance.

Some of us, however, need those interest payments to live on, and a theoretically correct portfolio that doesn't put food on the table doesn't work. While one can raise money by selling stock, those stock sales may come at the wrong time, when the market is down and the portfolio won't have time to recover. Thus, all things being equal, we may have to choose a higher proportion of bonds in order to meet our cash needs.

2. *Municipalities.* Local governments issue municipal (or muni) bonds, which are typically exempt from federal taxes.
3. *Corporations.* Companies issue bonds that are almost always fully taxable.

Two Types of Risk in the Bond Market

Let's face it—Kevin's not alone in perceiving bonds as something that makes stock indexing look exciting. Wall Street clearly understands this and has found ways to make bond investing exciting through fancy derivative products that promise enhanced returns with little risk. Underneath it all, however, are two types of risk associated with bonds—*default risk* and *interest rate risk.*

Default Risk

In the beginning of this chapter, Kevin refused my theoretical loan of a buck to his classmate, Randy, at a very handsome interest rate. This was because he suspected he'd never see that buck again. Kevin applied some sound if-then reasoning—as in *if* Randy doesn't return what he borrows at school, *then* he probably won't return my dollar. It's just that sort of reasoning that we adults often fail to realize.

Let me tell you a magical story about mortgage bonds. Not too terribly long ago, in a place called the United States of America, banks and mortgage companies were lending more than 100 percent of the value of a house to people without jobs and who sported rock-bottom FICO credit scores. Kevin would have seen *Randy* written all over them and avoided them like the plague. But the banks and mortgage companies didn't. In fact, it was easy for them to ignore any misgivings they might have had because they sold these loans to investment bankers. The investment bankers dressed these loans up with really fancy names, performed some "swaps" on the loans, and paid insurance companies to guarantee the loan payments. Next, they sold them as a bond-like investment, claiming that their high interest payments were accompanied by virtually no risk. Now that's what I call creating an illusion, one that would make David Copperfield *and* Cris Angel envious. And that illusion is the story of the subprime mortgage bubble that cost us hundreds of billions of dollars. The bottom line was that underneath all of the fancy packaging and all of the really cool-sounding names were loans to people who never had a prayer of being able to repay them. Such suspension of common sense would never have made it past a second grader, but Wall Street bit—hook, line, and sinker.

What lurked behind this subprime fiasco was the human desire that has coined many turns of phrase—*blood from a turnip, water from a stone,* or (in this instance) *getting something from nothing.* We wouldn't settle for a low rate of interest on a bond, so we tried to pretend we were actually buying high-credit instruments that also paid a high return. Of course, we all know the ending to the story; the whole kit and kaboodle came crashing down on us as the housing market bubble popped, as all bubbles do.

In reality, it's much harder to get something from nothing. Markets aren't stupid forever, and the higher the default risk, the higher the interest rates bonds must pay. Now that the mortgage market is back to normal, people with high credit scores and positive cash flow can borrow money for a much lower rate than those lacking both.

The same goes for the bond market. The U.S. government can borrow money at the lowest rate because it has the lowest default risk. Why? Because only the U.S. government can print money—legally, that is.[3]

Municipalities can also issue bonds. They aren't as secure as those issued by the U.S. government because municipalities can't print money. They can do the next best thing, however, which is to raise taxes. (Ah, to be a monopoly!) In many cases, muni bonds pay less than U.S. government bonds. This isn't because they are less risky; it's because they are exempt from federal income taxes and, if they are issued by the state you live in, usually exempt from state tax as well.

Next come corporations issuing bonds. Those large companies with strong cash flows and balance sheets can borrow money at low rates, but not as low as the U.S. government. They have to pay the money back the old-fashioned way—by earning the cash rather than just printing the money. Smaller companies with weaker cash flows and balance sheets issue bonds with higher interest rates because of the higher risk. These are also known as junk bonds. Rocket science, this isn't.

It's a human tendency to want to get the most return we can and I see many people chase yields to get a higher return. I think this is a huge mistake, even when it's done a whole lot more rationally than our largest financial icons did it during the subprime mortgage mess. Remember that one of the key roles of bonds is to stabilize our portfolio and protect us from a crisis in the stock market. In times of financial turmoil, lower-quality bonds may default and thus end up being as risky as stocks. It only takes the default of one or two risky bonds to more than erase the benefit of that slightly higher yield.

Let's say you have the option of buying either a bond with no default risk paying 5 percent, or one with only moderate default risk that pays you a handsome 8 percent return. Let's assume the one with moderate default risk will default only if:

- A new technology makes its products obsolete.
- A major terrorist attack, or $500-per-barrel oil price, brings us into a severe recession.
- The bond issuer is guilty of accounting fraud.

Admittedly, all of these events are rather rare, so let's say it will happen only once every quarter-century. When it happens, however, you lose 100 percent of your investment. Having a 4 percent chance (once in 25 years) of losing 100 percent of your investment translates into losing an average of 4 percent annually. Thus, the riskier bond has a long-term expected return of 4 percent (8% − 4%).

Whereas in the vast majority of the years it will return a full 3 percent more than the default-free bond, it actually returns less in the long-run. The biggest problem, however, is that you will likely lose your money just when you need it the most.

Interest Rate Risk

I didn't explain interest rate risk to Kevin, but this is an important concept I'll get to in a few years. When we buy a bond or bond fund, we are buying an income stream up to a fixed date, known as the *maturity date,* at which time we get paid back all of the money we invested. When we buy this instrument and interest rates go up, the value of our bond goes down. When rates go down, the value of our bond goes up.

It's important to understand why this happens, so let's take a look at an overly simplified example. Say I buy a bond today for $1,000 that promises to pay me back $1,050 in one year. The interest rate is 5 percent ($1,050 − $1,000)/$1,000. The value of the bond today is $1,000, calculated as follows:

$$\$1{,}050/1.05 = \$1{,}000$$

Now, let's say I hit a bad-luck streak and, immediately after I buy this bond, the Federal Reserve Bank issues an inflation warning and interest rates shoot up. Five seconds after I bought this bond, the same bond is now yielding 6 percent. A new bond would now be paying $1,060 in a year. The bond *I* bought, however, is going give me back only $1,050, so now the value of my bond is calculated as follows:

$$\$1{,}050/1.06 = \$990.57$$

or a decline of $9.43 from the $1,000 I paid.

Because interest rates went up by 1 percent, the value of my bond dropped by $9.43 or 0.94 percent. Of course, I don't have to sell the bond. If I keep it for the entire year, I'll get my $1,050 back and don't have the loss, right? Well, not so fast. Remember that the new bond is paying 6 percent, so I missed out on buying the $1,000 bond that would have paid me $1,060, or an additional $10.00. So, holding onto the bond has an *opportunity cost* of:

$$\$10/1.06 = \$9.43$$

It's no accident that the decline in value is exactly equal to my opportunity cost of holding it to maturity. Bond markets are extremely efficient.

What does all of this mean? Interest rate risk causes the value of a bond or bond fund to change whether you hold to maturity or sell it on the open market. Interest rate risk increases as the maturity date of the bond increases. There are some other determinants of interest rate risk captured by the term duration,[4] but this isn't a book on bond valuation. The concept of interest rate risk, however, is critical.

Capitalism generally rewards us for taking risk; interest rate risk is no different. The yield curve shown in Exhibit 7.1 illustrates that the longer the term of the bond, the greater the yield we should expect. Why? The longer you hold a bond, the more likely it is that either (1) the entity you loaned money to will become unable to pay you back; or (2) interest rate changes will negatively impact the value of your investment.

The yield curve has been known to be inverted, meaning that shorter-term bonds actually pay a higher amount than longer-term bonds. Generally, it is shaped as shown here in that bondholders are rewarded for taking on more risk. In my view, maturities of about five years tend to be the sweet spot on the risk/reward continuum. Buying bonds with maturities

Exhibit 7.1 Bonds: Yield vs. Maturity

The longer the maturity, the higher the yields typically paid by bonds.

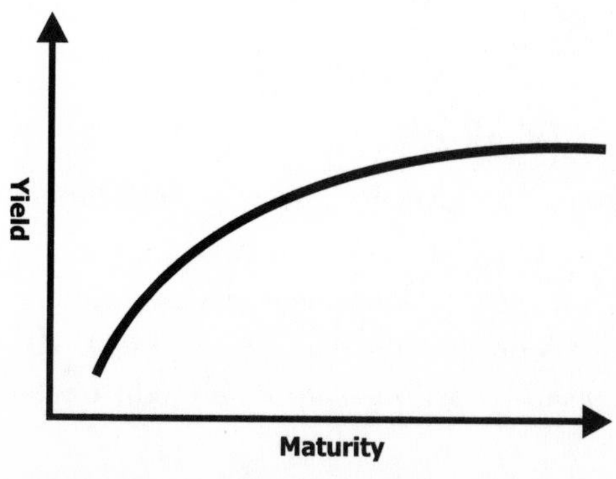

of 30 years is too risky, as any hyperinflationary period would wipe away much of the real value of the bond.

Don't get swindled by investment research that pretends to know what interest rates are going to do. Some may recommend long-term bonds because their award-winning research predicts that rates are going down and the value of the bonds will go up. The Federal Reserve gives us ample warning of what they will do with short-term interest rates, but they don't control long-term rates. Long-term interest rates are inherently difficult to predict and the top economists have correctly predicted the direction about 30 percent of the time—less than a coin flip.[5] By the way, this was particularly disappointing to me, because I thought I was unique in my dismal track record of predicting interest but now know I am in the same company as the nation's top economists.

Putting the Two Risks Together

Morningstar adapted the nine-box grid we showed to classify stocks and stock funds to illustrate both default and interest rate risk of bonds and bond funds. Exhibit 7.2 shows the bond style box; not surprisingly, long-term low-quality bonds pay the highest rates (lower right), while short-term high-quality bonds pay the lowest rates.

Bond Quality (default risk)

- *High credit quality.* Portfolio's average credit quality is AAA or AA.
- *Medium credit quality.* Portfolio's average credit quality is lower than AA but greater than or equal to BBB.
- *Low credit quality.* Portfolio's average credit quality is below BBB.

Exhibit 7.2 Morningstar Bond Style Box

This is an example of a high-quality intermediate-term bond.

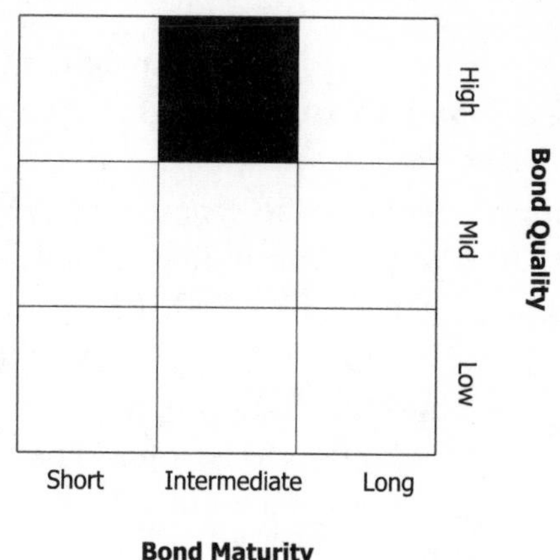

Bond Maturity (interest rate risk)

Bond Type	Short	Intermediate	Long
Taxable bond funds	0−3.5 years	3.5−6 years	6+ years
Tax-exempt bond funds	0−4.5 years	4.5−7 years	7+ years

To put it back in second-grader terms, Kevin lending the dollar for a day to his friend Brittany is the equivalent of a short-term investment-grade bond. Lending a buck to Randy for six years would be known as a long-term high-risk junk bond. We would expect this bond to have the highest yield to compensate for the highest risk the bondholder is taking.

Bond Mutual Funds and ETFs Are Better Than Bonds Themselves

While bonds are an important part of our portfolio, most of us can't buy hundreds of bonds to diversify enough. Owning a handful of bonds isn't diversification. Wall Street, however, would like you to believe otherwise, because there's usually more money in it for them. To perpetuate this myth, they have put out three strong but (in my opinion) faulty messages. Let's examine them.

Faulty argument #1: Bond funds change in value but holding a bond to maturity gets all of your money back. This falls under the category of true but completely misleading. Remember the example of the one-year bond I bought with impeccable timing seconds before the rates went up by a full percent? Whether I sold the bond or held it to maturity, I lost the exact same amount. The value of my bond dropped by $9.43 and my opportunity cost of holding the bond also was this exact amount. The value of owning the bond and getting your money back is a psychological value rather than an economic one.

Faulty argument #2: A laddered bond portfolio is superior in that it reduces interest rate risk. A laddered bond portfolio is a strategy of buying bonds with different maturity dates (buying bonds that mature in 2, 4, 6, 8, and 10 years from today, for instance). The stated reason for doing this is that, if rates are rising, maturing short-term bonds can be reinvested at higher rates. This argument is just plain false. What really matters is the average maturity of your total bond portfolio (or technically the average duration) and nothing more. If interest rates go up, you will lose the same amount of value. That loss in value will either show up in the decline in the price of the bonds or in the opportunity cost of receiving below-market interest payments until the bond matures.

Faulty argument #3: Bonds are just as marketable and liquid as bond funds. We are back to the true-but-completely-misleading category here. Yes, bonds are generally liquid, but this argument leaves out one of the industry's dirty little secrets: the cost of selling the bond. The brokerage house may tell you that it will cost you something like $10 to sell the bond, but they omit the fact that the difference between the price you sell it at (the ask price) and the price the buyer pays for it (the bid price) can be 3 percent or more. Selling a $10,000 bond can easily cost you $300 or more, which can be close to a year's interest payment.

The reason that these bid/ask spreads are so huge is because bonds are very thinly traded, especially municipal bonds. You will never actually see that cost show up on your statement, though it is quite real and you are most definitely paying it. So much for transparency in the industry. No-load bond funds, however, don't incur these trading costs when you sell. In addition, these funds can trade bonds with much lower commissions and spreads than individuals can.

Are We Forgetting International Bonds?

When Kevin and I had our discussion on spreading our eggs in the stock market, I explained that it was important to spread his eggs across the entire world by building a global portfolio. That's why he included an international stock fund. If the logic holds for stocks, why wouldn't it hold true for bonds? Why didn't I include a fourth fund—an international bond fund?

I wrestle with this question daily with my clients' portfolios and my own. Clearly, there are times when foreign bond funds significantly outperform Kevin's Total U.S. Bond Index Fund. Those happen to be times when the U.S. dollar is getting trounced by the euro and other foreign currencies.

Ultimately, I'm still leaning against international bond funds for Americans for the following reasons:

- Since the role of the bond fund is to provide stability, the foreign currency risk exposure from an international bond fund is too high. That is to say, we will spend down our portfolio using U.S. dollars rather than euros, yen, or other currencies. Whereas the foreign currency risk can be hedged, the costs of doing this are high.

- I haven't yet found a diversified total international bond fund with low costs. Thus, while I clearly see value in buying global bonds, the costs of entry are still too high for me relative to the price of buying a diversified U.S. bond index fund.

Buying Bond Funds

The case for stock indexing rests on simple second-grader mathematics, and the exact same mathematics is true for bonds. If the average bond fund is paying 6 percent and the average expense is 1 percent, then the average investor will get 5 percent. What is different here is that the inverse relationship between costs and returns is even more dramatic in bond mutual funds than it is in stock mutual funds.

Two studies in the *Journal of Investing* in both the taxable and tax-exempt bond markets reached the following conclusions:[6]

- There is a negative relationship between expense ratio and net return among bond funds with the same investment style.
- The expense ratio is a deadweight loss. A 1 percent increase in the expense ratio reduces net return by 1 percent.
- Loads are a deadweight loss.
- Among funds with the same style, lower-cost bond funds consistently produce better relative returns than higher-cost funds.

So, when you buy an expensive bond mutual fund, your odds of beating the lower-cost equivalent are even lower than when you try it with stock mutual funds. You'd really have to feel lucky. That's not to say that an expensive long-term junk bond fund can't beat a low-cost, short-term investment-grade bond fund, but that's an apples-to-oranges comparison. An inexpensive long-term junk bond fund will likely beat an expensive equivalent. Always remember that one of Wall Street's favorite illusions is comparing apples to oranges, or in some cases, apples to *parts* of oranges.

Chasing That Little Extra Yield

If you buy a bond fund, you might think you don't need to worry too much about default risk, since the fund typically owns hundreds of bonds. This, combined with our human desire to capture just a little more yield on our bonds, can lead to large errors.

Take, for example, the Schwab YieldPlus Ultra-Short Bond Fund (SWYPX, see Exhibit 7.3) and its performance, according to Morningstar. It was billed as a safe alternative to money market funds. In fact, in 2005 and 2006, the fund returned an extra 1 percent annually, versus the aggregate in its category, according to Morningstar. Naturally, the fund grew as investors rushed to get in.

Exhibit 7.3 Schwab YieldPlus (SWYPX) Performance

This fund was billed as a safe alternative to money market funds.

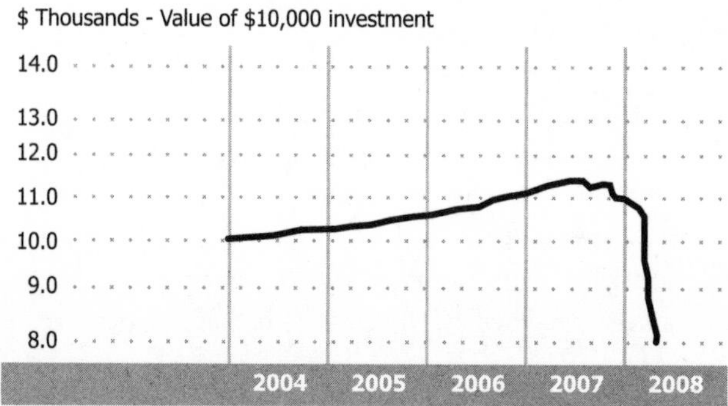

Then, at the end of 2007 and beginning of 2008, the fund dropped by more than 30 percent. What happened? This "safe" fund was actually highly exposed to subprime mortgages. Even Kevin could have told these fund managers that lending money to people who can't pay it back wasn't exactly going to stabilize the portfolio, though he would have said it differently.

This bond fund lost 30 percent of its value at a time when the stock market turned bearish. Our bond funds should be acting as shock absorbers during down stock markets and the last thing we want is a bond fund that is taking on more risk than our stock funds. Don't get greedy by chasing that extra little yield.

Applying the Golden Rule of Lending Money to Someone Who Will Pay You Back

The role of the bond portfolio is to stabilize our returns and possibly to provide income we can count on. In considering how much stabilization you want, set the proportion of bonds that's right for you and stick to it. Changing the allocation will likely increase risk and decrease return.

Don't get greedy by taking on too much risk in your bond portfolio, for the simple reason that it defeats the stabilization purpose. Junk bonds take on too much default risk, whereas long-term bonds take on too much interest rate risk. Especially during times of declining rates, we have a tendency to take on more risk to keep our income up. Don't do it. A second grader knows not to lend money to someone who may not pay him back, though we adults seem to forget that all of the time.

Buy bond funds rather than the individual bonds themselves. They provide diversification and dramatically decrease the costs of selling, should you need to sell. The argument that individual bonds eliminate interest rate risk is just another illusion courtesy of the Wall Street dream machine.

Always buy a low-cost bond fund, because what you don't pay in costs you receive in higher returns, without taking on more risk. Chasing the higher-cost, hot bond fund will yield the same dismal results we've seen from chasing hot stock funds. Second-grader math works for bonds just like it does for stocks.

Don't get sucked into muni bonds by blindly concluding you'll pay less taxes. It's not the amount of taxes you pay that matters; it's the amount of after-tax money you get to keep. If you are in the 35 percent tax bracket, a taxable fund paying 5 percent yields 3.25 percent after taxes (5% × (1 − 35%)). This would be more than an equivalent muni bond yielding 3 percent.

In deciding which bond funds to buy, always compare apples to apples. Looking the funds up on Morningstar.com is a great way to make sure they are comparable. I generally recommend bond funds that are intermediate term in length because it tends to be the sweet spot in the risk/return spectrum. I always stay in investment-grade quality since the role of the bond portfolio is safety and stabilization.

Exhibit 7.4 lists some intermediate bond funds I generally recommend to clients. These intermediate index funds provide exposure to the total bond market of Treasury bonds, government agency bonds, and investment-grade corporate bonds.

Exhibit 7.4 Total Bond Index Choices

	Symbol	Expense Ratio	Minimum Investment
Vanguard Total Bond Market ETF	BND	0.11%	1 share
Vanguard Total Bond Market Index Mutual Fund	VBMFX	0.19%	$3,000
iShares Lehman Aggregate Bond ETF	AGG	0.20%	1 share

There are also some low-cost nonindexed bond funds that work well (see Exhibit 7.5). The iShares Lehman TIPS Bond Fund and the Vanguard Inflation-Protected Fund are Treasury instruments that pay inflation plus a certain fixed percentage. They are a good way to hedge against inflation.

(Continues)

(Continued)

The Vanguard GNMA Bond Fund may sound scary because the *M* stands for *mortgage.* Fear not, they are backed by a U.S. government agency. They are not part of the subprime risk. These are not index bond funds, but are good low-cost intermediate bond fund alternatives to indexing.

Exhibit 7.5 Other Bond Choices

	Symbol	Expense Ratio	Minimum Investment
iShares Lehman TIPS Bond	TIP	0.20%	1 share
Vanguard Inflation-Protected Securities Mutual Fund	VIPSX	0.20%	$3,000
Vanguard GNMA Bond Mutual Fund	VFIIX	0.21%	$3,000

Keep your bond investing simple enough for a second grader to follow, and never buy an instrument that has a fancy name like "enhanced collateralized debt obligation investment unit trust." It's a loan that is so flimsy, you might as well give Randy the money.

Chapter 8

Better Than Bonds

"If the Teacher Promises You'll Be Paid Back, Then It's Okay to Lend Randy Money"

Now that Kevin more or less understood the risk–reward relationship in lending money, I threw in one more complication. I explained to Kevin that he had one more option when it came to lending money. I changed the facts from our discussion in the previous chapter. I asked Kevin whether he would lend the dollar to Randy today to get a $1.10 back tomorrow. But this time, I assured him that his teacher, Mrs. Hackman, would promise that Randy would pay him back the next day. Mrs. Hackman not only was Kevin's second-grade teacher, but had also been his preschool teacher, and she took a close second to my wife and me in his trust and affections. So, to

Kevin, Mrs. Hackman's promise meant more than a government guarantee.

Kevin asked, "But what if Randy forgets to bring in the money tomorrow?"

I responded that he didn't need to worry about that because Mrs. Hackman would pull out the $1.10 herself and pay him back immediately. "Would you lend the dollar to Randy, under these pretend circumstances?" I asked. "Sure," replied Kevin. "But why would Mrs. Hackman want to pay back money for Randy?"

To Kevin, the concept of someone, even his beloved teacher, paying back money that someone else owed, was a bit silly. But he had grasped that lending money to high-risk friends isn't so risky if it's backed by someone you can trust.

The Common Sense of Lending Money If It's Backed by Someone You Trust

As you may have deduced so far, I'm a dyed-in-the-wool indexer who believes that markets are relatively efficient. That doesn't mean, however, that I think markets are perfectly efficient. Case in point: Warren Buffett, whose decades of stellar performance are more than merely a short-term variation. I just think the odds of finding the next Warren Buffett are far too low to bet one's nest egg on.

But what if a market inefficiency was introduced by the U.S. government? And what if that inefficiency could be exploited only by the small individual investor and not by the usual big institutions? Well, such an inefficiency does exist in fixed income, and it's child's play to exploit, though it requires a little bit of time and effort.

This inefficiency comes in the form of the U.S. government guaranteeing our deposits in banks and credit unions. Member banks are backed by the Federal Deposit Insurance Corporation (FDIC) and member credit unions are backed by the National Credit Union Administration (NCUA).

Both the FDIC and NCUA are agencies of the U.S. government, and guarantee assets up to certain limits (which are discussed later in this chapter). Do not confuse either of these with the Securities Investor Protection Corporation (SIPC), which is a nongovernmental unit that insures clients of brokerage firms.

The U.S. Government Created Inefficiency in Fixed Income

In the previous chapter, we looked at two different risks in fixed income: default risk and interest rate risk in bonds. Both of these risks also exist in the world of banking when we lend our money to banks in the form of a savings account, money market, or certificate of deposit (CD). Obviously, a very large and well-capitalized bank would be less likely to go bankrupt than a small local bank or credit union, simply because the larger the institution, the better equipped they are to handle something like the subprime lending mess.[1] The larger, more secure bank would be able to borrow money for a lower rate since it has less default risk, which would mean investors would expect to earn a slightly lower return on certificates of deposit and open savings accounts at these large banks.

All of this is fairly logical and rational behavior and is exactly how things would be expected to work in a free market. It was, until the U.S. government stepped in and created the two agencies that guarantee our deposits up to certain limits, and effectively make the default risk of all member institutions zero. That is to say, the default risk of a CD is, for all practical purposes, no greater than the default risk of a U.S. Treasury bond.[2]

The Value of This Market Inefficiency

In the investing biz, we always come up with new terms to make investing seem as difficult to decipher as the Dead Sea scrolls. There is a term known as *alpha* that refers to the abnormal rate of return investors get on their investment, on a risk-adjusted basis. An investment that beats the market by 2.00 percent is said to have an alpha of +2.00. As mentioned, most dyed-in-the wool indexers correctly believe that alpha must be a zero-sum game. For every portfolio with a 2.00 alpha, there must be one with a –2.00 alpha. As you may have surmised by now, I look at things a bit differently. I believe that alpha can be achieved in the fixed income market—if you're willing to do a little work.

Let's look at a hypothetical example as of the time of this writing. Say a large institutional investor, call it Galactic Investments, Inc. (GII), wanted to invest a few billion dollars in a risk-free instrument for a period of five years. GII could turn to Treasury bonds and earn a dazzling 2.37 percent annual return. Of course, neither an institution nor an individual would have to pay state tax on this income, so let's assume they are in a very-high-tax state and have an effective annual yield of 2.63 percent. This would effectively be about a 15 percent state tax rate.

Now, Kevin could go out and buy a five-year CD. The average five-year CD was yielding 3.41 percent. The extra 0.78 percent that Kevin would earn more than the 2.63 percent effective yield for GII is, for all practical purposes, alpha. It's debatable whether that would be worth your time, or even Kevin's. But none of us have to settle for the average rate.

The FDIC and NCUA have effectively eliminated default risk as long as we stick to a member institution and keep below insurance limits. Firing up the Internet and doing a little searching turns up a 5.00 percent five-year CD! Kevin's computer skills are fast approaching mine, so, he can go out and buy this five-year CD and earn a whopping 2.37 percent excess return over GII. This translates to an extra return of 2.37 percent, as shown in Exhibit 8.1. In Investment jargon, we call this extra return *alpha*.

Exhibit 8.1 Example of Alpha: Treasury versus Highest-Paying CD

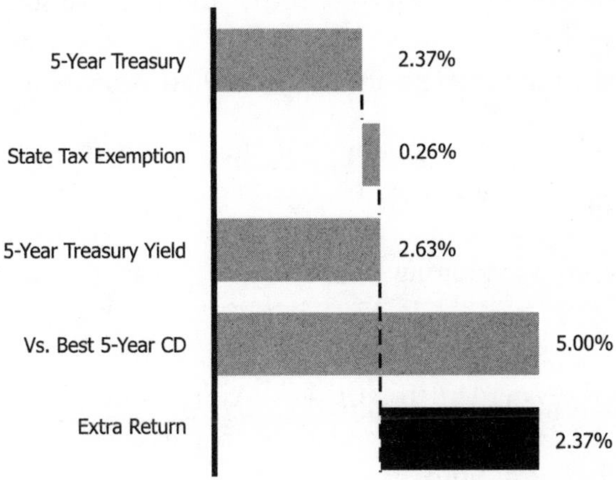

Why can't GII go out and buy this same CD? This government agency insurance creates a market inefficiency that only smaller investors can exploit. Individual accounts are insured only up to $100,000 on a permanent basis, and this wouldn't be meaningful for a large institution. While they could spread their money out, it would take 20,000 banks and credit unions to keep $2 billion insured. There aren't enough institutions around paying high yields. So, only small investors can benefit from this insurance.

In addition to the $100,000 individual account insurance, joint accounts are insured to $200,000 and retirement accounts are generally insured to $250,000.

Guideline to NCUA and FDIC Insurance Limits

- Taxable accounts are insured to $100K per institution for an individual account and $200K for a joint account.

- IRAs and Keoghs are insured for $250K each, in addition to the insurance on a taxable account.
- If you are letting your interest compound, make sure you keep your limits below these amounts.
- There are ways to increase the total insured funds at each institution but always confirm that all of your funds are insured.
- Go to www.NCUA.gov or www.FDIC.gov to learn more.

It's possible to get $2 million in insurance at each institution by titling accounts correctly. That's substantial for most of us but not so much for most multi-billion-dollar institutions. GII is shut out from exploiting this inefficiency that you, Kevin, and I can exploit.

As you remember, Kevin invested his fixed income portfolio in the Vanguard Total Bond Market Index Mutual Fund (VBMFX). At the time when this 5 percent CD was available, this bond fund was yielding 4.40 percent, thus only 0.60 percent less than the CD in question. To compare a CD to this fund isn't completely fair, since this total bond market fund is a combination of government-issued bonds (default risk free) and commercial bonds that do have some default risk (such as Enron and WorldCom, which were worth only pennies on the dollar after these world-famous bankruptcies). The five-year CD also has less interest rate risk than the total bond fund as its duration and average maturity are less (Exhibit 8.2).

Why These Attractive Rates Exist

All banks and credit unions use risk-management techniques. One of these techniques is matching the maturities of their loan portfolios (assets) to those of their deposits (liabilities). Sometimes they become exposed to certain maturities and need to close the gap by issuing CDs of a certain maturity.

Exhibit 8.2 The Five-Year CD Can Pay More and Have Less Interest Rate and Default Risk

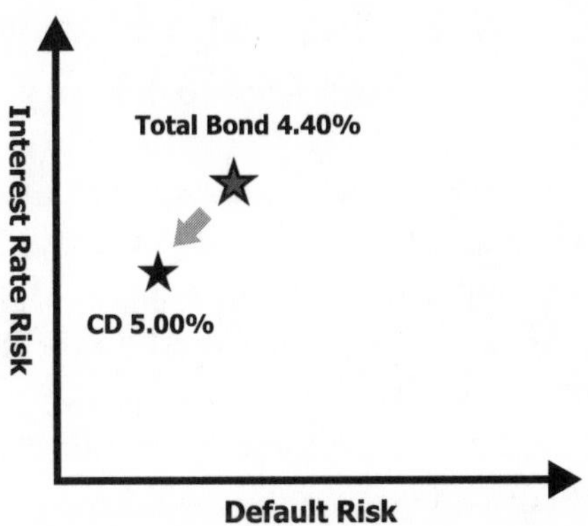

That's why you might see specials running such as a 7-month or 48-month CD.

In addition, it's not a level playing field between banks and credit unions. Banks must both return a profit to their shareholders in the form of dividends and pay income taxes. Credit unions are exempt from these obligations and can often offer superior rates. The credit union views the high CD rate as a way to return profits to its owners.

Finally, financial institutions will sometimes act irrationally. For example, one large credit union was recently offering a zero-closing-cost 5.00 percent APR mortgage, fixed for five years, while it was simultaneously offering a 6.00 percent APY five-year CD. Though technically not arbitrage, I did take advantage of irrational behavior from this credit union. As I closed this loan borrowing money at 5.00 percent and lending every penny back to them in the form of multiple CDs at 6.00 percent, I couldn't resist asking why they did this. Their response was "We make it up with volume."

Hopefully, my face didn't reveal what I was thinking at the time, which was something along the lines of "Are you serious?" I definitely wouldn't lend them money without that government guarantee.

Why These Above-Market Rates Last So Long

Economic theory predicts that any above-market rate would quickly disappear. If a small bank or credit union offered an attractive rate, information would spread rapidly and investors would quickly act to send their funds to the institution. Theory dictates that these rates would then quickly vanish as the institution received the needed funds. Yet these rates last weeks or months. There are two reasons for this.

First, the institutions paying the highest rates offer them directly to the consumer. CDs sold through brokerage channels have commissions that increase the costs for the financial institution issuing the CD. Therefore, they pay a bit less to the consumer.

Because directly sold CDs have the highest rates and brokers, advisors, and other financial salespeople have no incentive to find them, you are not going to hear about them from anyone else. The sales channel is very narrow and funds flow slowly into the institution, which makes the rates last a long time. Without the Internet, it would be incredibly difficult to find these rates and they would last even longer.

The second reason these rates last so long is that they are often offered by credit unions. It is widely believed that credit union membership is limited to a very small group. This was once true, but it is becoming easier and easier for anyone to get membership. Competitive forces are increasingly forcing credit unions to offer membership beyond the select groups they initially were created to serve. Many credit unions are now open to anyone, though you may have to pay a onetime $10-to-$25 fee to join an association and become eligible.

What to Look for in a CD

It may seem obvious that you want the highest-paying rate, but there is a little more to it than this. First, never even *think* about going for that higher rate from an offshore bank or any financial institution that isn't backed by either the FDIC or NCUA. This may or may not be fine for the risky portion of your portfolio, but is just wrong for the part meant to be your stabilizer.

Next, look at the terms of the early-withdrawal penalty. The word *penalty* conjures up some negative thoughts and we always seem to want to avoid them. I actually think penalties can be a good thing and there are times we want to pay them. Let me give an example.

Locking money up in a 5- or 10-year CD can be a very scary thing. What if you need the money earlier, or what if interest rates skyrocket and you're left with the opportunity cost of earning that lower rate for years to come? Is it really worth that 5 percent annual return? The answer is a definite *yes,* if you find the right one.

Early-withdrawal penalties seem to vary greatly. Some require you to forfeit interest you've earned in the past three months; some stretch that period to one year or longer. CDs with low early-withdrawal penalties are the ones to find. If a CD pays 5.00 percent and charges a three-month early-withdrawal penalty, you pay only 1.25 percent to get your money back. If interest rates skyrocket and suddenly go up to 7.50 percent, you can simply pay the penalty, invest in a CD paying the new, higher rate, and break even in just six months. (1.25 percent penalty/(7.50 percent − 5.00 percent)). A Treasury bond, however, would have dropped in value far more than

Exhibit 8.3 Shopping for High-Paying CDs

CDs with high rates and easy withdrawal penalties are the sweet spot.

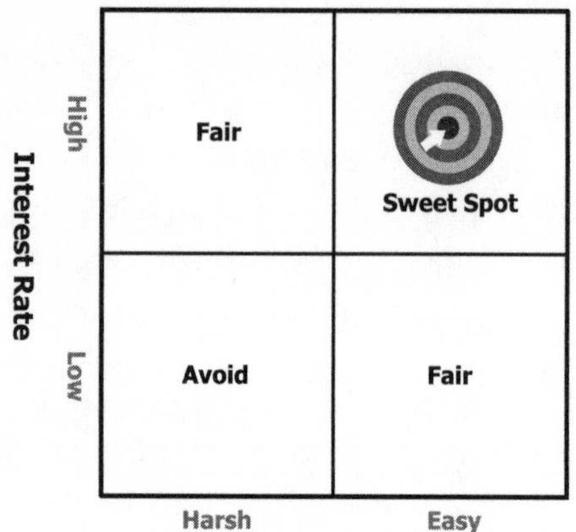

1.25 percent, so the right CD can have less interest rate risk than a Treasury bond.

Exhibit 8.3 shows what you want to look for in a CD. The sweet spot is a government-guaranteed institution paying the highest rates with the lowest surrender charge.

Enough Theory—Where Do I Find These Great CDs?

Finding the right institutions offering the right instruments does involve a little work, because none of those supposed financial fiduciaries looking out for your best interests are going to mention these to you. Bankrate.com is a web site that posts rates, though I've found the highest rates from other sources. One of those other sources is very low tech—the local newspaper.

A particularly great source is an Internet site called www.bankdeals.blogspot.com. Here, people post rates and give links to the institutions. The site contains a lot of useful information that's updated daily. Finally, an old-fashioned Google search of "highest CD rates" often comes up with some great rates as well.

Now, after you've found a great rate, a little due diligence is in order.

First and foremost is to make sure that the institution is insured by either the NCUA or FDIC by going directly to the agencies' own web sites. Do some due diligence. Anyone could set up a web site that looks legitimate and posts the FDIC logo. Make sure you go directly to the FDIC or NCUA web site and make sure it is indeed a member institution.

Next, call the institution and make sure it will hold that rate while you are sending the funds. The last thing you want is to send the institution your hard-earned money only to find out that the great rate had expired and they opened your account at a much lower rate.

Guide to CD Due Diligence

- Always make sure your funds are insured by going directly to either www.NCUA.gov or www.FDIC.gov. Never get greedy by chasing a higher yield from an uninsured institution.
- Speak to someone at the institution and confirm that they will hold this rate until you are able to get your funds to them.
- Check out the early-withdrawal penalty. Penalties of six months or shorter are generally acceptable.
- Make sure you are dealing directly with the institutions. Many sites fail to mention they charge a hefty fee, which, of course, reduces your return.
- Try not to choose the option of letting the CD automatically renew. You want to be reminded that it's coming due

so you can again shop for the highest rates. Sometimes, you will have no choice.

- Always mark the maturity date on your calendar and, a few weeks earlier, be ready to shop for new rates yielding above Treasuries.

Finally, make sure your deposits are within the insurance limits. It's possible for a family of three to get up to $2 million per institution by titling the CDs various ways and having some funds in your retirement account. If you have an estate plan, check with your attorney as changing the titling of these accounts can conflict with your plan.

What Can Go Wrong?

This strategy can also easily backfire. It's important to understand that most of these CDs will automatically renew upon maturity. Many institutions are counting on *stickiness,* meaning that you will renew your CD at a lower rate in the future. The institutions will inform you that your CD maturity is nearing, but it's easy to mistake it as junk mail. If you overlook it, you may find your CD has rolled over at a much lower rate. It is critical that you write down the maturity dates and start looking for the best rates again when those dates get near.

Is It Worth the Trouble?

The answer to this is a definite *maybe.* It all depends on three things: the amount of money you have to invest, the spread between an equivalent bond investment and the highest-paying CD, and the value of your time. Take the example of Kevin earning 5.00 percent on a CD versus a Treasury effective yield of 2.63 percent over a five-year period; Exhibit 8.4 shows the differences in return.

Exhibit 8.4 Earnings from Treasuries versus CDs

Investment	2.63% Treasury	5% CD	Five-Year Alpha Value
$10,000	$1,386	$2,763	$1,377
$100,000	$13,860	$27,628	$13,768
$1,000,000	$138,601	$276,282	$137,680

Whether it's worth your time is a value judgment that I'm not qualified to make. I am willing to say, however, that spending a few hours researching a high-paying CD will provide a greater economic value than clipping coupons. Yet, many people will spend hours saving a few dollars and then let real money slip away by passing on these CDs.

Have I Committed Heresy?

There are some slight differences between CDs and Treasury bonds, so some would debate whether this is truly beating the fixed income market. I believe it is certainly additional return far and above any additional risk:

- *Liquidity.* Treasuries are more liquid as they are easily negotiable.
- *Interest rate risk.* CDs are often superior since some have minimal surrender charges. If interest rates spike, the holder of the Treasury would have to either sell at a lower price or hold and receive lower interest payments. The CD holder could minimize loss by paying an early withdrawal and reinvesting at the higher rate.
- *Default risk.* Treasuries are insured directly by the U.S. government, whereas CDs are insured by agencies of the U.S. government.

And what about simple arithmetic? Have I violated the rule that alpha must be a zero-sum game? I'm going to argue that I haven't. There are some key differences between public markets, such as the stock and bond markets, and private markets, such as certificates of deposit.

I've noted several times in this book where failures have occurred because people thought they were smarter than the market. The little extra yield of the Schwab Yield Plus ended up costing investors a bundle, as noted in Chapter 7. And let's not forget Lehman Brothers' "vigilance on risk" that put them out of business months after reporting record profits. With this strategy, however, we are not making the same mistake of saying we are smarter than the market. We are only taking advantage of a market inefficiency created by the government. That doesn't help billion-dollar investors, and no one except us investors can make money by selling.

Applying the Golden Rule of Lending Money If It's Guaranteed by Someone Trustworthy

This isn't a strategy that works for those who want to invest on autopilot and Kevin's not ready to monitor CD rates and maturities. It does take some effort to find the right CDs and stay on top of the maturity dates. And you are not likely to find an investment professional to help you identify the top-paying CDs because there is nothing in it for them.

But do not underestimate the value of earning even an extra 1 percent on the fixed income portion of your portfolio. It can make a huge difference. Let's take a look at a theoretical 60 percent stock and 40 percent fixed income portfolio. An efficient equity portion with a 0.20 percent expense ratio would underperform the market by 0.20 percent, whereas the fixed income portion yields a +1.00 return. As shown here, that equates to a risk-adjusted combined return of +0.28 percent versus the market:

(60 percent equity × −0.20 percent return) + (40 percent fixed income × +1.00 percent) = +0.28 percent market return

Later, when we talk about constructing the entire portfolio, we will see what that will do to the withdrawal rate when it comes time to start living on your nest egg. You'll see how this strategy alone will get you to financial independence a year earlier!

My advice is that if you have more than $10,000 to invest in fixed income and are willing to commit a few hours a year, start looking for these CD rates. Spend a few minutes a day on www.bankdeals.blogspot.com and start getting educated. Compare those rates to rates you see advertised in the local paper. Start comparing those rates to national averages of CDs with similar maturities. These averages can come from many different sources, such as www.bankrate.com.

When you see a rate that looks attractive, give them a call or go to their web site and find out what their early withdrawal penalty is. If the penalty is a year or longer, you probably want to avoid it. If it says something like "economic loss," then avoid it even more. That's a fancy way of saying it's unlimited. Make sure to read the CD terms and keep a copy. Relative to prospectuses and insurance policies, they are actually very short and simply written.

Next, make sure you qualify to buy this CD. Sometimes banks want only local customers, or credit unions don't offer a way for anyone to join. Confirm that you are not being lured into a *teaser* rate. Warning signs are institutions that:

- Give you a rate that can change at any time, even after you've opened the account.
- Give you this great rate but limit the deposit amount to a low maximum like $1,000. An extra 1.00 percent on $1,000 yields only an additional 10 bucks a year—hardly worth it.
- Tie your great rate to something like a credit or debit card. All they are doing is subsidizing one product with another.

If everything looks good up to this point, then start researching the institution on the FDIC.gov or NCUA.gov web site. Make sure it is legitimate. Be careful not to exceed insurance limits. There is no need to take uncompensated risk by going over these amounts. If local, go visit the institution to set up and fund the CD. If out of town, call the institution and confirm the rates and arrange the fun-fest of filling out all of the paperwork and funding the account. Then always confirm that the account was set up and opened at the agreed-on rate.

(Continues)

(Continued)

Finally, mark the maturity date on your calendar, as well as a reminder three weeks earlier. You'll want to start researching rates well ahead of the date your CD matures. If you find a higher rate, let that institution know because it will often match the rate in order to hold onto your funds. Try to select an option that doesn't let your CD automatically renew as it will likely be at a rate lower than your alternatives at that time.

Finding these rates may not be as exciting as other endeavors, such as trying to find the next hot stock or mutual fund. What it lacks in excitement, it will more than make up for in ease and profit. If the government offers a guarantee for the taking, and you're willing to invest a little time, my advice is to take it. Kevin will not be ready for this strategy for a while, but it might be right for you.

Chapter 9

Simply Brilliant or Brilliantly Simple—Building Your Portfolio

"Don't Bet Your Lunch Money"

Most days, Kevin brings lunch from home, but sometimes he feels like buying it at the school cafeteria. On these days, Kevin's mom makes sure to give him $2.75, to cover lunch and a drink. Kevin carefully puts the money in a special hidden compartment in his backpack where it will be safe.

One Saturday afternoon, Kevin and I sat down for another father–son investment lesson. I asked Kevin why he took such care with his lunch money. He clearly knew I knew the answer, but humored his old man by stating the obvious: "I won't get lunch if I lose it!"

"*Aha!*" I exclaimed in fake surprise, thinking to myself that my thespian skills (or lack thereof) would not have Broadway beating down my door anytime soon. I then asked Kevin, "If you could invest one dollar when the school bell rings, and have a seventy-five percent chance it would be worth two dollars when the lunch bell rings, would you risk it?"

Initially, Kevin seemed pretty excited about the prospect of doubling his money. He gave it some more thought, though, and asked what happened the other 25 percent of the time. I said, "You'd lose the dollar."

He immediately responded, "I'd only have a dollar-seventy-five left and would have to go without lunch that day?" "Well, yes," I responded.

Now it was Kevin's turn to give me a lesson on how important it was to eat regularly and healthy. Skipping a meal was out of the question, no matter how much money could be made.

Kevin's mom was listening in and proudly said, "That's a great choice. Health is always more important than wealth."

Kevin looked pretty pleased with himself. "That was the easiest lesson yet," he said, as he scrambled off to the playroom.

I think he meant that it was the shortest lesson yet.

The Common Sense of Holding on to Your Lunch Money

Investing is much more than making an investment decision that maximizes our wealth. It also involves minimizing the chances we will run out of money. The theoretical option I gave Kevin to invest his lunch money on average would have turned his \$1.00 into an expected \$1.50 (\$2.00 × 75%) probability in only four hours. This would seem to be a clearly winning proposition that any good economist would recommend taking.

While Kevin understood the mathematics of the proposition, he also realized the penalty that he'd have to pay if he lost—namely no lunch for the day. That was a price he correctly decided was too high to pay and he passed on my hypothetical proposal.

What Kevin valued was that he had enough money to meet his needs, which in this instance was to enjoy his lunch and stay healthy. He had enough money to meet this goal and had no need to take the risky proposition I offered.

When it comes to investing and deciding how much of our portfolio we should put in the stock market versus more secure bonds, this second-grader analysis is exactly what we should do.

How Much Risk Is Right for You?

There are many investing myths, like the one that says that asset allocation determines 90 percent of your return. This happens to be true in a theoretical world only. In the real world, costs explain far more of the variation. Nonetheless, if you are committed to the low-cost portfolio, then asset allocation is the next critical decision you have to make. Simply put, stocks are riskier than fixed income in the short-run and the question of risk is critical.

The reason we take risk is that we expect to be compensated in the form of higher returns. In fact, the very foundation of capitalism is the quid pro quo of taking a smart risk with the expectation of getting a greater return in the long run. That's what the stock market is all about.

Historically, the stock market has yielded a long-run annual return of about 10 percent, while fixed income has yielded a bit over 5 percent. Many people, including myself, don't think returns will be so handsome going forward. In my view, I've shaved 2 percent off the stock market to yield a long-term 8 percent return. I suspect that risk-free bonds

Exhibit 9.1 The Real Growth of $1,000

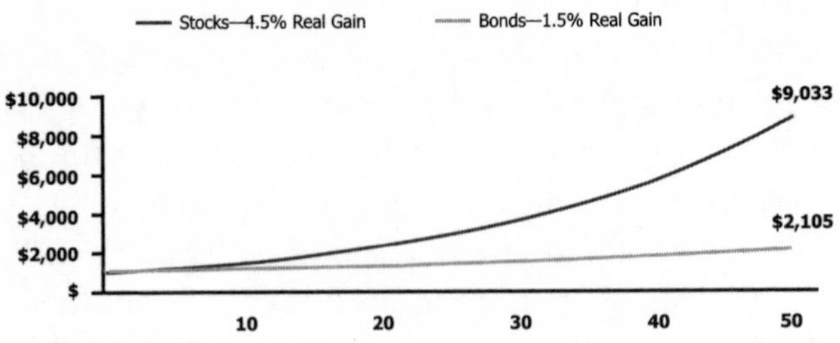

will get somewhere around 5 percent. If inflation comes in at about 3.5 percent, that means our stocks will give us a long-term 4.5 percent real (after inflation) annual return, with bonds yielding only a 1.5 percent real annual return. (And my wife calls me a *pessimist*—can you believe that?)

As you can see in Exhibit 9.1, $1,000 invested over long periods of time grows much more rapidly invested in stocks than it does in bonds. And, of course, the growth is never this steady.

Should you have 10 percent of your money in the stock market, or 90 percent? Probably somewhere in between, but determining the answer must be based on the following two factors:

1. Your *willingness* to take risk.
2. Your *need* to take risk.

These two areas of risk are very different, and let me show you how.

What's Your Willingness to Take Risk?

Do you toss and turn all night like a chicken on a rotisserie when the market goes down 3 percent? Or are you more likely to look at your portfolio, or the market, as often as you change the oil in your car? These are indicators of your willingness to take risk.

The traditional way most planners, including myself, measure one's willingness to take risk is with a risk-profile questionnaire. They ask such questions as:

> If my stocks lost 50 percent of their value, I would:
> a. Sell all that is left.
> b. Sell some.
> c. Do nothing.
> d. Buy more stocks.
>
> In a year where my stocks gained 50 percent and my bonds lost 10 percent, I would:
> a. Sell all bonds to buy stocks.
> b. Sell some bonds to buy stocks.
> c. Do nothing.
> d. Sell some stock to buy bonds.

The implication is that we can measure your willingness to take risk by asking you a series of questions and seeing how you respond. If only it were that simple.

Over the years, I've personally taken dozens of these risk-profile questionnaires and have received feedback telling me I'm a thrill seeker who should have 100 percent of my assets in the stock market. The funny thing is that I've also had some results telling me I'm a walking weenie, too scared to lose a dime. Often, these different conclusions have come from surveys I've taken within days of each other. What gives?

It turns out that our willingness to take risk isn't easy to quantify because it is difficult to measure and very unstable. Take the question of what you would do if your stocks lost 50 percent of their value. I ask this question of my own clients, but I'm aware that the purely theoretical nature of the question tends to garner purely theoretical answers from most people. Yes, intellectually we all know that if stocks lost half their value it would be a good opportunity to buy low.

Unfortunately, I've never found a way to ask the question where I could also replicate the anxiety they would be feeling. Even painting the picture of seeing half of their stock portfolio disappear, along with the dreams of having enough money to pursue their wants and desires, seems to generate the same intellectualized answer. When I meet with the client, I try to drive home this point, but it's still only theoretical pain.

The truth is that we're all fair-weather investors. We tend to think of ourselves as risk takers in good times when the market is booming. The great feeling we get from seeing our portfolio grow makes us want to put more in the stock market so it will grow faster. We forget the pain we felt during the last bear market, and this selective amnesia allows us to kid ourselves as to what sort of risk taker we are. It's a form of the "labor pain" phenomenon, which is the ability women have to forget the physical ordeal of giving birth from one child to the next. I suspect if women didn't have this ability, we would be a world of one-child families.

If the market is traveling downward, taking our hard-earned money with it, we are feeling some real psychological pain. As I previously mentioned, studies show that we have an asymmetrical attitude to investing. That is, the pain we feel from losing $10 hurts twice as much as the pleasure we receive from gaining that same amount. In behavioral finance, this is known as *prospect theory,* and helps to explain why our willingness to take risk is both so hard to measure and so unstable. It also explains why the more we look at our portfolio, the more conservative our portfolio will tend to be.[1] Since the market is up about as often as it is down, on a daily basis, we get twice as much pain as we do pleasure.

The bottom line is that any survey that pretends to tell you what your asset allocation should be is likely flawed. At best, it's only an indicator. Financial planner Ross Levin puts it well: "We all have the same risk profile: We want market returns in up markets and money market returns in down markets."

If only it were that easy.

What's Your Need to Take Risk?

Most of the effort in understanding investment risk seems to be focused on our willingness to take risk, which is very hard to measure. On the other hand, the need to take risk is just as important and far easier to measure. Let's look at a couple of examples.

A 70-year-old single woman came to me with a $4 million portfolio, nearly all in stocks. She had a very simple lifestyle, spending roughly $60,000 per year. By far, her most important goal was to make sure that she had enough money to live comfortably for the rest of her life. She clearly had a high willingness to take risk and it served her well in building up her nest egg. But, much like Kevin having met his lunch-money goal, this woman had met her retirement goal and had no need to take as much risk as she was taking. She could accept a lower expected return on her portfolio to maximize her chances of meeting her primary goal.

In another instance, a 60-year-old man came to me with only about $100,000 in a nest egg, mostly in bonds. He was a high-income earner but hadn't managed to save because he had a lavish lifestyle. Obviously, he had no chance of retiring while supporting his current lifestyle, but he had a very high need to put 90 percent of this money in the market. He also happened to have a need to change his lifestyle, yet this isn't so easily solved, mathematically.

Risk and Your Asset Allocation

The first step in selecting the allocation that is right for you is to have a realistic understanding of what can happen in the short term.

Exhibit 9.2 shows worst annual performance of a mix of a global stock portfolio with a bond portfolio. Note how much

Exhibit 9.2 Annual Average Historic Return versus Worst Single Year, 1970–2007 Global Stock and Bond Portfolio

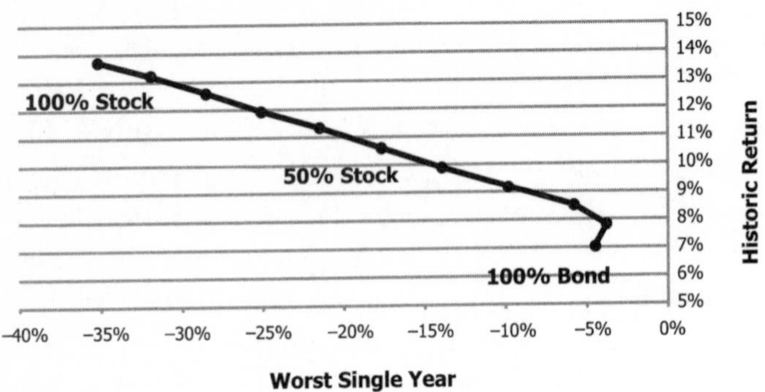

Source: Paul Merriman, FundAdvice.com

the annual downside risk has varied, from a low of a 4 percent loss with 10 percent stocks to over a 35 percent loss with a 100 percent stock portfolio. Considering this is less than 40 years of history, the stock market can actually do worse than the loss shown here. These short-term losses represent the price of admission to participate in the capital markets. Without this pain, we won't get the long-term stock market gains.

Even a common 60 percent equity and 40 percent bond portfolio has lost over 21 percent in a given year. Studies show that a large proportion of investors who lose this amount will react by selling stocks to reduce future exposure to losses. People who do that will be selling low and probably never should have allocated that much to stocks in the first place.

Many people correctly point out that, over a 10-year period, the downside risk of a 100 percent stock portfolio has tended to be no greater than the downside risk of a 100 percent bond portfolio. Exhibit 9.3 shows the worst 10-year performance of the U.S. stock market.[2] Stocks have lagged inflation

Exhibit 9.3 Worst 10-Year Real Annual Performance: T-Bills, Bonds, and Stocks (1802–2006)

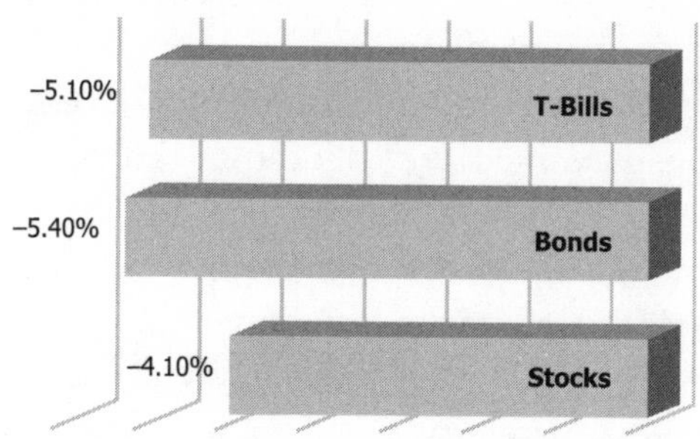

SOURCE: Jeremy Siegel, *Stocks for the Long Run,* McGraw-Hill, 2008.

by as much as 4.1 percent annually over a 10-year period, but bonds and T Bills have done even worse. Sure, stocks can have large real declines over 10-year periods, but so can bonds.

This would seem to argue that there is really no long-term stabilization role for bonds. In fact, we can get the superior long-term gains of the stock market along with the lower long-term levels of risk. Life is good.

There are two problems with that argument. The first is that very few investors have the wherewithal to sit through that down year, or two or three down years, in the market. With impeccably terrible timing, most of us will sell and move out of stocks near the bottom of the stock market. We will sell our stocks after they have lost 25 percent and then buy them back after they have reached new highs. This loss brings with it enough real pain to send us running to the medicine chest. Oh, to be a second grader and have the luxury of not caring.

The second problem is that even nearly 200 years of history doesn't guarantee that this will always happen in the future. In fact, in Japan, the Nikkei index is only about half of where it was in 1990. It could happen to a global portfolio as well. While it isn't likely, author Larry Swedroe advises never to confuse the unlikely with the impossible.[3]

As a general rule of thumb, however, I think the mathematical answer is to put any funds you won't need for more than 10 years into the stock market. Unfortunately, we have to realize that we are not mathematical creatures. Let's take Nobel Laureate, Harry Markowitz, the founder of modern portfolio theory who quantified asset allocation through something known as the *efficient frontier.* Rather than calculating the covariances of asset classes (math) to create the most efficient and economically rational portfolio for himself, he instead split his retirement account at 50 percent stocks and 50 percent bonds.[4]

Even the most mathematical of us shift gears into acting as a human being when it comes to our investments. Human beings have emotions, and bonds have a key role in stabilizing our behavior so we don't move in and out of the market.

As previously discussed, the more we move into and out of the market, the lower our returns end up being. Thus, a portfolio that consistently stays at 50 percent stocks is likely to outperform one that averages 70 percent stocks, but constantly changes that mix. That's because the investor will in all likelihood time the changes wrong.

What about Investments That Give the Best of Both?

The world is rarely black and white. Investments come in more flavors than common stock and bonds. There are instruments such as *preferred stock* that are equities that have some bond-like characteristics. There are also securities called *convertible debt* that have some equity-like characteristics. I could write another book about all of these instruments that go all the way to sophisticated derivatives.

Lucky for me, I don't have to write this exciting book. All I need is one sentence: "Just say *no.*" Hybrids make great cars but aren't as consumer friendly when it comes to investing. It's not that there is anything inherently wrong with preferred stock or convertible bonds; it's just that an individual investor with less than $10 million can't get enough to buy a diversified portfolio. Most of us can buy them only through mutual funds. And because they take a lot of management, they are usually the most expensive of the mutual funds out there. That leads me back to costs, and we all know that high costs are a loser's game.

How Many Eggs Do I Put Overseas?

Kevin now knows that the United States is merely part of the entire world. Once you decide how much stock market risk you want to take, the next step is to allocate between the United States and international. Here I recommend one-third of one's total equity portfolio be in international stocks. For Kevin, who is 90 percent stocks, this means that 60 percent is in the United States and 30 percent in international. For an investor who is 60 percent in the market, that would mean 40 percent in the United States and 20 percent international. You get the drill.

How did I arrive at this 2/3 U.S. and 1/3 international allocation? I didn't use a magic formula; rather I used some judgment. The world stock market value is roughly 45 percent United States and 55 percent international. Pure market cap weighting would have only 45 percent United States rather than two-thirds. The judgment I use is that we U.S. residents are going to spend most of our money in U.S. dollars rather than euros, pounds, or yen. Thus, taking on too much foreign currency risk is something we want to avoid. If you live outside the United States, disregard this argument and overweight stocks in the currency of your home country a bit.

Many people feel that one-third of one's equity portfolio in international stocks is way too high, whereas others feel it's not nearly enough. That actually makes me feel pretty good about my choice, but let me address two faulty arguments:

Faulty argument #1: You don't need international stocks, because American multinational companies have a large percentage of their operations overseas. *This gives you enough international exposure.* To see the flaw in this logic is easy. During the five years between 2003 and 2007, the U.S. stock market earned a handsome 91 percent return, but international stocks returned 187 percent. The very fact that the returns differentials could be this large between U.S. and international stocks shows that you don't get enough international exposure by just buying U.S. stocks.

Faulty argument #2: One should overweight international stocks, because most of the world's economic growth will come from overseas. I certainly agree with this argument, but that does not translate into international stocks outpacing U.S. stocks. That's because it's not exactly a secret that countries like China and India are growing faster than the United States, and this knowledge is already priced into the market. This is the same phenomenon as Google being priced at much higher multiples than Ford, because we know Google has better economic prospects. Remember that beaten-up value stocks tend to make better investments than the star growth stocks. The same may be true in that the fastest-growing economies might not be the best investments.

Finally, it's important to buy international stocks for the right reasons. I've been using the *1/3-international* spiel for many years. The typical response several years ago was "I can't go that high." After stellar years for international stock performance, however, the typical response changes to "Why only a third?" Can you say "performance chasing"? That's the wrong reason to put international in your portfolio, and those that do it for that reason are likely to sell when it's no longer the hot flavor.

What Portfolio Allocation Is Right for You?

This is the part of the book where I wish I had a questionnaire you could take that would tell you to put 73.278 percent of your portfolio in stocks and the rest in bonds and cash. But I'd bet you the price of this book that if you revisited that same questionnaire three days later, it would tell you that you should have something like only 32.722 percent of your portfolio in stock. The best I can do is offer you some pointers.

Get in Touch with Your Feelings

As a typical guy, I'm not so good at talking about my feelings. But getting in touch with your feelings is perhaps the most important part of asset allocation and reaching your financial goals. Maybe that's another reason women make better investors.

Carve out an hour of your time when your investments are doing particularly well. Write down how you are feeling about your financial goals and your ability to take risk. State what you would do if the market went down 30 percent, and whether you are in it for the long run. Then do the very same thing at a point in time when your investments are doing particularly poorly. Talk about these feelings with someone you trust.

My hunch is that you will end up with two very different pictures of your ability to take risk. You may feel invincible during the good times, and ready to stuff your nest egg in a mattress during the bad times. The *aha!* moment will come when you see how differently you feel about risk. Don't feel bad; it merely means you are human.

Now, keep both pieces of paper. At any time you are considering either buying or selling a large proportion of your stock portfolio, pull your writings out and see what you said you would do in both the up market and the down market. Comparing how you feel today with how you felt in other times may help you make a more logical decision.

Examine Your Past Behavior

We could certainly do an exercise today of writing down how we felt in October 2002, when the market lost nearly 50 percent of its value from its high in 2000. We could do the same for October 2007, when the market set new highs. Yep, that would be great, except for the fact that we investors tend to have very short memories. And because our memories are short, we end up making the same mistakes. For this reason, it's very important to get your feelings down in writing.

If you just aren't the sort to commit your feelings to paper, the next best thing is to examine how you actually behaved during those times. Were you far more allocated toward stocks in October 2007 than you were in October 2002? Did you do what most investors did and pour money into the stock market after it had gone up and then sell after it had plummeted? If so, it means you took on more risk than you were actually willing to take.

These two exercises aren't exactly a fun-fest, especially if you are a guy. If you read the Guy Manual, it clearly states that we aren't "feelings friendly." Personally, I blame it on the Y chromosome. However, I think you'll find these exercises far more useful than taking a 143-question risk profile that pretends to measure something as complex as human emotions. Remember that staying with your asset allocation is every bit as important as choosing the right one in the first place.

Getting to Your Allocation

Once an asset allocation is selected, is it better to just buy it and get it over with, or better to use a method known as *dollar-cost averaging* (DCA)? DCA is buying a fixed dollar amount of a particular investment on a regular schedule, regardless of the share price. More shares are purchased when prices are low, and fewer shares are bought when prices are high.[5] For example, if you wanted to buy $120,000 of the total stock market index fund, you could buy it all today or use DCA and buy $10,000 a month for the next 12 months. While I disagree with those who use math to show that dollar-cost averaging delivers superior returns to investing all at once, I do believe that dollar-cost averaging has significant psychological advantages. You don't have to worry about any worst-case-scenario market timing such as buying at the top of the market.

If you dollar-cost average in over a long period of time, say two or three years, you are actually more likely to stay in the market. If the market goes down, you'll feel better that you didn't sink it all in at once, and because you're buying more shares at a lower price. For that reason, I often recommend this technique.

Advanced Portfolio Construction

Real-life complexities often make portfolio construction more difficult. Say you want to build a total U.S. stock portfolio but your 401(k) offers only an S&P 500 index fund. What do you do?

There are completion indexes, such as the Vanguard Extended Market Index Fund (VEXMX) or ETF (VXF), which own the entire U.S. stock market except for the S&P 500. Because the S&P 500 represents roughly 80 percent of the U.S. market value, you could build the total U.S. market as follows:

401(k) account: S&P 500 Index Fund	$8,000
Taxable account: Extended Market Fund	$2,000
Total United States	$10,000

Between the 401(k) and taxable accounts, you own the entire United States. This technique also works if you have large gains in certain taxable accounts that you don't want to realize. You build total portfolios around these holdings.

Rebalancing the Portfolio: Market Timing That Actually Works

Kevin already understands that if you buy things when they are on sale, you can get more with your allowance. He also noted in Chapter 4 how silly adults act when it comes to investing. He'd rather buy when stocks are down and sell a bit when they are up. This simple, but again not-so-easy, method is known as *rebalancing.* For example, if you've decided on a portfolio that is 60 percent stocks and 40 percent fixed income, that means you need to buy more stocks if they decline and sell some if they've been hot. Exhibit 9.4 shows that we'd have to be selling during the go-go days in the late 1990s, buying during the half-off sale between 2000 and 2002, and start selling again during the five-year raging bull between 2003 and 2007.

You will notice that rebalancing has two traits:

1. It goes against every human emotion we have in investing. Given that our emotions constantly fail us when it comes

Exhibit 9.4 Total U.S. Stock Market

Rebalancing forces us to sell stock during up periods and buy during down periods.

to investing, doing the opposite of how we feel may not be such a bad idea.

2. It forces us out of the ranks of the faux contrarian and into the less-traveled ranks of the true contrarian. That is, since investors consistently chase what's been hot, rebalancing forces us to sell some of what's hot and buy some of what's not.

When you stop to think about it, rebalancing is a systematic way of buying low and selling high. In a weird sort of way, it's market timing that actually works.

Rebalancing, however, is not for the faint-of-heart. Bear markets are a part of investing and so is human nature. At the time of this writing, the Bears are clearly in the short-term control of the stock market, and Kevin isn't earning the 10 percent on his stocks that we had hoped for. So, what's he doing? A whole lot of nothing. Unlike adult investors who are withdrawing money from stock mutual funds, Kevin is barely aware when the market is down.

Applying the Golden Rule of Not Betting Your Lunch Money

The uncluttered mind of a second grader has many lessons for us adults. Kevin knew not to bet his lunch money because the goal of that money was to buy lunch. His mom gave him $2.75, which was exactly the amount he needed to meet that goal. He kept it in a safe place because there was no need to risk it. An economist would say there was little reason for Kevin to try for a small financial gain at the risk of not having enough money for lunch.

Now I could have gone over another scenario with Kevin. Suppose his mom had goofed and only put $1.75 in his backpack. If he had discovered

(Continues)

(Continued)

this just before class started, he would have realized he was $1.00 short of the lunch money he needed. This time, if he were offered the same investment opportunity in the beginning of this chapter (to have a 75 percent chance of doubling the dollar), I suspect he would have taken it. He would have gone from a 0 percent chance of meeting his goal of having enough money for lunch, to a 75 percent chance. He would have had a need to take such a risk.

The same lessons apply to our nest egg. The closer you are to reaching your financial goals, the more conservatively you want to invest, so more high-quality fixed income is appropriate. Don't take risks if you don't need to. However, a conservative portfolio of mostly fixed income might be lucky to keep up with inflation, after paying income tax. If that portfolio return is certain to fall short of your goals, then you must take more risk, much like Kevin's having to "invest" some of his lunch money if he was short.

As rule of thumb, money you need in the next 5 or 10 years generally should be invested in fixed income. The stock market is far too risky for money needed in the short-term—and yes, even 10 years can be considered short-term. Take this risk only if you have no other way of meeting your goal.

Always keep at least 10 percent of your nest egg in bonds or fixed income. It has very little impact on your long-run returns and can lower overall risk. Never be so sure of your risk tolerance that you put everything in the stock market. Even low-cost diversified index funds have substantial risk. Conversely, always keep at least 10 percent of your nest egg in equities. Not only will that 10 percent in equities bump your return, it also tends to lower your overall short-term risk. That's because the stock market often does well in years that bonds get beat up.

Look at your past behavior and get in touch with your feelings. If you are picking your allocation during an up market, you may not be as big of a risk taker as you think. If you happen to be setting your allocation during a down market, you may want to force yourself into taking a bit more risk than you feel like at the time.

Put about one-third of your stock portfolio in international stocks. Do it because we live in a global economy. Don't do it because international stocks have recently outpaced U.S. stocks.

Just say *no* to instruments like preferred stock or convertible bonds. When someone says the word *derivative*, don't believe that they are smarter than the market and are delivering market-like returns with less risk.

Once you pick an allocation, stick to it like glue. Don't let the siren song of emotions cause you to wreck your retirement ship on the rocks, and sway you to go in and out of the market. The Wall Street wizards will always be optimistic in an up market and pessimistic during a down market. My advice is to ignore them. The more you move in and out, the lower your returns are likely to be. Sticking with the allocation you select is every bit as important as selecting it in the first place. As they say, "If you can't be right, at least be consistent."

Kevin has a huge advantage over us adults in that he doesn't look at his portfolio very often; in fact, now that I think about it, he has yet to look at his portfolio at all. At this point, the money isn't real to him. Though a second grader doesn't want to lose money any more than an adult does, it just doesn't hurt him like it does us. We must deal with the pain, and how we deal will separate an investor from a speculator. Building the nest egg is a marathon where endurance counts. Sprinting will merely leave you tired and out of the race.

While selecting the asset allocation is a difficult task, remember that building the portfolio is much simpler. The ultra-simple second-grader portfolio (Exhibit 9.5) and the advanced (but still simple) second-grader portfolio (Exhibit 9.6) can work with any level of risk that you select.

Exhibit 9.5 Second-Grader Portfolio

	High Risk	**Medium Risk**	**Low Risk**
Total Bond Index or CD	10%	40%	70%
Total U.S. Stock Index	60%	40%	20%
Total International Stock Index	30%	20%	10%
	100%	*100%*	*100%*

Remember to rebalance periodically—perhaps when any of your asset classes varies by more than 10 percent from its target. For example, if your

(Continues)

(Continued)

target is 20 percent for international stocks, rebalance if your actual allocation becomes less than 18 percent or more than 22 percent.

Exhibit 9.6 Advanced Second-Grader Portfolio

	High Risk	**Medium Risk**	**Low Risk**
Total Bond Index or CD	10%	40%	70%
Total U.S. Stock Index	54%	36%	18%
Total REIT Index Fund	6%	4%	2%
Total International Stock Index	27%	20%	10%
Precious Metals Fund	3%	0%	0%
	100%	*100%*	*100%*

Here are some rules, meant to be as simple as possible, for rebalancing. Because taxes are involved, we have to violate the KISS (keep it simple, stupid) rule:

1. Don't wait until you are out of balance and put new money in the asset class underweighted. If you are in the accumulation phase of your life, you are probably putting money in a 401(k) or IRA. You may be investing after-tax dollars as well. Periodically take a look at your overall allocation. If you are a bit overweighted in international stocks, consider putting all new money in bonds and U.S. stocks until you hit the correct balance. Take a look at your accounts every 6 to 12 months.
2. When you have to sell to rebalance, always look to your tax-advantaged accounts first. When you need to adjust your overall allocation, it's best to do it in a tax-efficient way. A good place to start is in your tax-deferred accounts. You can buy and sell anything in your 401(k)s, IRAs, and the like without paying the tax collector.
3. Next, look to long-term capital gains. If you can't do the rebalancing within the tax-deferred accounts, you are going to pay the tax collector. Realize the long-term gains first, since they're taxed at a lower rate, which minimizes your tax hit.
4. What if you have to take a short-term gain to rebalance? Consider breaking the tolerance rule if you have to recognize a short-term

capital gain. If you are in a high tax bracket and realizing a short-term gain will result in a large tax bill, consider waiting a bit. If you are only a bit out of the tolerance zone and you are about to hit that magic year-and-one-day on the investment, consider waiting until that short-term gain becomes long term.

Admittedly, these rules are a bit of a simplification. In fact, the phrase *simple tax rules* is an oxymoron. More on taxes in the next chapter.

Investing is simple, but it isn't easy. I tell people to "dare to be dull.[6]" Sure, it's dull to own the entire world in a handful of ultra-low-cost index funds. The daring part, however, is to have enough guts to rebalance and buy stocks when they are down. Dare to go against the herd and buy when they are selling. Everyone seems to know this works, but few can actually do it.

Remember Kevin's advice: Buy your candy when the price goes down. If you think like a second grader, you won't even know you are going against the herd. And always remember the words of Warren Buffett: "Be fearful when others are greedy and greedy when others are fearful."

Chapter 10

Investors Who Love to Pay Taxes, and the IRS Who Loves Them

"Don't Pay Taxes If You Don't Have To"

Kevin once asked me how much we pay for him to attend his school. Since Kevin attends public school, I responded without thinking, "Nothing."

"You mean it's free?"

"Not exactly," I replied; "we pay through our taxes."

"You and Mom pay taxis?" he asked, picturing yellow checkered cabs rather than the IRS.

"No, not *taxis;* I mean *taxes. T-a-x-e-s,*" I corrected.

Anticipating the next question, I told him that everybody who earns a certain amount of money per year pays taxes to the government. This money goes to build the schools and pay his teacher and principal. It also goes to build the roads and pay our police and firefighters to protect us. I told him that Mom and I pay taxes every year for this and he will have to as well, some day.

Being the curious kid that he is, Kevin asked how much his mom and I have to pay. A *lot,* I assured him.

"Does everybody pay the same?" he asked.

"No," I said, "people will pay different amounts based on how much money they make and other things."

"Then how do people know how much to pay?" Kevin wondered. I filled him in on a scary thing known as the *tax code,* which determines how much we pay, though no one actually knows how it works.

"But you're a CPA," he replied, assuming I was an authority on such matters. I didn't have the heart to tell him that although I maintained my CPA credentials, I hadn't cracked a tax code since the early days of the Reagan Administration. At this point, it was *I* who wanted to end the lesson and watch *SpongeBob SquarePants.*

I went on to explain that most of the taxes we paid were on the income we make. Part of that income comes from the earnings on our investments. "You mean we don't get to keep all of the money we earn from my portfolio?" Kevin asked glumly.

"I'm afraid not," I told him. I did make him feel better by telling him that Mom and Dad would pay the taxes until he was all grown up.

"Want to know what we can do to lower taxes on our investments?" I asked and he nodded. My wife rolled her eyes at the prospect of me trying to explain capital gains, dividends, ordinary income, and the alternative minimum tax to an 8-year-old. Kevin saw this and amended, "How about just a little?" Smart kid, isn't he?

"Okay," I began, "there are only two tax lessons you need to learn, and they are both pretty easy." In lesson #1, I told Kevin to pretend he made $100 and had a choice of two tax rates—one at 15 percent and the other at 28 percent. You could see him calculating the math, and he quickly realized that I was giving him a choice of paying $15 or $28. He took the 15 percent rate.

Now I told Kevin that the second lesson was a bit more complex. "If you owed the tax man some money, and he gave you the choice to pay it now or pay it years from now, which would you choose?" This was much more difficult to contemplate, because Kevin is very conscientious about returning borrowed items quickly. Doing so is one of the habits that is highly encouraged at school.

So, before he could answer, I gave him some more guidance. "Let's say you owed the government a hundred dollars, but they gave you a year to pay it to them. If you took the year, you could open a CD at the credit union and they would pay you back one-hundred-and-five dollars just in time to pay the tax man. You'd pay the tax man one hundred dollars and get to keep the five bucks. Would you do it?"

"Yeah!" exclaimed Kevin.

I had to go one more step in this lesson. I told Kevin that the government would tax him on the $5 he made, so he would have to pay them about $1 and would only get to keep $4. I noted to Kevin that, in the end, he actually paid a dollar more in taxes since he paid a total of $101, when he could have paid only $100. "Yeah, Dad, but I got an extra four dollars," he reminded me.

Kevin thought the lessons of paying taxes at the lowest rate, and not paying until you have to, were both pretty easy. Yet I explained to Kevin that, when it comes to investing, we adults usually pay more in taxes than we have to, and pay them sooner than we have to. Kevin gave me the "no-way" jaw drop and said, "So, adults like to pay more expenses *and* more taxes?" I nodded.

"Pretty silly, Dad."

Tell me about it, kid.

The Common Sense of Not Paying More Tax Than You Have To

I'm certainly not going to make the case that tax-efficient investing is child's play. Let me just say straight up that I've outsmarted myself more than once when it comes to tax planning. I've also been warned that it's impossible to write a simple book about investing and cover taxes. Yes, *taxes made simple* is clearly an oxymoron.

Nonetheless, taxes are just too important to ignore, because the two lessons of paying less taxes and paying them as slowly as possible can create even more wealth for you than low-cost investing alone. And the most beautiful thing is that low-cost investing happens to be incredibly tax efficient.

Lesson #1: Keep Your Tax Rate as Low as Possible

In general, the government taxes our investment income at two different rates:

1. *Ordinary income rate (higher).* This rate is applied to any interest income we receive on our taxable bonds, such as Kevin's Total Bond Index fund, and for reportable gains we've made on our investments held one year or less. Income from REITs is also taxed at this higher rate.
2. *Preferred income rate (lower).* This lower rate is applied to income received in the form of (most) stock dividends, and to gains on investments held for more than one year.

Admittedly, this is a gross oversimplification and there are all sorts of exceptions to the rules of thumb listed here. It's important to note, however, that even when ugly monsters like the alternative minimum tax (AMT) raise their heads, the preferred income tax rate is still lower than the ordinary income tax rate.

For purposes of this example, let's assume that the ordinary income tax rate is 28 percent and the lower preferred (long-term capital gain and dividend rate) is 15 percent. Now let's put Kevin's two stock funds up against Wall Street.

When it comes to pretax return, it's an unfair game to match Kevin's funds up against those expensive funds managed by the experts—the cost advantage of Kevin's portfolio is simply too large a hurdle. For purposes of discussing taxes, however, we will give them the benefit of the doubt and assume that they perform just as well before taxes. I don't believe this for a minute, but I want to separate the case for tax-efficiency from the case for low-cost investing.

So let's look at what happens when an index fund investor using Kevin's stock index funds competes with a fictitious fund run by, let's call it, Galactic Wealth Management. Let's assume that both funds earn 8.5 percent for the year and we start with $10,000. Thus, both Kevin and Galactic earn $850 before taxes. Further, let's assume both investors are happy with their investments and hold them for the long run.

Both Galactic and Kevin's funds will pay out some dividend income. Let's assume both have a 2 percent dividend yield, which equates to $200 on the $10,000 investment. Everything is equal so far, but things are about to change. This is merely the calm before the storm.

Surely Galactic Wealth Management will talk about its tax-efficiency in its glossy brochure, but talk is cheap. Some of the ones that hype the most tend to be the least efficient. See, you don't have to sell a fund to be taxed on it. If the fund you own sells its stocks for a gain, the government wants its share. And guess who they turn to? You, of course.

In my research, I've found that the typical mutual fund holds a stock on average for about one year and four months. That means that 75 percent of its holdings at the beginning of the year will be gone by the end. This 75 percent is known as the mutual fund's stock *turnover rate.* Data on separately managed accounts by private money managers is much more difficult to obtain, though I've seen turnover that seems to be pretty much in line with this 75 percent amount. Let's assume that Galactic has this same turnover. Broad index funds, however, have virtually no turnover. There are dozens of variables that will determine how much of the gain will be passed on to shareholders of Galactic, but Exhibit 10.1 shows a pretty common scenario of how their $850 gain may be broken out.

Notice that Galactic had a $162 unrealized gain. That means it still holds the stocks that increased in value and won't pass this gain on to the investor until either Galactic sells these stocks or the investor sells Galactic. For now, the Galactic investor has paid the tax collector $135 in taxes and is left with $715 in after-tax gains ($850 – $135).

Now, let's compare this to the investor using the broad index fund approach. The broadest stock index funds, such as those used in the second-grader portfolio, have virtually no turnover. No turnover means no capital gains to pass on until you sell them. Exhibit 10.2 shows the tax impact to this investor.

Exhibit 10.1 Tax Impact—Galactic Wealth Management

Income	Amount	Tax Rate	Taxes
Dividend income	$200	15%	$30
Short-term capital gain	$244	28%	$68
Long-term capital gain	$244	15%	$37
Unrealized gain	$162	0%	$ 0
Total	*$850*		*$135*

Exhibit 10.2 Tax Impact—Simple Index Funds

Income	Amount	Tax Rate	Taxes
Dividend income	$200	15%	$30
Short-term capital gain	$ 0	28%	$ 0
Long-term capital gain	$ 0	15%	$ 0
Unrealized gain	$650	0%	$ 0
Total	*$850*		*$30*

The *aha!* I'm shooting for is that the index fund approach is far more tax-efficient than Galactic. The index fund strategy leaves you with only $30 in taxes versus the $135 paid in the Galactic fund. The index fund investor has $820 to reinvest versus only $715 for Galactic.

So, the indexer has an extra $105 to invest that first year and, in subsequent years, starts harnessing the power of compounding. Through compounding, she will likely get an even bigger amount in each subsequent year. This ever-growing tax savings is reinvested and generates further tax-efficient gains. The Galactic investor, on the other hand, is doing more than his far share to pay off the tax deficit.

Kevin easily grasped the value of lowering the bill owed to the tax collector. Why can't Wall Street learn it?

Lesson #2: When the Government Wants to Lend You Money Interest-Free, Take It!

There is a bank out there that is willing to lend us money. And it's at an interest rate that looks too good to be true—0 percent annually. It *is* true, and we can take advantage of this interest-free loan by using such tax-deferred vehicles as 401(k)s and IRAs. With these vehicles, the government is basically saying that it will let us hang onto the money we owe it and, in the process, let us reap the financial reward.

Take a taxpayer in the 28 percent tax bracket. If he decides to put $10,000 into his 401(k), his tax bill will be lower by $2,800. Now, say he puts that $2,800 in a safe fixed-income investment and earns 5 percent. At the end of the year, this taxpayer now has $2,940 ($2,800 × 1.05), or an extra $140 on the money that would have gone out the door in taxes.

Over time, this can add up to real money. Let's look at what happens over 20 years. At this same safe 5 percent rate, the $2,800 grows to $7,429. The tax collector will take $2,080 ($7,429 × 28%), leaving $5,349 in after-tax dollars. Pretty sweet, considering our taxpayer made this from only $2,800 that really wasn't his to begin with. Remember, this was the $2,800 in taxes he deferred by putting $10,000 in his 401(k).

This could certainly backfire if the taxpayer ends up in a higher tax bracket later on. But, while we can't control what tax rates will be in the future, we can control, at least in this case, *when* we have to pay those taxes. We can withdraw the funds when our income is the lowest and have a better chance of paying less in taxes.

By the way, the best way to protect yourself from an increasing tax rate is not to avoid tax-efficient investing; it's to diversify against what Congress may eventually do with tax rates. If you think you will be paying at higher tax rates when you withdraw the money, consider Roth IRAs or Roth 401(k)s. They don't give you the tax deduction immediately, but do allow all of your earnings to be withdrawn completely tax free. Since most of us don't know our future tax situation, I often recommend putting some funds in a traditional IRA or 401(k) and some in a Roth IRA or 401(k). This diversifies us against what Congress may eventually do to tax rates.

Finally, other vehicles offer some short-term tax efficiencies. These are namely insurance vehicles such as annuities, equity-indexed annuities, and whole-life policies. I'm going to address these in the next chapter. For now, let's just say I generally advise that these be avoided like the plague.

Asset Location, Location, Location

We finance types talk about asset allocation ad-nauseam. I must admit that it's much more fun than talking about taxes. Come to think of it, even a root canal (minus the anesthesia) may be more fun than tax talk. But locating our assets where they are most tax-efficient can be every bit as important as asset allocation. As a matter of fact, it can result in more wealth, whether the market goes up, down, or sideways.

Here I'm talking about which types of investments belong in your taxable accounts versus your tax-deferred retirement accounts. In most of the accounts I see, people have tended to put their stocks in their tax-deferred accounts and bonds in their taxable accounts. The logic behind this conventional wisdom goes something like this: Retirement accounts are long-term and should be invested in equities. You are likely to spend from your taxable accounts earlier, so they should be invested in more secure bonds.

In addition, we tend to think of our taxable money as more "real," so we want to use more caution in investing it. After all, we can't really tap that retirement money for many years.

My position is that this is exactly opposite of what we should be doing. That is to say, we should be overweighting stocks in our taxable accounts and putting bonds in our tax-deferred accounts. I sometimes get the "are you crazy?" look from clients when I tell them they have tax-engineered their accounts backwards.

That's because stock index funds are very tax efficient, while fixed income and CDs are taxed immediately and at the highest ordinary income rates. Even income provided by the total bond fund is taxed immediately at the highest income tax rates. So, placing fixed income in the taxable accounts fails to:

- Utilize the lower tax rates on qualified stock dividends and long-term capital gains.
- Defer paying the taxes on your stocks.

Let's take a simple example of someone with a $200,000 investment portfolio who wants 50 percent in fixed income and 50 percent in stock. Now let's assume that half of it is in a taxable account and half is in an IRA. We'll also assume the equities will earn 8.5 percent annually and his fixed income earns 5 percent. Finally, let's say he is in the 28 percent tax bracket.

If this investor does as most people do, and places the fixed income in his taxable account and equities in his IRA, then, after 20 years, and after paying all taxes, he has amassed $571,000. But if he reverses the location of those assets, he now has $629,000, or $58,000 more! Asset location matters, as shown in Exhibit 10.3.

By merely reversing which accounts the investor held his stock and bond funds, he was able to dramatically increase his return without increasing risk one iota. What's going on here is that the IRA account is eventually going to be taxed as ordinary income whether you are invested in stocks, bonds, or anything else. Withdrawn in retirement from your IRA or 401(k), the gains on your stock portfolio are taxed at the higher ordinary income rate. If they're held in a taxable account, however,

Exhibit 10.3 Asset Location, Location, Location

Placing stocks in taxable accounts and bonds in tax-deferred accounts leaves more after-tax money for you.

Tax Engineering	**20 Year After-Tax Value**
Typical Tax Design $100K **bonds** in **taxable** account **and** $100K **stocks** in **tax-deferred** account	$571,000
Efficient Tax Design $100K **bonds** in **tax-deferred** account **and** $100K **stocks** in **taxable** account	$629,000

Assumes 8.5% annual growth for stocks and 5% annual growth for bonds. Tax bracket = 28%.

they'll be taxed at the lower long-term capital gains rate. Combine this with the terrible tax inefficiency of bond funds, and it's a no-brainer: You want both your fastest-growing and most tax-efficient investments outside of your IRA account.

This strategy is particularly appealing for those who believe that future tax rates will be higher than today's. Let's assume that our investor finds himself in the 38 percent tax bracket when he withdraws his funds, rather than the 28 percent bracket he is currently at. The investor with bonds in his tax-deferred account now ends up with only $603,000 but the other strategy leaves only $520,000. This leaves an extra $83,000 for the investor who locates his holdings in the most efficient accounts.

If you're wondering what the outcome would be if the investments grow at two different rates of return, the answer is that *it doesn't matter.* Under nearly any scenario, we are better off to place tax-efficient investments in our taxable account, and tax-inefficient investments in our tax-deferred accounts.

Now I'm not advocating holding stocks only in your taxable accounts. You clearly want enough cash or access to cash to meet any emergency needs. I typically recommend having access to 6 to 12 months' cash. But let's do a worst-case scenario where you need to raise some cash by selling stock in your taxable account. Let's see what happens. Say, after one year, you need $20,000 immediately.

Selling the stock in your taxable account leaves you with two problems to solve. The first problem is the taxes you are likely to have to pay on any gains you're realizing. This isn't great news, but if you've held the investment for over a year, you'll be taxed at the lower long-term capital gains rate. In this scenario, you're still better off than if you had held your bonds in the taxable account, paying ordinary income tax on their interest payments every year. And if you're realizing short-term capital gains, it's a wash, as they're taxed at the same ordinary income tax rate.

The second potential problem is that you are forced to sell at an inopportune time. What if you sold the stock funds at the bottom of the market? This problem is easily solved. You could just simultaneously sell some of your bond funds in the 401(k) account and buy the appropriate amount of stock funds.

Advanced Tax Planning—Tax-Loss Harvesting

There is one additional investment tax strategy known as *tax-loss harvesting*. If, for example, you buy the Vanguard Total U.S. Stock Index Fund and the stock market declines, you can get some benefit out of your misfortune in the way of a tax deduction.

You can sell this fund and simultaneously buy another fund such as the Fidelity Total U.S. Stock Market Fund. The IRS won't allow you to buy back the exact same fund within 30 days and you don't want to be out of the market for that timeframe. A different fund, however, is just fine. The IRS will not allow you to take a loss in your taxable account if you buy the same security simultaneously in you IRA account. Here, a qualified tax advisor can save you from a costly mistake.

You need to make sure that you can use this tax loss because they can be used only to offset other gains plus an additional $3,000.

Applying the Golden Rule of Paying Less Taxes

Where do you go from here? First, determine how much risk you want to take and build your asset allocation according to that amount of risk. Then, determine where to put the assets. There's an old saying in real estate, that to be successful, it pretty much comes down to location, location, location. The same goes for investing, since location is also an important component to building wealth.

For your taxable accounts, I suggest stock index funds. For your tax-deferred accounts, consider CDs, taxable bonds, REITs, and other investments taxed at the highest rates.

Take my advice and do a little t
assets in the right locations, you'll gu
you get there.

Take every dime the government
maximizing tax-deferred investing, usi
or a host of other government vehicle
match. I match any amount Kevin put
knows better than to miss out on that
haven't learned that lesson.

The only reason not to max out tax- ... that you have the opportunity to instead invest in a Roth 401(k) or Roth IRA. Which is better, the traditional or the Roth, depends on what Congress eventually does with the tax code. Trying to predict what Congress will do, though, is more difficult than timing the market. For that reason, I recommend that most people use both.

Finally, the mother of all investing tax efficiencies is engineering our portfolio to locate our assets where we get to keep more and pay the IRS less. As a general rule, locate assets as follows:

Taxable Accounts	Tax-Deferred Accounts
Broad stock index funds	Taxable bonds
Low-turnover stock funds	REITs
Tax-managed funds	CDs
	High-turnover stock funds
	Fun gambling stock accounts

Note: While muni bonds are overused, they would be held in a taxable account.

Admittedly, putting conservative assets like bonds and CDs in our tax-deferred accounts just doesn't feel right. Remember, however, that our feelings usually fail us when it comes to investing.

As far as what's best for your Roth IRA or Roth 401(k) account, there is, unfortunately no rule of thumb I can give here. It depends on many complex factors. Remember, I said *investing* was easy enough for a second grader, not taxes.

Chapter 11

Nightmare off Wall Street—The Scary Tale of Trick-or-Treat Investing

"If the Game Is Too Hard to Understand, I'm Not Playing"

To this point, I felt I had adequately explained to Kevin about the advantages of investing. Now I thought I would take a stab at explaining the disadvantages. How does one impart to one's 8-year-old that there is no shortage of schemes out there that are emotionally appealing and yet ultimately result in separating us from our money? Admittedly, eight years old might have been a bit young to learn this lesson, but what the heck.

I bet you're wondering whether I ever do anything other than give finance lectures to my son. Well, as a matter of fact,

I do. As mentioned, we play some board games, and one Saturday night in particular we were preparing to do just that when an idea struck—maybe I could explain the *scheme* concept by *using* our board game.

Before I get to that, though, let's talk about the social waters that children navigate. I think anyone who either has raised young children, or teaches young children, or coaches young children, and so on, will relate. Their little society is actually quite organized, democratic, and purist. When playing a game, a consensus is reached on what game will be played and what the rules will be. Any player not abiding by the rules is deemed a cheater and must face the consequences, which are either *get with the program* or *get told on*. And getting told on at school means one must face the wrath of the *teacher.* Now, unless the cheater in question is looking to occupy a slot on the *America's Most Wanted* list some day, having to deal with the teacher is an intimidating consequence and quite a deterrent to bad behavior.

Okay, back to game night. It was my turn to choose the game, and I went with Monopoly. We selected our game pieces: Kevin was the car, I was the top hat, and my wife was left to choose between the thimble and the iron.[1] I was the banker, so I divvied up the money and handed Kevin the dice.

We made a couple of loops around the board, buying property, passing Go and collecting $200, and so on. As we started on our third lap, I put my plan into action.

"Since it's our third time around the board, there are some new rules," I stated. My wife shot me a quizzical look, and I responded with a "work with me" look.

Kevin asked, "What new rules?"

"Well," I said, "first off, this time when you pass Go, you don't get two hundred dollars."

"Why?" Kevin asked.

"I've got some new rules and it's in this rule book," I assured him. I pulled out a 473-page annuity disclosure and told him it was my new rule book. "You can look at it if you want," I said. He took one look at the microscopic print in the brochure and declined.

Around the board we went again as I turned the game of Monopoly on its ear. Landed on your property with two hotels? Nope, don't have to pay if you're the top hat. Stuck in jail and want to use your Get Out of Jail Free card? Sorry, only if you have hotels on all your properties.

When I saw Kevin reaching critical mass (even my wife looked like she was about to throttle me), I let the cat out of the bag. I told him that I made up a game with rules only I could understand and that he had no chance of winning so as to demonstrate what also happens in some investing. I told him that there were lots of nasty investments out there that had all sorts of promises but rules that were unfair and that not a single player ever understood. I even explained that it would cost players a lot of money if they wanted to quit playing this game they couldn't win. Kevin wondered why anyone would play such a game, while Patty just gave me that look again and said, "Does *everything* have to be a life lesson?" She said that like it's a bad thing.

For now, I just thought I'd reinforce something Kevin's mom and I have already told Kevin. "What do you say when a stranger comes up to you making all sorts of great promises?" I asked Kevin.

"I turn around and walk away—I'm not supposed to talk to strangers."

The Common Sense of Staying Away from Something Too Good to Be True

There have been times when I've actually been successful in getting consumers to realize their expensive mutual funds have underperformed the broad index. Unfortunately, these consumers will sometimes get out of those expensive funds only to buy something far worse.

There are a lot of people in the financial industry who understand the mathematics of investing and preach the need to keep costs low and tax efficiency high. They will *tsk-tsk* the greed of Wall Street, and warn people to stay away from mutual funds, even using Jack Bogle's criticisms of the industry to support their arguments. But then they'll turn around and use these truths to sell you something even worse. And you won't even know what hit you.

Top Misuses of Jack Bogle's Work

Jack Bogle gave any second grader the tools to beat Wall Street, but his tools can also be misused to sell the Wall Street Fantasy. He recently provided a list of some of these misuses:

1. Using his criticism of the mutual fund industry to sell stuff that is even worse.
2. Taking indexing "Hollywood" by carving out hundreds of ETFs so narrow that they more resemble active mutual funds that carry all the risky excitement of a Batman thriller.
3. Using index funds for pure gambling, such as ETFs that short the market or heavily levering debt so short-term swings could wipe out your position.
4. Using broad market indexing as an active trading strategy to time the market.
5. Claiming to be a low-cost mutual fund by comparing their expense ratio to the average fund, rather than a low-cost index fund.

Before you get sold, you'll get wined and dined in the highest fashion. Your invitation to a "free" investment seminar will be beautifully engraved. The seminar will be at one of the most elegant hotels, and will be serving the finest prime rib and shrimp, with an open bar. The seminar will be staffed with really nice people who will talk to you about what money means to you and offer to help you achieve your goals. So what's the problem?

You may have heard the statement, "There's no such thing as a free lunch." Well, there's no such thing as a free seminar, either. Those really nice people have one goal and one goal only—to close a sale, which will surely transfer a good portion of your wealth to them. And it's quite legal.

Whether you get a "free" meal in the bargain or not, it's important to take a look at some of the things that will come your way. The financial industry is constantly coming up with so many new and seductive products that it would be impossible to go over all of them. I'm going to give you something much better though—a tool that will slice through all of the hype, glossy brochures, and misstatements. This handy, dandy tool is simply *common sense.* Let's take a look at some of the nasty stuff, with the obvious goal being to avoid it like the plague.

Insurance Investing Is Great—For Your Agent, That Is

When I use the term *Wall Street,* I'm referring to the entire finance industry. This part of Wall Street has been particularly creative in coming up with brilliant products that make multimillionaires—among those who sell them. Unfortunately, they are not so good for us consumers. These are products that come in 64,000 flavors with names like equity-indexed annuities, variable annuities, universal life, and whole life. They have really sexy names that are meant to make the investor feel good and have peace of mind, as they build wealth for those who sell them.

I once got a call from the marketing arm of an insurance company. They went on and on about how much money, as a financial planner, I could make selling their annuity. Just when it seemed like it couldn't get any better, they told me I could double my commission by selling the version with the longer surrender period (the number of years consumers would have to wait to get their money back without a hefty charge).

When I could take no more, I asked whether it was in my clients' interest to double my commission by selling them annuities with longer surrender charges. The call abruptly ended.

Lest anyone think I'm some anti-insurance wacko, I'm not. People need health insurance, auto insurance, and other forms of insurance to protect themselves from losses they can't afford to incur. Life insurance is also necessary to protect loved ones. After all, if you're the only income generator and something happens to you, your spouse and children could be left to deal with financial hardship. I'm all for life insurance in cases like this. Insurance in general is an integral part of managing your risk. What I am critical of is insurance *investing.* Take the brochure I received that advertised a type of fixed annuity called an equity-indexed annuity (Exhibit 11.1).

Exhibit 11.1 Advertisement for Equity-Indexed Annuity

Advertisements like this are common.

The stock market is way too dangerous to invest without a safety net!

- Enjoy stock market–linked returns without stock market risk.
- Permanently crashproof your retirement funds.
- Receive guaranteed income for life.
- Retro-pick the #1 market index as if you owned your own time machine.
- Bonus 7% upon signing up.
- Checkbook access to your money.

Guaranteed Income!

When I spoke to the agent, I was told I'd get 100 percent of market returns on up years and no loss on down years. I'd get to weight my returns based on which index performed the best between the Dow, S&P 500, and the NASDAQ.

Though I knew in my heart of hearts that this had to be bunk, my adrenaline was rushing like a raging river. A neuroeconomist might say my brain was reacting much in the same way as a drug addict anticipating cocaine. I wanted to believe everything in the document was true.

The good news is that I found every single word in the sales pitch was 100 percent true! The bad news is, while it was the *truth,* it was anything but the *whole truth.* In fact, after reading all of the footnotes and conducting my own extensive analysis, I found this "safety net" product would actually give you only 25 percent of the stock market return. I even spoke to two senior officers of the multi-billion-dollar insurance company behind this product. Their terse response was, "We have reviewed the materials for completeness and accuracy and the company is comfortable that it is consistent with its standards." Guess that's another Christmas card list I'm crossed off of.

Let me tell you, I think this is nasty stuff. Yet the insurance agent (now permitted to call himself a *financial planner*) who distributed this marketing campaign told me every one of his "clients" fully understood what they had bought. *Riiiiiight,* of course they did.

And while you may need a PhD to understand these products, you don't need much to either sell or buy them. In fact, the agent that I spoke to sincerely believed it was the whole truth. Why? Because his income was dependent on his believing he was selling something good. As Upton Sinclair put it, "It's difficult to get a man to understand something if his salary depends on his not understanding it."

Why Insurance Investing Doesn't Work

How the promise of market returns without risk translated to getting only 25 percent of the market return is very technical, and there would be no way to explain it in a brief chapter. Thankfully, we don't have to. We can use some logic simple enough for a second grader to understand.

Kevin once told me a story about a kid in school who was selling dueling cards. For those who haven't heard of these cards, they are a part of a marketing monster that ties in a cartoon about martial arts warriors with a type of trading card, as well as action figures, video games, and anything else they can come up with. The young entrepreneur was selling cards that cost 25 cents at Wal-Mart for 50 cents in the schoolyard. Kevin chose to buy the cards directly from Wal-Mart and bypass his friend acting as an intermediary between Wal-Mart and the students in class.

The same goes for any insurance investment. The insurance company is also acting as a financial intermediary and invests your premiums. Do they invest in something magical? It turns out that the vast majority of their portfolios are invested in some pretty plain and conservative portfolios. I've looked at two of the giants, and their $100-billion-plus portfolios are invested in roughly 89 percent fixed income, 7 percent stocks, 1 percent real estate, and 3 percent "derivatives and other." Don't get me wrong, I think it's appropriate that insurance companies invest your premiums conservatively. I'm merely pointing out that we consumers could have built a virtually identical portfolio ourselves. This even includes derivatives, though I don't recommend them.

Unfortunately, the return to the policyholder won't likely be as good as if they had built the portfolio themselves. See, the insurance company must take the earnings from this conservative portfolio and then carve out:

- Broker commissions
- Marketing costs

- Other operating costs
- Taxes
- Insurance company profits

What's left over goes to the policyholders in the form of dividends or income. The obvious point is that buying the portfolio directly, using ultra-low-cost vehicles, would have avoided the extra costs associated with this financial intermediary (the insurance company). (See Exhibit 11.2.)

I have many clients who bought these "permanent" insurance policies before they knew any better. I am put in the unenviable position of being the bearer of bad news as I show them their dismal returns. I then must deliver more bad news in that these products, so easy to buy, are terribly difficult and expensive to get out of, in part because of their "surrender charges." Because the insurance companies pay the agent generous commissions to lure you into these products, they need you to stick around long enough to earn that money back. If you end up leaving before that point, those surrender charges kick in, insuring that they get their money back.

Exhibit 11.2 You Can Invest Your Money Directly in Stocks and Bonds, or Indirectly Through Insurance Companies with Extra Costs

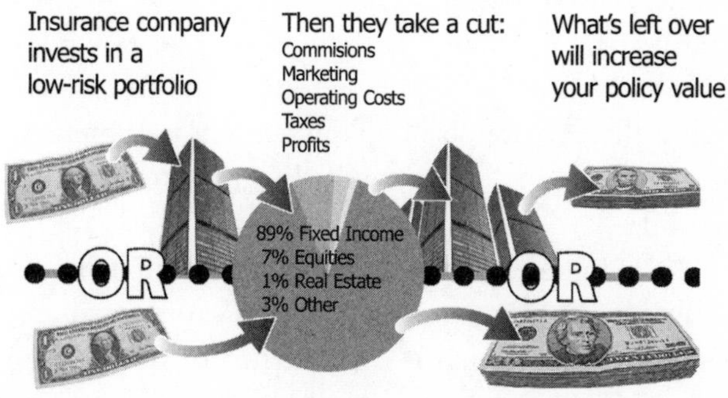

As one financial planner put it, "Insurance preserves wealth, investments create wealth and confusing the two is a sure way to financial disappointments or outright disaster." When it comes to building wealth, my advice is to bypass the insurance intermediary and buy direct. In all but a few cases, I recommend staying away from whole life, universal life, and anything in the general vicinity of an annuity.

If you need life insurance, buy low-cost term insurance. If you take the savings from what you would pay with "permanent insurance" and invest the rest directly, you are likely to be far better off. Don't fall for the old line, "Why would you want temporary insurance when you can buy permanent insurance for your family?" Bypassing the insurance company and investing directly will build up a portfolio that eliminates the need for insurance when your term policy ends.

Investment Newsletters

I recently received a newsletter advertisement similar to the one in Exhibit 11.3. For only $299.99, you can subscribe to this newsletter and won't have to settle for the boring returns I've told you about. Well, not so fast. Given the hundreds of investment newsletters out there, some are going to beat the market and earn above-average returns. It's just a simple law of averages that if enough people make enough predictions, then some are going to get it right. Even a broken clock is right twice a day.

Mark Hulbert, of Dow Jones MarketWatch, has been tracking investment newsletters since 1980 and writes his Hulbert Financial Digest, which is a newsletter of newsletters. He currently tracks the performance of about 180 newsletters. While he can point out which of the newsletters has the best performance, is it really worth knowing?

Exhibit 11.3 Market Newsletter Ad

Advertisements such as this are hard to resist.

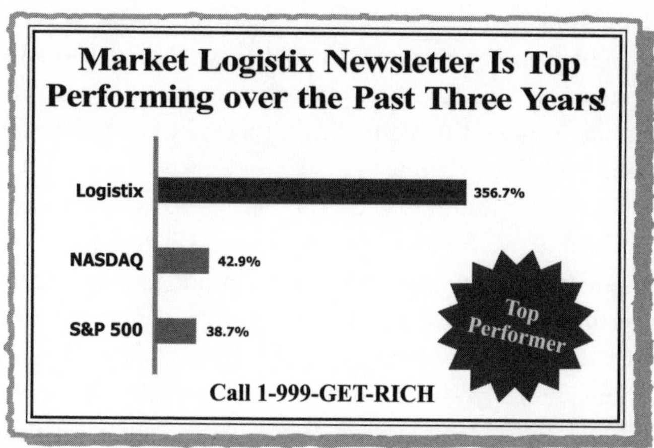

What if you had invested $10,000 in a portfolio in 1980, following the advice of the top-performing letter over the prior year, and then changed it each year to the top newsletter for the prior year? Would you be worth millions? According to Mr. Hulbert, your investment would actually be worth just a few pennies. The top-performing newsletters get to the top by taking on a ton of risk. That risk eventually catches up to the investor. You will note that the ad in Exhibit 11.3 for the newsletter wasn't just touting a hot year. It had a "long-term" track record of three full years. Since I don't consider three years to be long-term, let's look at newsletters with the best 10-year track records. Surely the sustained performance is much more meaningful. Would following the advice of the newsletters with the best long-term track records have padded our portfolios?

According to Mr. Hulbert, the best of the newsletters underperformed the broad stock market indexes going forward. This means you would have been better off owning the entire market and settling for the market averages. And this result didn't even include the trading costs and the tax-inefficiencies of the market newsletter strategy.

Taylor Larimore, co-author of *The Bogleheads' Guide to Investing* (John Wiley & Sons, 2006), was once a market-timer and published a market-timing newsletter. Taylor learned the futility of market timing and readily confesses that his former newsletter is his greatest embarrassment. Taylor's favorite portfolio is now the same three total market index funds I recommended for Kevin.

Maybe it's just me, but if I developed some proprietary model that allowed me to earn above-market returns by picking the winners and dumping the losers, I'm not such an altruist that I'd go through the trouble of writing a newsletter and trying to market it to investors. It seems to me that I could make a whole lot more money by applying the strategy to my own investing. Or, if my advice really earned above-market returns, I think I'd benefit more by selling it to a few institutions for millions of dollars rather than peddling it across the country for $299 a pop.

If you want to get rich with newsletters, then I recommend that writing a newsletter would be a much better strategy than investing your nest egg according to their advice. It's human nature to believe these newsletters are offering insights that will make us rich, but actually they are far more likely to lead to underperformance. Don't waste your money to jeopardize your portfolio. The second-grader portfolio is far more likely to outperform going forward.

For now, I've actually been thinking of writing my own newsletter:

> **Second-Grader Newsletter—issue #1:** First, buy the whole market at the lowest costs and greatest tax efficiency. Second, do nothing.
>
> **Second-Grader Newsletter—issue #2:** See issue #1.

Any guess as to what issue #3 will say? This newsletter may not be exciting, but it will beat nearly all of the others out there!

Investor Education and Software

> Learn how to trade stocks and options with confidence and skill! You'll know when to buy and when to sell. No one cares more about your money than you do, so learn to put your future in your own hands. Our high-profit-with-low-risk techniques have been taught to hundreds of thousands of investors in countries throughout the world. Come to our free investor education class.

Did you say *free*? I'm there! What have you got to lose except for a few hours of your time? As it turns out, plenty, because once you are there, you are going to be seduced. Their proprietary class and software will make you rich. Just listen to the speaker who took the class and now spends only one hour a week trading from his yacht in the Bahamas. I found myself so seduced that there was clearly a piece of me that wanted to suspend reality and follow this nonsense.

At the free "investor education seminar," you'll be presented with another seemingly riskless offer: Come to the two-day training course and, if you're not satisfied, we'll refund your money on the spot. All you need to do is pay $1,999 for the training course and $300 for the first-period subscription to the proprietary software. If not satisfied, they really will refund the full $2,299 then and there.

The problem is that you are unlikely to want your money back when you have this opportunity. You've just spent two days learning how to use this really cool-looking program that tells you when to buy and sell based on how many green or red arrows are on your screen. And you've just heard about the millions of dollars that have been made by the folks teaching this class. You are unlikely to say "No, thanks."

I've spent some time researching one of these products that claims to be able to tell you which stocks to buy and which to sell. It would be easy for this company to show the performance of those it recommended to buy versus those it recommended to sell. The firm declined to provide this data.

Now, back to second-grader common sense. All of these database programs have gobs of, well, data. If they actually worked, the companies would be easily able to show the statistical validity of their proprietary software. Again, it could just be me, but it would seem that they could sell this software to a Wall Street firm for billions of dollars just by showing it gave even a 1 percent above-market return. So, why would they instead be traveling to remote corners of the world to pitch it to people in dank hotel conference rooms?

One of these companies is a publicly traded small-cap company. It would be snapped up by some Wall Street firm for several times its current market value by just showing its software added any value.

Let's say I didn't convince you with this simple second-grader logic. Let's assume that this software really did work and did beat the market by a consistent 5 percent per year. Since they have spread this software to hundreds of thousands of investors, what do you think would happen to a stock that just got assigned more green up arrows? It would go up, of course. So you'd better be the first to discover the arrows or you will be following the herd, yet again. To put it another way, if you do discover a technique that beats the market, you'd better be the only one to know about it. If others do, it's toast.

There are many of these products out there under the guise of "investor education." They all have one thing in common—revving up your emotions to get you to suspend simple common sense.

Hedge Funds

Hedge funds are investment pools that are relatively unconstrained in what they do. They are relatively unregulated

> (for now), charge very high fees, will not necessarily give you your money back when you want it, and will generally not tell you what they do. They are supposed to make money all the time, and when they fail at this, their investors redeem and go to someone else who has recently been making money. Every three or four years, they deliver a one-in-a-hundred-year flood.[2]

A typical hedge fund manager is paid 2 percent of the asset value and 20 percent of any money made on the portfolio. There is nothing wrong with sharing a portion of any windfall gain, but there is an inherent conflict in the manager sharing none of the pain.

If the hedge fund manager loses a portion of your money, he doesn't share in your loss. It doesn't take a Mensa member to see that would create the incentive for the manager to take as much risk as possible with your money.

So, why were we so surprised when these hedge funds blew up? Because we suspended reality and bought the sales pitch that these hedge fund managers were smarter than the market and the funds would always go up. We yet again believed what we wanted to believe in that we could get market returns with far less risk.

Avoid Gurus Giving Self-Serving Advice

The financial industry has no shortage of self-serving advice. They can twist logic into a pretzel if it will get you to hand over your hard-earned money to them. I'm going to just give you a couple of examples, and then we'll apply some second-grader logic that will protect you from falling prey to these and others.

Pretax Retirement Plans Are Bad

Pretax retirement plans do not save income taxes. In fact, you end up paying far more in taxes, which is just what the government wants.

Perhaps the most egregious argument I've heard against investing in tax-deferred retirement accounts is that you shouldn't do it. And why, you may ask? Because you just end up paying more in taxes, which is exactly what the government wants. Let's examine the argument a bit.

The Value of Tax-Deferral

Let's look at a hypothetical example, where you have the option to put $10,000 in your 401(k) account or pay taxes on your income today and then invest in the most tax-efficient index fund. We'll keep the same 28 percent ordinary income tax bracket and 15 percent capital gain and dividend tax rate.

If you pay the taxes on the $10,000 income today, you'll be out $2,800. However, you'll get the taxes over with, and then pay taxes at the lower rates and deferring the capital gains tax for decades. You'll have $7,200 left to invest ($10,000 – $2,800). However, the 401(k) gets to keep this $2,800 for now, but will pay at an ordinary income tax rate eventually. We'll assume that both accounts earn an average of 8.5 percent and are cashed in after 20 years.

Voila, the results do show that the 401(k) strategy results in paying more taxes—$14,314 versus only $7,095 for the "pay the taxes now" strategy. You may know where I'm going; my response is "So, what?" The much more important fact here is that the 401(k) option leaves you with an extra $5,267 dollars, even after paying these higher taxes.

The second-grader approach of paying the tax collector later works, because, in essence, the government gave us an interest-free loan of $2,800. In the example, we kept that loan for 20 years and then paid it back. Sure, the government took a chunk of it in the form of more taxes, but the extra $5,267 isn't chump change.

If this money had been invested in lower-returning fixed income accounts, then the results would still be skewed toward the 401(k) account. That's because the earnings on the $7,200 are taxed at ordinary income tax rates. The 401(k) account ends up with nearly the same amount of after-tax dollars.

Will you end up paying more in taxes if you put your money in a tax-deferred 401(k)? *Almost certainly* is the answer. But is that a bad thing? Kevin didn't think so. Remember the example in Chapter 10, where Kevin had the choice of paying $100 in taxes now or putting it into a CD and earning 5 percent, where he would have $105 at the end of the year? True, he had to pay $101 in taxes at the end of the year, but he chose to pay the extra buck in taxes because he got to keep $4 he wouldn't have otherwise had ($100 + $5 CD interest – $101 taxes). The lesson here is that it's not the amount you pay in taxes that matters; it's the amount you have left after paying taxes that is critical.

Now, it's quite possible that tax rates will be higher when we withdraw our money. Again, I say that this isn't the right question to ask. Overall, tax rates certainly can go higher (and I think they will), but this doesn't mean that our effective tax rates will go higher. If we withdraw the money from our retirement accounts when we no longer have earned income, we are likely to be paying taxes in the lower tax brackets. Let's look at the example in Exhibit 11.4.

Exhibit 11.4 Ten Percent Tax Increase

A tax rate increase doesn't mean your rate will increase if your income at retirement is lower.

Tax Bracket	Current Tax	Higher Tax
1	**10%**	**20%**
2	**15%**	**25%**
3	**25%**	**35%**
4	**28%**	**38%**
5	**33%**	**43%**
6	**35%**	**45%**

In this example, I've played Scrooge and raised tax rates by 10 percent across the board. You can see I have no career in politics. Note that the person who went with the 401(k) plan was in tax bracket 4 and deferred taxes at 28 percent. Now, tax bracket 4 is at 38 percent. Not to worry—when that person needs the money for retirement, she is likely no longer working. That means she might find herself in tax bracket 2 and paying only 25 percent when she withdraws the money.

Even if she does find herself in the same tax bracket 4, she actually still ends up slightly better off. The value of the interest-free loan (the tax deferral) is greater than the cost of her tax rate going from 28 percent to 38 percent. I haven't even mentioned a customary employer match here. The argument for tax-deferred investing is conclusively strong even without an employer match, but if you are walking away from any employer match, you are just throwing money away.

The argument to stay away from tax-deferred investing is usually pitched by some of the, how should I put this, *questionable* "financial planners" out there and is very self-serving. If you don't invest in your 401(k), the planner can sell you another product that he can make money on. Can you say "permanent insurance"?

If your goal is to reduce taxes, just quit your job and stop making any income. If you have a more logical goal of maximizing your after-tax dollars, tax-deferred investing is a critical tool.

Maximize Your Mortgage

The most expensive way to own a house is with cash. Take out the largest mortgage you can and pay it back slowly.

"Mortgage interest is your friend, not your foe." I have heard two arguments to support this absurd advice. The first goes as follows: If you get a 6 percent mortgage and are in the 28 percent tax bracket, you are paying only 4.32 percent on it after taxes. Even a bond pays more than that, so at even 5 percent you are better off. The problem here is that the argument conveniently leaves out the fact that the 5 percent earnings on the fixed income are also taxable. At the 28 percent tax rate, that leaves you with only 3.60 percent. So in actuality, you are borrowing at 4.32 percent and earning only 3.6 percent.

Now, the typical response to this reality check is to say you shouldn't invest it in conservative bonds. You should get stock market returns of 8.5 percent or more. While I believe this is possible, I just don't believe it can be done without dramatically increasing risk. The stock market is far from being an actuarial certainty. Remember that the first step in investing is selecting the amount of risk that is right for you. Does it make any sense to select an asset allocation and then maximize your mortgage and increase your stock holdings proportionally? What you have done is take on a ton of risk that you are likely to pay dearly for when things don't pan out.

The second argument of the "debt is your friend" proponents is that houses will always go up in value, so you are maximizing your return by borrowing as much as you can. As we've all seen, real estate doesn't always increase in value at a double-digit pace. But that doesn't matter when it comes to this argument. While I may not know whether the value of your house will go up or down next year, I can tell you with a 100 percent degree of confidence that it will have nothing to do with how you finance it.

How do I know about these techniques? I get calls from mortgage brokers asking me to team up with them. All I need to do is send them my clients and they will free up the equity in their houses. Then, I can take the money and sell them an investment such as one of those products giving the upside of the market without the downside risk. It's a "win-win!" A win for the broker and a win for me maybe, but a *no-win* for the consumer.

Applying the Golden Rule of Staying Away from Something Too Good to Be True

Never underestimate what I call the broader Wall Street ability to find new, creative, and emotionally appealing ways to transfer your nest egg to theirs. Your brain is wired to *want* to believe these are true. Before jumping in, put your toe in the water and think like a second grader.

The very first rule is that you must be able to explain what you are doing to a second grader. Albert Einstein once said, "If you can't explain it simply, you don't understand it well enough." Make sure you can explain the following:

1. *How does the product work?* I make it a rule never to buy a financial investment I couldn't describe to an average second grader. In almost every case, a simple investment is better. Complexity creates costs and costs take from your return. I have had many clients come to me with insurance investments, but I've never had one who understood what it was he bought. Take Kevin's advice: "If I don't understand the rules, I'm not playing the game."
2. *How do others make money when you buy the product?* Millions of us seem to believe that an insurance company could invest in low-paying bonds and yet pay us higher returns. We forget to ask ourselves this question and take the bait—hook, line, and sinker. When you understand how others are making money from you, you are more likely to figure out that the better way is to buy direct. Never buy anything indirect when you can bypass the intermediary and eliminate the profit others are making from you.
3. *Does it pass the smell test?* Take the rose-colored glasses off and ask yourself why you are being pitched a product. I was just called by a stranger offering to put me in an oil well deal where the driller had hit on all 35 of his last 35 wells! I noted to the caller that, with such a track record, he must have thousands of investors wanting him to take their money. He certainly wouldn't be cold calling people like me. Whether it's oil wells or "investor education" software, ask yourself if they'd be pitching it to you if it were really so good. If it looks too good to be true, it probably is.

4. *What is your exit strategy?* Any product that is easy to buy and hard to get out of should raise a red flag. If there are charges to get out of the product, be especially skeptical. If you hear the word *surrender* as in *surrender charges,* tip your hat and leave.

Here's a little rule of thumb to apply when next you are invited to an investment seminar: The value of the investment advice is inversely related to the quality of the food and libations. Also, *never* buy a product immediately. Give yourself some time to understand the pros and cons of the investment. Discuss it with your friends, or a second grader if you happen to have one around. Remember, invest in haste, repent in leisure.

Look for some warning signs of a bad or even fraudulent investment:[3]

1. It looks too good to be true.
2. It's good only for a certain amount of time, like "today only."
3. It involves signing something you haven't read and understood.
4. The person selling it uses religion or some other bond to build a rapport with you and win your trust.

Kevin was taught early on that if a stranger comes up to him offering candy, he should politely say "No, thanks" and walk away. That lesson is a good one for us adults when it comes to investing.

Chapter 12

Increase Your Return No Matter What the Market Does

"If You Pick the Low-Hanging Fruit, You Don't Have to Climb the Tree"

Every autumn, we hop in the car for a visit to the Happy Apple farm. It's a popular spot for suburban families who want their children to have that traditional harvest experience. And by traditional, I mean some Disney movie version of it. The friendly farmer giving guests a hayride may look the part with his flannel shirt, overalls, and straw hat, but he's not pulling us with horses or a tractor; it's more like some monster ATV. And when we're dropped off at the pumpkin patch from which we select our annual Halloween pumpkin, the pumpkins, in a variety of sizes, are cut and laid out in the fields so that even the smallest guest can just pick one up. The apple orchard is probably closer to reality since the fruit is still on the trees to be picked, which is what Kevin and I were doing one crisp morning in early October.

As we walked through the orchard, paper bags in hand, Kevin stopped at one tree and picked an apple from a low branch he could reach. I asked him why he picked that particular apple.

"It looked like it would taste good," he said.

I pointed to an apple higher up in the tree and observed that it looked pretty tasty, too. "How come you didn't pick that apple?" I asked.

"I'd have to climb the tree to get that apple, Dad. All I had to do for this one was reach over and pick it," he said.

And that was the lesson of the low-hanging fruit.

The Common Sense of Picking the Low-Hanging Fruit

When it comes to our personal finances, we are often staring at that red, juicy apple at the top of the tree. We don't take notice of the three apples right in front of us that are just as ripe and much easier to get to.

A True Story of Low-Hanging Fruit

A wealthy couple once came to me looking for help in their portfolio. While there were many expensive investments in their portfolio, I first focused on the $2 million they had in their money market account earning only 1 percent. I also noticed they had a $600,000 mortgage at 5 percent.

In an analysis any second grader could have done, I pointed out that they could save by paying off the mortgage. In fact, they could net

$24,000 annually by merely paying off the mortgage [$600K × (5% − 1%)]. "Oh, I couldn't do that," replied the wife, "I just wouldn't feel like an adult." I had no response to that one.

At least I could make them aware that there were money market accounts paying far more. So, I noted that if they put their cash in a money market account earning 3 percent, they would be $40,000 better off every year [$2M × (3% − 1%)]. "But we'd have to change brokerage accounts," the husband chimed in. That was off the table, too, apparently.

The bottom line was that between paying off the mortgage and putting their cash in a higher-paying, safe money market account, they could have saved $48,000 annually* irrespective of how the market performed.

This was a very smart and well-educated couple. They understood the mathematics of what I was telling them. Also, they weren't so wealthy that $48 grand was immaterial to them. What was stopping them from picking the low-hanging fruit was a very powerful force known as *inertia.* We humans say "change is good" but, in reality, we just don't like change. Not only did this smart couple fail to grasp the obvious advantages of what I suggested, they declined to pick the fruit even when it was pointed out.

*Calculated as follows: $600K × (5% − 1%) + ($1.4M × (3% − 1%).

So far, this book has concentrated on specific ways you can dramatically improve your odds as an investor. This chapter is going to give you steps to take that will create wealth for you whether the market goes up, down, or sideways. They're yours for the picking.

Where to Find Low-Hanging Fruit

Now, I'm not saying everyone has $48,000 in low-hanging fruit, or even close to it, but it's a rare occurrence that I don't find *some.* Though every case is different, here are a few areas to look at to see whether you have some easy pickings.

Cash

Have you ever read something like "the average money market account is paying 1.08 percent and the average one-year CD is paying 2.03 percent"? It amazes me that there always seem to be institutions paying two to three times the national averages. According to traditional economic theory, we consumers would quickly move our money from average-paying accounts to the highest-paying accounts, which would of course drive those averages up.

In reality, the average consumer settles for the average rate. As explained in Chapter 8, it's child's play to find the highest-paying CD and money market rates. While the couple with the $2 million in cash earning 1 percent was extreme, I find nearly all of us to be somewhat, well, *lazy* might be a tad judgmental, so I'll say *action impaired*. We let our cash gather cobwebs in some bank, when we're really only making money for the financial institution. Remember, each 1 percent on each $10,000 is worth $100 to you—far more than the price of this book. Start searching the local newspaper and go to bankrate.com and bankdeals.blogspot.com.

Debt

Most of us carry some debt, whether it's a mortgage, home equity line of credit (HELOC), car loan, or credit card interest. If you, like the couple mentioned earlier, happen to be fortunate enough to have enough cash sitting around to pay off all of your debt, you probably should do it. In 99 percent of the cases, you'll be better off. If you're this fortunate, congratulations! You can go ahead and skip the rest of this section.

For the rest of us, it's important to remember that the goal is to pay the least amount of after-tax interest that we can. Don't worry, I'm not going to make value judgments as to how you got in debt. I will, however, give you some ideas on how to get out of it.

Some interest is tax-deductible and some isn't:

Tax-Deductible Interest	**Non-Tax-Deductible Interest**
Mortgage interest	Auto-loan interest
HELOC interest (up to certain limits)	Credit card interest

A *HELOC,* by the way, is a home equity line of credit extended to a homeowner that uses the borrower's home as collateral. Once a maximum loan amount available is established, the homeowner may draw on the line of credit at his or her discretion. Interest is charged on a predetermined variable rate, which is usually based on the prevailing prime rate (up to certain limits). It's critical to know what the maximum is that you can borrow with your HELOC and that the bank doesn't have the right to freeze your credit if it thinks the value of your home is declining.

In virtually every case I've analyzed, the non-tax-deductible debt is the most expensive and the one we want to work on first. Take an example of someone in the 28 percent tax bracket where both the mortgage and the auto loan are at 6.00 percent. Assuming the taxpayer itemizes on his return, the mortgage will cost the consumer only 4.32 percent (6% × (1 − 0.28) while the auto loan isn't tax-deductible and will cost the full 6 percent.

Here are some rules of thumb in paying off debt:

1. Pay down the most expensive non-tax-deductible debt first. This is usually the credit card debt. Sources to pay down the debt can be low-yielding cash in your savings or a HELOC. I've seen people getting new credit cards every six months to take advantage of teaser rates that may not charge interest for the first few months. This may work in the short-term but, for right or wrong, changing credit cards regularly will pound your FICO score. The FICO score is a credit score that lenders and insurance companies

look at when they decide how much to charge you. So I don't recommend this strategy.

2. Continue looking for your cheapest and your most expensive pieces of debt. Look to increase a cheap source to pay off an expensive one.

Again, cases vary, but let's take a look at an example of how debt can be restructured to pick low-hanging fruit, with the assumptions shown in Exhibit 12.1. We will assume that the Apple family is in the $28 percent tax bracket.

The Apples have $50,000 in cash earning 3 percent, which nets them $1,500 before tax and $1,080 after taxes. This cash happens to be six months' worth of living expenses and they have been told to keep this amount safe for emergencies, such as the loss of a job. The Apples also have $290,000 in debt with annual rates ranging from 6 to 18 percent. The lowest-rate loans happen to also be tax-deductible, which is most typical. They are paying a total of $22,000 in interest. After taking into account the deduction they get for the mortgage and the HELOC, they are paying $18,248 in after-tax interest.

So, they are netting a total after-tax payment of $17,168, which comes from the $1,080 they earned on cash, less the $18,248 they paid. Now let's go looking for fruit by lowering their interest payments.

Exhibit 12.1 Apples' Cash and Debt

Account	Rate	Balance	Income/Costs Pre-Tax	Income/Costs Post-Tax
Cash	3.00%	$50,000	$1,500	$1,080
Mortgage	6.00%	$(200,000)	$(12,000)	$(8,640)
HELOC[1]	7.00%	$(20,000)	$(1,400)	$(1,008)
Auto loans	8.00%	$(40,000)	$(3,200)	$(3,200)
Credit card	18.00%	$(30,000)	$(5,400)	$(5,400)
Debt		$(290,000)	$(22,000)	$(18,248)
Total		$(240,000)	$(20,500)	$(17,168)

[1] HELOC total available line is $100,000.

Exhibit 12.2 Step 1: Savings from Paying off Credit Card

Account	Rate	Balance	Income/Costs Pre-Tax	Income/Costs Post-Tax
Cash	3.00%	$(30,000)	$(900)	$(648)
Credit card	18.00%	$30,000	$5,400	$5,400
		$—	$4,500	$4,752

First, we'll start by paying off the credit card debt with the cash in the savings account. You may be thinking I'm playing Russian roulette with their emergency account because of that old rule of keeping six months' cash on hand. I think a better rule is that we should always have access to six months' cash. So, as long as we keep enough available credit in the HELOC, we'll be okay. Thus, step 1 saves the Apples a cool $4,752 after taxes (Exhibit 12.2).

The next most expensive debt is the auto loan at 8 percent, which is also not tax-deductible. We'll use another $10,000 in cash here, so that we are left with $10,000 cash. We've now drained the Apples' cash account by $40,000, so we need to leave access to that much cash in our HELOC account. We can tap another $30,000 in the HELOC to pay off the auto loan. The HELOC rate is only 7 percent and is tax-deductible. This will save the Apples another $1,472, after taxes (Exhibit 12.3).

Now the Apples are left with Exhibit 12.4. By merely restructuring a few areas, they have lowered their interest costs

Exhibit 12.3 Step 2: Pay off Auto Loan with Cash and HELOC

Account	Rate	Balance	Income/Costs Pre-Tax	Income/Costs Post-Tax
Cash	3.00%	$(10,000)	$(300)	$(216)
HELOC	7.00%	$(30,000)	$(2,100)	$(1,512)
Auto loans	8.00%	$40,000	$3,200	$3,200
		$—	$800	$1,472

Exhibit 12.4 Apples' New Cash and Debt

Account	Rate	Balance	Income/Costs Pre-Tax	Income/Costs Post-Tax
Cash	3.00%	$10,000	$300	$216
Mortgage	6.00%	$(200,000)	$(12,000)	$(8,640)
HELOC[1]	7.00%	$(50,000)	$(3,500)	$(2,520)
Auto loans	8.00%	$—	$—	$—
Credit card	18.00%	$—	$—	$—
Debt		$(250,000)	$(15,500)	$(11,160)
Total		$(240,000)	$(15,200)	$(10,944)
Original		$(240,000)	$(20,500)	$(17,168)
Difference		$—	$5,300	$6,224

[1] HELOC total available line is $100,000.

and will save $6,224 annually, or more than $500 a month. This savings isn't dependent on the stock market or even cutting living expenditures. It's just low-hanging fruit for the taking.

I'd be willing to bet that I haven't convinced some of you to draw down the $50,000 in cash to a measly $10,000, and break the rule of always keeping six-months' cash. Remember, however, that the Apples could always tap that additional $40,000 via the HELOC, if needed. In the meantime, they are saving the 7 percent payment on the HELOC and only giving up the 3 percent they were making on the cash. However, the Apples have to have the discipline not to run that credit card balance back up.

Equities

I know I've drilled in the fact that high-cost mutual funds are unlikely to outperform the low-cost equivalent mutual funds. But, while moving from the high-cost mutual fund to the low-cost index fund is a good thing, it isn't technically low-hanging fruit. The high-cost fund can always get lucky and can end up beating the odds. Low-hanging fruit must be virtually a sure thing.

But why do high-cost index funds and ETFs exist? As noted earlier, an expensive S&P 500 fund has virtually no chance of beating a low-cost S&P 500 fund. They follow the same index and you are all but guaranteed to underperform by the amount of the cost differential. It's rather like making a left turn to the gas station with $6.00-a-gallon gas, when the one on the right had the same gas for $2.00 a gallon. We wouldn't do it because we can see the pump calculating every painful penny being taken from us. Because we can't see how much the expensive index fund is taking from us, we don't feel the pain and don't react.

Technically, there can be additional differences between these index funds, known as *tracking error.* This means that the index fund or ETF didn't own the exact index and varied by a bit. My own research shows that the more expensive the index fund, the more it is likely to underperform even after taking into account these extra fees. In fact, in 2003, every extra dollar in fees destroyed about $1.24 in return. Jack Bogle says you get what you don't pay for, but when it comes to index funds, it may actually be *worse* than that.

Don't settle for just any index fund. Find the lowest-cost equivalent fund out there. If your expensive index fund is in a tax-deferred account, make the change today. If it's in a taxable account and you have a gain, you have a decision of either paying taxes today or paying higher fees for years.

The Mother of All Low-Hanging Fruit: Asset Location

We've already covered the largest of these sources in Chapter 10. Locating our investments where they are most tax efficient can often increase return by more than all of the other sources of low-hanging fruit combined. Remember that you first need to select an asset allocation that is right for you.

Next comes the location of those assets in taxable versus tax-advantaged accounts, which pretty much run the opposite of your instincts. Stock index funds and stocks are very tax efficient and better in your taxable accounts. Your tax-deferred IRA accounts are better suited for your bonds, bond index funds, REITs, and anything taxed at the highest rates.

Other Sources of Low-Hanging Fruit

There are many other sources of low-hanging fruit, but they take more exploring. For example, if you are now paying for a child in college, you may have the option of having the government subsidize it via a 529 plan. In Colorado, for example, the state grants a 4.63 percent tax deduction for money deposited to a college 529 savings plan. Colorado also doesn't have a minimum time the funds are required to be deposited in the plan.

So, the parent could either pay $10,000 to the college directly, or put it in the 529 plan money market account for a day. They then get a tax savings of $463 ($10,000 × 4.63%). With the current costs of college, these are some pickings that are both easy and meaningful. Of course, a much better way to use a 529 plan is to start building it early and let it grow tax-free. Remember that costs matter here, as well. Be sure to look up whether your state gives a tax-deduction for contributions to 529 plans and see whether there is a minimum period the funds need to be invested. Go to www.savingforcollege.com or Google your state's 529 college plan and go directly to their site.

Another source for seniors is to reapply for social security benefits. Larry Kotlikoff, economics professor at Boston University, has written about one of my favorites. A little-known law allows beneficiaries to pay back all benefits without any interest and then reset social security payments shortly afterwards. So if you took it at age 62 and, in a few years, you are still in good health, you can repay it and then take the higher benefit. And if you are nearing the early social security age and thinking about waiting for the higher benefit—don't! Take the money and put it in a safe investment, like a money market account or TIPs. Later, you can pay it back without interest and then opt for the higher payment.[1] Be sure to monitor whether Social Security is looking at closing that loophole.

One final source I've found in the finance arena is in the costs for insurance. After a couple of decades with the same insurance company, I was getting every discount under the sun for my home, car, and umbrella line. Even with those discounts, my premiums were going up. Finally, I got off my duff and fought the inertia that kept me complacent. At the risk of sounding like a commercial, I saved a ton on my insurance, without lowering my coverage. I send many of my clients to that same insurance agent.

Beyond what I've talked about in this chapter, there are many ways to save, but that's not what this book is about. One of my mottos is "Never pay retail!" My wife says I'm cheap, but I prefer the term *value oriented.* Every dollar saved can go into your nest egg and help you reach financial independence that much sooner.

Applying the Golden Rule of Picking the Low-Hanging Fruit

Take it from Kevin: Picking a ripe apple within reach is easier than climbing the tree. So carve out some time and start looking for your fruit:

- Is your cash working as hard as it can for you, or is it making your financial institution rich?

(Continues)

(Continued)

- Can you get rid of your most expensive debt, either with your cash or with less expensive debt?
- Are you in an expensive index fund that is guaranteed to underperform the least expensive equivalent index fund?
- Do you have your highest-taxed assets located in your tax-deferred accounts? It may feel good to have cash in taxable accounts, but it will cost you more.
- Are you paying an expensive bill on a regular basis without checking to see whether there are alternative options at a much lower price?
- Are their some tax savings that you are missing, such as the example of paying the college via the state 529 college plan?

Remember that the obvious isn't always so obvious. Find that low-hanging fruit and, if you're hesitant to pick it, ask yourself why. You may be fighting one of those mental models like "every adult should have a mortgage." You may also be fighting inertia.

Chapter 13

Keep It Simple, Stupid (KISS)

"Why Do Grownups Have to Make Things So Complicated?"

Kevin and I like to call the Internet "the great big book of everything," which is based on Kevin's favorite Disney show, "Stanley," about a boy his age who loved animals and had a magical scrapbook he called "the great big book of everything." Granted, the Internet isn't some magical place you can jump in and out of like Stanley can, but calling up information on any subject at the click of a mouse runs a close second. In any case, it was here that I decided to begin our final investment lesson.

Our first search was Sir Isaac Newton. I briefly explained the three laws of motion, and told Kevin that Newton was believed to have had the greatest impact in the history of science.[1] Kevin was duly impressed and said, "He must have been really smart." I responded that he certainly was, and perhaps even a genius. Then I showed him my favorite Sir Isaac Newton quote:

> Truth is ever to be found in simplicity, and not in the multiplicity and confusion of things.[2]

Next, we looked up Albert Einstein. I told Kevin that many people believe that he was the smartest person who ever lived. I explained to him that he invented what was called the *theory of relativity.*

"The theory of relatives?" asked Kevin. I smiled and wondered what Einstein might have theorized for some of *my* relatives.

"No," I responded. "Einstein's theory was about time, not people. But he also had interesting things to say." I actually had several quotes in mind, but pulled up this one:

> If you can't explain it simply, you don't understand it well enough.

"So what were Sir Isaac Newton and Albert Einstein talking about?" I asked.

Kevin's eyes lit up as he noted the common link and answered, "That it's good to make things simple?"

"*Bingo,*" I replied.

At this point, I think Kevin was hoping this lesson was over, but we still had to apply two lessons that these geniuses taught us on investing. It was Albert Einstein who once noted that the most powerful force in the whole universe was the power of compound interest. Since we had already covered this a bit earlier, I held out a dollar bill and noted that if he invested this and earned 10 percent annually, he'd have over $45 dollars by time he was my age.[3]

Next, I told him that if he gave 2 percent away to helpers, then the 8 percent annual return would be only $22 in 40 years. And finally, if he was like most investors and underperformed by an additional 2 percent, then his 6 percent annual return would turn into only about $10.

"Wow," Kevin said. "Albert Einstein was right about that!"

Now, we turned to Sir Isaac Newton and his first law of motion, known as the *law of inertia.* It states that "an object at rest tends to stay at rest, and that an object in uniform motion tends to stay in uniform motion." Okay, so I condensed it a bit. I explained that if his portfolio was moving in the right direction, he could harness that power of inertia. All you need to do, I explained to Kevin, is nothing. He looked a little confused. Second graders are still pretty literal with the English language, so he wasn't sure how one *did* nothing.

I tried again. "How about—once your portfolio is moving in the right direction, you can harness the power of inertia and then you don't need to do anything." It was less catchy, but he got it that time.

I wrapped up by telling Kevin that he owned the world with the lowest costs and was paying the tax collector as little as possible. In doing so, he had harnessed the two most powerful forces in the universe: the powers of compounding and inertia.

"That's it?" asked Kevin.

Yes, you have now graduated and will beat Wall Street over any period of time. Your U.S. stock fund will beat Wall Street, and so will your international stock fund and your bond fund. It's that simple, as Newton and Einstein might have said.

Kevin responded, "Investing sure is easy!"

"It is for a second grader," I said.

Then Kevin asked, "So why do grownups have to make it complicated?"

"Good question, Kev," I said, which is usually what I say when I don't have an answer. So, I responded like any parent would to a child's good question that there was no good answer to:

"You'll understand when you're older."

The Common Sense of the KISS Principle

Confucius once said, "Life is really simple, but we insist on making it complicated." The point is that, when it comes to investing, brilliance is not about creating the next derivative investment in the hope that it outsmarts the market. These derivatives have two things in common:

1. They are close to impossible to understand.
2. They consistently blow up in the investor's face.

If the Wall Street brokerage firms were really so good at giving investment advice and managing risk, why did they write down hundreds of billions of dollars' worth of derivative investments? Why did it take taxpayers to bail them out? The answer is clear in that they didn't understand what they were buying and how these instruments worked. They were too busy building the next scheme and forgot that behind these fancy collateralized insured debt obligations were millions of loans to people who couldn't pay them back.

In short, they forgot the KISS principle.

What impact can second-grader investing have on you? Exhibit 13.1 shows that a second-grader portfolio can grow 4.1 percent faster than a typical Wall Street portfolio. First, cut costs from 2 percent to 0.2 percent. If you are in the 33 percent combined tax bracket, that will save you 1.2 percent, after taxes. Next, don't generate capital gains and pay unnecessary taxes to Uncle Sam. This may gain you another 1.4 percent annually. By controlling your emotions and not following the herd, you can gain another 1.1 percent annually. This may be the hardest single thing to do, and I admit I'm not nearly as good as Kevin in tuning out the market

Exhibit 13.1 Additional Annual Earnings from Second-Grader Strategies

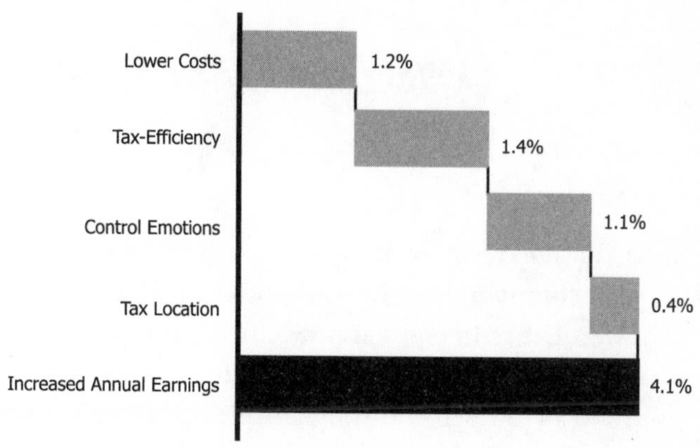

media. Finally, you may get another 0.4 percent annually by just placing assets in the right location. None of this is rocket science.

The fixed income side of your portfolio can net you about 2.8 percent in additional annual return. That's from a combination of cutting costs, finding the highest-yielding CDs, and keeping your fixed income within your 401(k) or IRA accounts. Thus, a portfolio of 60 percent stocks and 40 percent fixed income could average an additional 3.6 percent return. This is a combination of the 4.1 percent additional return on stocks and a 2.8 percent bump on fixed income.

What could this simple investing do to your life? I've found my typical clients can achieve their financial independence roughly one year sooner for every 0.25 percent annual performance increase they do to their portfolio. Every 1 percent reduction allows them to pursue whatever fulfills their life four years earlier. You heard me right, second-grader investing that yields an additional 3.6 percent annually really can move up your financial independence by about 14 years! (Exhibit 13.2.)

Exhibit 13.2 Impact of 1 Percent Performance on Financial Freedom

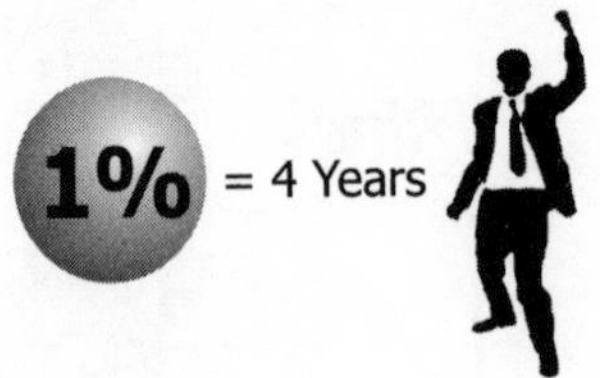

Albert Einstein really knew what he was talking about when he said that compounding was so powerful. If you're already retired, however, it can be just as powerful. Increasing return by 3 percent annually can increase your safe rate of withdrawals from your portfolio by 50 percent. You can spend half again as much on whatever you'd like by using the second-grader approach.

Switching to a simple portfolio will not be easy, though. Any change you make will require you to fight Newton's law of inertia. That is to say, even if you recognize you are on the losing side of compounding, you will still need to change the motion you are moving in.

Kevin, like most children, accepted that Einstein and Newton knew more than he did and embraced their wisdom. He was happy to take their word on the powers of compounding and inertia, and wanted to harness both.

Investing really is simple enough for any second grader to do. We need only remember two lessons:

1. Don't play a loser's game by paying money for one expert to outsmart another expert. In investing, you actually get what you don't pay for. As Albert Einstein put it, "Sometimes one pays most for the things one gets for nothing."
2. Don't put all of your eggs in one basket. We live in a global economy, and spreading our investments across thousands of companies via low-cost index funds does the trick.

Exhibit 13.3 Second-Grader

The secret to successful inv

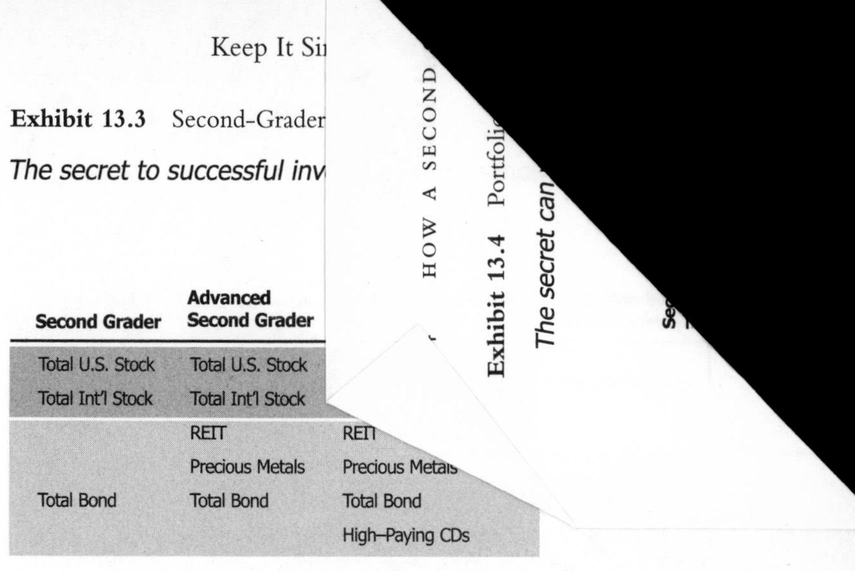

Second Grader	Advanced Second Grader	
Total U.S. Stock	Total U.S. Stock	
Total Int'l Stock	Total Int'l Stock	
	REIT	REIT
	Precious Metals	Precious Metals
Total Bond	Total Bond	Total Bond
		High–Paying CDs

Exhibit 13.3 shows the simple solution that takes into account Albert Einstein's power of compounding and Sir Isaac Newton's law of inertia.

The second-grader portfolio owns the entire world. The advanced second-grader portfolio throws in a few REITs and precious metals and mining funds. Am I violating advice from Einstein and Newton? Possibly; I couldn't convince Kevin, which makes me wonder whether I'm outsmarting myself.

The alternative second-grader portfolio may be right for those willing to go off autopilot and find the highest-paying federally insured CDs to substitute for part of their bond index fund. It's not a free lunch in that you have to stay on top of the CDs and keep track of maturity dates.

Finally, remember that taxes are costs, too. Where we locate these assets is critical and, in my experience, we usually get it backwards. Broad stock index funds are beautifully tax efficient on their own and appropriate for the taxable portfolio. Bonds, CDs, REITs, and precious metals and mining stocks throw off gains at ordinary income and are better off in your IRAs and 401(k)s.

Which of the three simple portfolios you select probably isn't going to make that much difference. They are all broad, low-cost, tax-efficient portfolios. What's more important is

with Different Levels of Risk

work for any level of risk.

ond Grader	Aggressive	Moderate	Conservative	
Total U.S. Stock	60%	40%	20%	Taxable accounts
Total Int'l Stock	30%	20%	10%	
Total Bond	10%	40%	70%	Tax-deferred accounts
	100%	100%	100%	

Advanced Second Grader	Aggressive	Moderate	Conservative	
Total U.S. Stock	54%	36%	18%	Taxable accounts
Total Int'l Stock	27%	20%	10%	
REIT	6%	4%	2%	Tax-deferred accounts
Precious Metals	3%	0%	0%	
Total Bond	10%	40%	70%	
	100%	100%	100%	

Alternative Advanced Second Grader	Aggressive	Moderate	Conservative	
Total U.S. Stock	54%	36%	18%	Taxable accounts
Total Int'l Stock	27%	20%	10%	
REIT	6%	4%	2%	Tax-deferred accounts
Precious Metals	3%	0%	0%	
Total Bond	10%	40%	70%	
High Paying CDs				
	100%	100%	100%	

determining your willingness and need to take risk. Once you pick it, stay with it. Don't react to your gut instincts and especially to the gurus giving you short-term forecasts.

Which level of risk is right for you is something you'll have to decide, with or without help. Guidelines for the three portfolios are shown in Exhibit 13.4.

Simple Investing Isn't Easy

I've been asked a million times: If investing is really this simple, why don't more people do it this way?

First, we adults, myself included, have a tendency to overcomplicate things. This is especially true if something is important to us. Like it or not, money is very important to us and I make no apology about that. It gives us the freedom to do what we want in life and we're always looking for ways to get that freedom sooner. Unfortunately, as herd animals, we humans tend to do all of the wrong things in pursuit of that goal.

Second, Wall Street does its level best to constantly play on our emotions and make us believe that investing isn't simple at all. It's way too complex for us Average Joe investors. In fact, Wall Street charges us $350 billion a year to make rocket science out of brilliant simplicity. They continually feed us the message that we reside in the rarified air of above-average Lake Wobegone. It's critical that we stick our common sense in a drawer so that we won't figure out that investing is a zero-sum game.

Learn about the subject of behavioral finance. Jason Zweig's book, *Your Money and Your Brain* (Simon & Schuster, 2007), will teach you to be a better investor. The logical side of your brain may recognize the street signs of simplicity, but the emotional side will surely steer you off course, or off a cliff. Unfortunately, it's hard to know which side of your brain is in the driver's seat when you are making a decision.

It's Okay to Have a Little Fun

The biggest problem of the second-grader portfolio is that it just isn't any fun. Believe it or not, there are times when a little voice in my head says, "Come on, Allan, live a little, have some fun. You know you want to." And I do want to, because beneath this dull exterior beats the heart of the *gambler.* Even yours truly gets the occasional urge to buy that risky stock in the hopes of a 1,000 percent return, and sometimes I just can't resist acting on that thrill-seeking urge.

That's why I carve out a small piece of my portfolio for, perhaps, the only fun I have in investing. I call it my *gambling portfolio.*

Now everybody should have the right to craft his or her own system to outsmart the market. Mine is buying stocks that have fallen from grace and that I think have about a 50–50 chance of going bankrupt. They are usually trading for a few dollars and those that don't go bankrupt might just get a 10× return.

Rules for My Gambling Portfolio

1. Gambling is gambling, whether it's investing or blackjack. I bet only what I can afford to lose.
2. Keep perspective on my wins and losses and the territory they go with—my own version of "what happens in Vegas, stays in Vegas" (or ought to).
3. Never confuse luck with brilliance.
4. Always remember rule #1.

Of course, if I thought my approach to beating the market really worked, I'd keep it close to my vest and never reveal it to anyone, much less put it in a book. But this gambling portfolio provides me with some fun and gives me the ability to conveniently forget my losses and have pride in my gains. As Paul Farrell put it so succinctly, "If you have two brains, you may need two portfolios."[4]

Write a Contract between You and Your Money

One of the best ways to keep investing simple and avoid being a victim of Wall Street is to put it in writing. Exhibit 13.5 is an example of a contract to keep you investing like a second grader.

Exhibit 13.5 Investment Policy Contract

I, ______AJAY ISSAR.______,
hereby state that I am an investor, not a speculator.
I hereby agree to:

- Keep my portfolio costs dirt low.
- Own the entire world rather than chase what's hot.
- Invest for the long-term and not time the market.

I have thought about the risks and rewards of investing and agree to the following asset allocation:

Asset Class	Allocation
U.S. Stocks	_____%
International Stocks	_____%
Fixed Income (Bonds & CDs)	_____%
Alt Assets (REITs & Precious Metals)	_____%
	100%

I will keep this portfolio allocation for the long-term as I understand that the more I change this allocation, the greater the likelihood that I will be chasing performance and lowering my return.

The only time I will make changes in my portfolio is to rebalance to get back to the stated allocations above. I realize this means I have to buy more of the asset that has done the worst, and to sell some of the asset that has done the best. I further note that this will go against my instincts but will rebalance whenever any asset allocation becomes __% off my target allocation above.

I understand that paying people to beat the market is betting against second grader arithmetic and know my odds of disproving this math are very low.

(continued)

I further understand that financial experts will continue to tell me how to invest my money and will explain why markets have behaved as they have in the past. I will be tempted to take that advice and may even get an irresistible urge to outsmart myself by making changes. When I get those irresistible urges, I will let them pass.

The only exception to the above will be what I term my "gambling portfolio." This will consist of $________ representing only ____% of my portfolio. If I do poorly with this portion of my portfolio, I will not put more funds into this gambling portfolio. If I do well, I will not assume it was my brilliance and will also not put more funds into this gambling portfolio.

I hereby state that no one cares more about my money than I do. I will hold this portfolio until the following date which is at least ten (10) years from the date of this contract:

________________________________, 20__

With my signature below, I am agreeing to the terms of this contract and will regard this as a legally binding contract. Any violation of the terms set forth in this contract is likely to result in the following damages:

- Pushing back my financial freedom by several years.
- Dramatically lowering the amount I can spend in retirement.

I hereby agree to fully accept the consequences for any default on the terms in this contract.

Signed: **Date:**

____________________ ___________, 20___

Witnesses:

____

____

My Parting Words to Wall Street: "Thank You!"

A Wall Street analyst once asked me what I thought of some of the up-and-coming companies in a particular industry. I explained to him that that I didn't believe in what he was doing in trying to pick winning companies. I proudly told him that I was an indexer.

He looked at me as if I had just told him I had wallpapered my house with aluminum foil to block out signals from outer space! The next comment out of his mouth, I was sure, would be how idiotic I was to be an indexer, especially since his job was to beat it. Can you believe people call *me* argumentative? But the throw-down never happened; instead he put my philosophy in perspective and me in my place. He pointed out that it was people like him who kept the markets efficient. Without analysts telling people what stocks to buy and sell, we wouldn't have a working market. I realized he had a more than valid point and that it was I who was completely wrong.

The irony is that, if everyone invested in index funds, there would be no trading on stock exchanges. Markets would collapse and liquidity would disappear. It was obvious to me that he was 100 percent correct and we owe thanks to all of those professionals who try to add value in the zero-sum game of investing.

So Wall Street plays a critical role for passive investors. It gives us a free ride in investing, in that we can share in the benefits of the marketplace without paying our share to keep it working. We indexers owe a great debt to Wall Street, and should anyone from Wall Street actually be reading this book, please know that you have my gratitude. I might even try to establish a National holiday—maybe something like "Take an Active Investor to Lunch Day." It's the least we can do.

Applying the Golden Rule of Second-Grader Investing

If you can apply the golden rules of the second-grader portfolio, you may be able to move up your financial independence by more than a decade. It's that powerful.

My advice is to *think like a second grader* and remember the *SECOND* acronym:

*S*imple
*E*motionless
*C*osts matter
*O*bvious
*N*asty stuff
*D*iversified

- *Simple.* If you can't explain your investment strategy and every product in your portfolio to a second grader, you are probably doing something wrong. Don't outsmart yourself. Be brilliant like Einstein and Newton, and apply the KISS principle.
- *Emotionless.* We are not in control of our emotions, but the more we can separate them from our investing, the better off we will be. Kevin has a huge advantage in that the money in his portfolio isn't real to him yet. Investors who believe they are acting logically are the ones who are making the biggest emotional mistakes. If you are getting excitement from your portfolio, you are setting yourself up for a big fall. When you get that irresistible urge to do something, let it pass.
- *Costs matter.* The average dollar invested in the market will earn the market return, less costs. This is dependent only on simple second-grader arithmetic. Remember, however, that taxes are costs as well. Index funds keep both expenses and taxes at their lowest.
- *Obvious.* Always take a step back and apply some not-so-common common sense. Put yourself in the shoes of the people selling you a product and ask how they make money. Ask yourself:
  - Can everyone really be above average?
  - It the product is so good, why are they offering it to me?
  - If they really knew how to beat the market, why would they be telling people?

- *Nasty stuff.* Remember that Wall Street will always be developing new products and sales techniques to separate you from your money. You will want to believe this stuff works. Falling prey to it will set back your financial goals. Before jumping in, make sure you truly understand it. If an investment professional contacts you with something too good to be true, say what Kevin says: "I'll have to check with my parents first."
- *Diversification.* Spread your nest egg across the globe. Chasing what's hot is sure to disappoint. There will be more bubbles and the only way I know to avoid them is to own the world. If you are betting on sectors or even countries, you are speculating rather than investing.

Investing is that simple. Unfortunately, it will never be easy for us adults. The best we can do is to imagine ourselves as second graders and try to think like them. Look back at the second grader's golden rules of investing and make sure you are following them.

I wish I could be like Kevin and not follow the market daily (or 10 times daily, to be more accurate), or need the buzz of my gambling portfolio.

Never Forget the Purpose of Money

In spite of the lip service that is paid to believing that money doesn't buy happiness, we all seem to be on the treadmill of acquiring as much of it as we can. The disappointment sets in when we find that the raise we got, or that windfall profit, doesn't actually make us happier for long periods.

In actuality, acquiring twice the money doesn't bring with it twice the happiness. Research shows that the relation between happiness and money looks something like Exhibit 13.6. Who else remembers Maslow's Hierarchy of Needs from freshman psychology? Well, it demonstrated that satisfying our physical needs, such as food and shelter, is pretty much what drives us. Once those needs are met, we are faced with meeting the need at the tippy-top of the pyramid, which is *self-actualization*.

Exhibit 13.6 Relationship between Money and Happiness

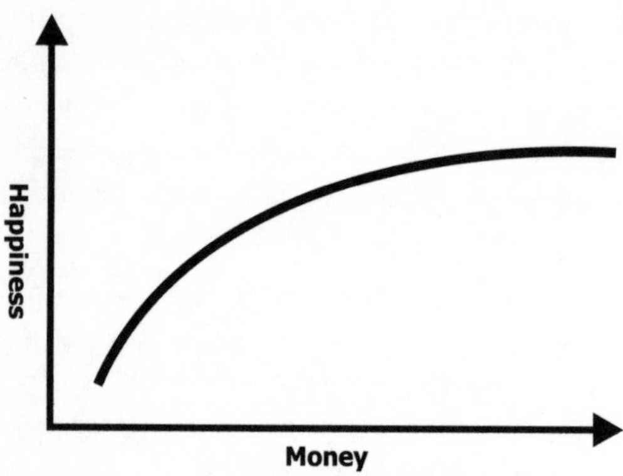

That's no easy task in the human condition. So, if you don't have enough to pay the bills and put food on the table, you will likely be stressed and miserable. Yet, once your finances reach a secure level, each additional dollar brings less and less reward.

In his final (and 1,009th) column in *The Wall Street Journal,* Jonathan Clements reminded us all of the three purposes of money:[5]

1. Having money makes us worry less about money. That alone improves our lives.
2. Money can give you freedom to pursue your passions. (I actually once had a real job in corporate America.)
3. Money can buy you time with your friends and family. Studies show that regularly seeing friends and family can provide a huge boost to happiness.

For now, Kevin, Patty, and I wish you an exciting life. We just hope you get it from somewhere other than your investing. Always remember, the goal of your nest egg is to give you the freedom to do exciting things, not to provide the excitement itself.

Kevin's Postscript

Hi, I'm Kevin. I'm in fifth grade now, but when I was in second grade, my dad said he was going to teach me about investing. I was thinking, "Huh?," because I thought that was for adults. Dad said it was really easy to understand, even for kids. My dad is good at explaining things to me, especially math things. Whenever I need help with my math homework, I always ask Dad. Anyway, Dad explained investing to me and I understood it, which was really cool. Together we invested my money from my grandparents.

Since then, I really haven't done anything with my portfolio. I just let it grow. Doing nothing is the key to investing. To me, investing is simple. Adults always overcomplicate and overreact, which are bad things in investing if you want your money to grow.

When I was in fourth grade, a teacher taught me "The Stock Market Game™." We each picked three stocks that we thought would do well over the next few weeks. Kind of like putting all your eggs in three baskets. I didn't do so well. It was fun, but I bet that if people invest real money like the game, they won't do so well, either.

Last year, my dad and I watched a show called *Mad Money* with a guy named Cramer. I thought Cramer was short-tempered and a bit crazy. Because he was yelling so much, I didn't even understand what he was saying except that he told every caller they were looking at things the wrong way. I did like the sound effects. I wouldn't want to watch that show again. I'd rather watch cartoons like *SpongeBob* or *Chowder.* They're easier to understand and they're funny.

So, here are some things I have learned about investing since second grade.

First, don't always look at what the market is doing. It tells about what it is doing only in the *short term* and you want to focus only on the *long term.* If you look at the market all the time, like my dad, you'll get stressed out over nothing. It's funny that Dad looks at the market a lot, because he tells people not to look at it. Uncle Mike says that Dad is like the doctor who tells people not to smoke, but he smokes.

Second, if people tell you they know what the market is going to do, like tomorrow or the next day, don't listen to them. It's impossible to tell what the market will do over a short period, although it's easier to tell what it will do in the long term.

Third, remember that investing is simple, so don't overcomplicate things when you invest. If investing were complex, then I wouldn't have been able to understand it in second grade and make the *second-grader portfolio.*

When we first were writing this book, the market was pretty good. Now everybody knows that it is really, really bad. My dad always checks what the market is doing, but now when he does it he looks less grumpy and more like he has a bad headache. I'm still going to do what I did before it got so bad, and that is nothing. I don't worry about what's going to happen because I think it will get better after awhile since it always does. So I hope everybody won't worry and get scared and sell, because they'll lose their money that way. Let's all just do nothing together!

Don't believe people who tell you the stock market will never come back. I learned in Junior Achievement that companies grow and it really doesn't matter how they are doing right now. So, if you worry, do something that takes your mind off of it, like watching SpongeBob or watching paint dry. Even that's better than stressing out.

Good luck, and thanks for reading this book. Because the book was something we did together, Dad says my share of any money will go into what he calls a *529 college account.* That's really good, because I'm going to be a doctor, and you need a lot of college for that.

Notes

Introduction

1. Adapted from Penelope Wang, "The Best Investment in 10 Years: Get in While You Can,"*Money* (April 2008).
2. 2000 letter to shareholders.
3. Calculated from Morningstar data.
4. In a once-unthinkable move, the Federal Reserve Bank provided an emergency loan in March 2008 that wiped out the vast majority of the stock's value as it was acquired by JPMorgan Chase.

Chapter 1 The Claw Will Take Your Money

1. Another possible explanation is that Kevin inherited my lack of skill in playing these arcade games.
2. John C. Bogle, "The Relentless Rules of Humble Arithmetic," *Financial Analysts Journal* (November/December 2005).
3. At the time of the budget submission, the projected deficit was $410 billion.
4. Both five-year periods through August 8, 2008.

5. William F. Sharpe, "The Arithmetic of Active Management," *Financial Analyst's Journal* 47/1 (January/February 1991): 7–9.
6. John C. Bogle, Bogle Financial Markets Research Center and Wealth Logic Analysis from the Federal Reserve Flow of Funds Report.

Chapter 2 Own the World

1. At this point, I chose not to go into the differences between publicly owned companies and privately owned ones.
2. John C. Bogle, *The Little Book of Common Sense Investing* (Hoboken: John Wiley & Sons, 2007).
3. "The Ultimate Investment Club," *Money* (October 2003). Performance was for the 12 months ended August 31, 2004.
4. "Google Goes to the S&P 500," TheStreet.com, March 23, 2006.
5. Okay, I conveniently left out the U.S. government and their right to print money.
6. Paul Merriman, "Fine Tuning Your Asset Allocation," FundAdvice.com, March 18, 2008. Between 1970 and 2007, a 100% global equity portfolio earned a 13.7% annual return while a 90% Equity/10% fixed income portfolio earned a 13.2% annual return.

Chapter 3 The Advantage of Having Wall Street Marketing Blinders (and Where Can I Get Some?)

1. I was amazed that in the new millennium magicians are still doing the rabbit-in-the-hat trick, although sometimes they get creative and use another rodent. At this party, I think it was the hamster-in-the-hat trick.
2. Taylor Larimore, Mel Lindaur, and Michael LeBoeuf, *Bogleheads Guide to Investing* (Hoboken: John Wiley & Sons, 2007).
3. Zvi Bodie, Dennis McLeavey, and Laurence B. Siegel, "The Future of Life-Cycle Saving and Investing," *Research Foundation Publications* (October 2007).
4. As of the date of this writing, there was no such ticker symbol as WSMC.
5. From the Bear Stearns web site (March 17, 2008).
6. Lehman Brothers 2007 Fact Book. Performance was for fiscal year ending November 30, 2007.

7. Stephen Dubner, Freakonomics web site, April 2, 2008.
8. John C. Bogle, "The Relentless Rules of Humble Arithmetic." *Financial Analysts Journal* (November/December 2005).
9. According to Dimensional Fund Advisors, from 1926 to 2004, the S&P 500 returned 10.4% annually, government bonds yielded 5.5%, and the CPI came in at 3.0%. Post–Great Depression, the CPI has averaged 4.0% since 1945.
10. A simple calculation with an 8% return being taxed at the 25% combined state and federal tax-rate. This would be a combination of ordinary income, short-term gains, and long-term gains.
11. AAII mailing. AAII Business Wire, dated October 15, 2002 stated "AAII members report investment returns that are on average 4% higher than that of the stock market as a whole.".
12. Daniel Bergstresser, John Chalmers, and Peter Tufano, "Assessing the Costs and Benefits of Brokers in the Mutual Fund Industry" (Harvard Business School Finance Working Paper No. 616981, October 1, 2007).
13. Christopher Carosa, "Passive Investing: The Emperor Exposed?" *Journal of Financial Planning* (October 2005).
14. Allan Roth and Christopher Carosa, "Results of Appeals Process," *Journal of Financial Planning* (July 2006).
15. "Notice of Retraction," *Journal of Financial Planning* (May 2007).
16. Paul Farrell, "Boo-Yah This: 'Lazy Portfolios' beat 'Mad Money'," MarketWatch, November 13, 2007.
17. Some might disagree with this characterization.

Chapter 4 Adults Behaving Badly

1. George Santayana, *The Life of Reason,* vol. 1 (Charles Scribner's Sons, 1905).
2. Geoffrey Friesen and Travis Sapp, "Mutual Fund Flows and Investor Returns: An Empirical Examination of Fund Investor Timing Ability," *Journal of Banking and Finance* (September 2007).
3. To date, the record answer is 95%.
4. Lipper Average is the average performance for the category of mutual funds over a period of time being measured.

5. Ola Svenson, "Are We All Less Risky and More Skillful Than Our Fellow Drivers?"*Acta Psychologica* 47/2 (February 1981): 143–148; doi:10.1016/0001-6918(81)90005-6.
6. Brad M. Barber and Terrance Odean, "Boys Will Be Boys: Gender, Overconfidence and Common Stock Investment," *Quarterly Journal of Economics* (February 2001).
7. First defined by Ellen Langer, "The Illusion of Control," *Journal of Personality and Social Psychology, 1975.*
8. Selena Maranjian, "Butter in Bangladesh Predicts the Stock Market," Motley Fool, September 20, 2007, www.fool.com/investing/general/2007/09/20/butter-in-bangladesh-predicts-the-stock-market.aspx.
9. Jason Zweig, *Your Money and Your Brain* (New York: Simon & Schuster, August 2007),

Chapter 5 Can You Beat a Second Grader's Portfolio?

1. I'm guilty of comparing a total market to the S&P 500, but I have no data for the total U.S. stock market during this period.
2. The concept of beating the odds many times in a row is similar to Kevin's math, but the calculations are more complex because, in the comparison of multiple funds, the amount each fund beats the index is relevant, rather than just a win/lose outcome.
3. Geoffrey C. Friesen and Travis R.A. Sapp, "Mutual Fund Flows and Investor Returns: An Empirical Examination of Fund Investing Timing Ability,"*Journal of Banking and Finance* (2007).
4. The Stock Market Game is a trademark of the Foundation for Investor Education, www.stockmarketgame.org.
5. Per SMGWW.org (accessed February 23, 2008).
6. Mathew Emmert, "Vegas Psychology," Motley Fool, March 29, 2004, www.fool.com/investing/general/2004/03/29/vegas-psychology.aspx?terms=mathew+emmert+know+the+odds&vstest=search_042607_linkdefault.

Chapter 6 Beyond the Second-Grader Portfolio

1. Per Barclay's iShares for the three-year period ending January 31, 2008.
2. Ibid.

3. Ibid.
4. Ibid.
5. Per Vanguard correlation calculator for 3- and 10-year periods as of June 30, 2008.

Chapter 7 Bonds—Your Portfolio's Shock Absorber

1. To my knowledge, there was no one actually named Randy in Kevin's second-grade class.
2. Investopedia.com.
3. Of course, printing money isn't free; it causes inflation and the decline of currency value.
4. The *duration number* is a calculation involving present value, yield, coupon, final maturity, and call features. It's the geometric present value average length of time the bondholder receives cash payments of interest and principal.
5. Bianco Research.
6. William Reichenstein, Baylor University, "Bond Fund Returns and Expenses: A Study of Bond Market Efficiency,"*Journal of Investing* (Winter 1999); Dale L. Domain, University of Saskatchewan, and William Reichenstein, Baylor University, "Predicting Municipal Bond Fund Returns,"*Journal of Investing* (Fall 2002).

Chapter 8 Better Than Bonds

1. Not that any of the large Money Center Banks successfully avoided the subprime lending scheme.
2. Technically, the Treasury is backed directly by the U.S. government, whereas the CDs are backed by agencies of the U.S. government.

Chapter 9 Simply Brilliant or Brilliantly Simple— Building Your Portfolio

1. Richard Thaler and Cass Sunstein, *Nudge* (New Haven, Conn.: Yale University Press, 2008), 121.
2. Jeremy Siegel, *Stocks for the Long Run* (New York: McGraw-Hill, 2002).

4. Larry E. Swedroe, *Rational Investing in Irrational Times* (New York: Truman Talley Books—St. Martin Press, 2002).
5. Jason Zweig, *Your Money and Your Brain (*New York: Simon and Schuster, 2007).
6. Invostopedia.com.
7. DARE TO BE DULL® is a registered trademark of Allan Roth & Company, LLC and used frequently in my financial planning practice.

Chapter 11 Nightmare off Wall Street—The Scary Tale of Trick-or-Treat Investing

1. For the sake of domestic harmony, I refrained from making the obvious jokes.
2. Duff McDonald, "The Running of the Hedgehogs," *New York*, April 9, 2007. Cliff Asness of AQR Capital.
3. Developed in conversations with Colorado Securities Commissioner Fred Joseph.

Chapter 12 Increase Your Return No Matter What the Market Does

1. Taken from case study by Laurence Kotlikoff, Boston University. More information can be found at www.esplanner.com/Case% Studies/double_dip.pdf..

Chapter 13 Keep It Simple, Stupid (KISS)

1. "Newton Beats Einstein in Polls of Scientists and the Public," *The Royal Society* (retrieved on October 25, 2006).
2. J. E. Force, *Newton and Religion*, Springer; 1 edition (December 31, 1999), p. 244.
3. Forty years. Kevin was 8 years old and I was 48.
4. Paul B Farrell, Ph.D., *The Lazy Person's Guide to Investing* (New York: Warner Books, Inc., 2004).
5. "Parting Shot: What I Learned from Writing 1,008 Columns," *Wall Street Journal* (April 9, 2008).

About the Author

ALLAN ROTH is the founder of Wealth Logic, LLC, an hourly-based financial planning and investment advisory firm, that advises clients with portfolios ranging from $10,000 to $50 million. His expertise is in portfolio construction and performance benchmarking, and is frequently quoted in the financial media. An Adjunct Finance Faculty Member at the University of Colorado at Colorado Springs and Colorado College, he teaches behavioral finance at the University of Denver's Graduate Tax Institute. Mr. Roth is a CPA and CFP with an MBA from the Kellogg School at Northwestern University. During the course of his professional career, he has held the position of finance officer for multibillion-dollar companies, and has been a consultant at McKinsey and Company. Roth writes a personal finance column for the *Colorado Springs Business Journal.* Despite these credentials, Roth still claims the ability to keep investing simple.

Roth trademarked the slogan, *"Dare To Be Dull,"* to convey his belief that investing should be just that: dull. His personal mission is to convince one investor at a time that getting any sort of emotional charge out of investing is a sure sign that we're doing something wrong. Only by daring to go against our emotions do we have a shot at doubling our real return. More information can be found on his web site at www.DareToBeDull.com.

Index